Poverty and Inequality among Chinese Minorities

Despite recent economic advances, the number of poor people in China is huge. Chinese minorities constitute less than 10 per cent of the Chinese population yet they constitute 40 to 50 per cent of the poor. This book investigates poverty and inequality among Chinese ethnic minorities, focusing in particular on two important questions: Have the minorities shared the fruits of spectacular economic growth in China during the past two decades? Is their backwardness due to ethnic and cultural factors or to extremely low incomes?

The book examines the different factors explaining poverty; the relationship between poverty and ethnicity; poverty indicators that permit a comparison between minorities and non-minorities (or the Han majority); and economic and demographic characteristics of minorities and their educational, occupational and gender profiles. It considers whether special measures in favour of minorities introduced by the Chinese government have contributed to an improvement in their standard of living. International comparisons are made with other developing countries such as India, which also has substantial ethnic minorities and similar preferential policies.

Throughout, special attention is given to literacy and basic education and access to health services, showing that low literacy and poor access to health services aggravate poverty among Chinese minorities. The study concludes that poverty among minorities, lack of education and limited access to health services is due more to *economic* than ethnic or *cultural* factors. Overall, this book provides a detailed examination of a critical issue in contemporary Chinese society. It fills a gap in the existing economic literature, since no major work to date has dealt with the subject of poverty among Chinese ethnic minorities.

A.S. Bhalla is a former Fellow of Sidney Sussex College, Cambridge, and former Special Adviser to the President of the International Development Research Centre (IDRC), Canada. He is co-author of *Poverty and Exclusion in a Global World* (1999, 2004; Japanese edition 2005) and *The Employment Impact of China's WTO Accession* (2004); and author of *Uneven Development in the Third World* (1992, 1995).

Shufang Qiu is an Economic and Business Consultant based in Cambridge, UK. He has worked for the Chinese government on economic reforms. His research interests include poverty alleviation, WTO and economic transition in China.

Routledge studies on the Chinese economy
Series editor: Peter Nolan, *University of Cambridge*
Founding series editors: Peter Nolan, *University of Cambridge*
and Dong Fureng, *Beijing University*

The aim of this series is to publish original, high-quality, research-level work by both new and established scholars in the West and the East, on all aspects of the Chinese economy, including studies of business and economic history.

Poverty and Inequality among Chinese Minorities

A.S. Bhalla and Shufang Qiu

Routledge
Taylor & Francis Group

LONDON AND NEW YORK

First published 2006
by Routledge
2 Park Square, Milton Park, Abingdon, Oxon, OX14 4RN

Simultaneously published in the USA and Canada
by Routledge
270 Madison Ave, New York NY 10016

Routledge is an imprint of the Taylor & Francis Group

Transferred to Digital Printing 2009

Typeset in Times by
Rosemount Typing Services, Auldgirth, Dumfriesshire

British Library Cataloguing in Publication Data
A catalogue record for this book is available from the British Library

Library of Congress Cataloging in Publication Data
Bhalla A.S.
  Poverty and inequality among Chinese minorities / A.S. Bhalla and
Shufang Qiu
     p. cm. – (Routledge studies on the Chinese economy ; 22)
  Includes bibliographical references and index.
   1. Minorities–China–Economic conditions. 2. Minorities–China–
Social conditions. 3. Minorities–Education—China 4. Ethnology–
China 5. Race discrimination–China. 6. China–Ethnic relations. 7.
Poor–China. 8. Racism in education I. Qiu, Shufang. II. Title.
III. Routledge studies in the Chinese economy : 22.

  HC427.95.B48 2005
  339.4'608900951–dc22   2005025862

ISBN10: 0–415–30840–2 (hbk)
ISBN10: 0–415–55523–X (pbk)

ISBN13: 9–78–0–415–30840–3 (hbk)
ISBN13: 9–78–0–415–55523–4 (pbk)

To our children Ranjan, Arman and Shirley

Contents

Figures

Tables

Preface

The book was prepared within the framework of the research project on Sino-Indian liberalization at the Sidney Sussex College, University of Cambridge, where one of the authors, A.S. Bhalla, was a Fellow. The project examined the processes of economic liberalization that occurred in India and China, and its implications for external and domestic policies including poverty reduction.

The present volume is devoted to the study of poverty and inequality in China with special reference to ethnic minorities. Wherever appropriate it makes international comparisons with other countries (e.g. India) with diverse and significant ethnic minorities and similar preferential policies for their betterment. The choice of minorities is guided by the fact that there is little socioeconomic literature on the subject at present. In fact, we know of no economic work on minorities; much of the literature is concerned with their history and culture.

Chinese minorities constitute less than 10 per cent of the total population, yet they represent 40–50 per cent of the absolute poor. To the best of our knowledge, there is no study dealing with the evolution of poverty among the minorities. Thus, we hope that the volume will make a modest contribution to the existing literature on ethnic minorities in China.

We examine how the rural poverty among Chinese minorities has evolved and whether special measures in their favour have led to any appreciable positive impact on their standard of living. We attempt to answer two main questions:

(1) Have minorities shared the fruits of economic growth in China and in the interior provinces?
(2) What has been the evolution of the poverty situation of minorities in the West region where they are mostly concentrated? Is it ethnicity and cultural factors or extreme poverty that explains their backwardness?

GDP per capita grew rapidly between 1978 and 1996 in all the Chinese provinces, which suggests that benefits of growth were widespread. But it is not clear how different ethnic groups, compared to the Han majority, have benefited from this unprecedented growth. It is somewhat paradoxical that the autonomous regions (where a large proportion of minorities live) are often quite rich in natural resources but their populations remain quite poor. Over 39 per cent of China's forest areas are located in these regions, which produce substantial quantities of minerals, notably, iron, manganese, copper and lead. Despite natural richness most of these areas are poor because of low land fertility, mountainous terrain, inadequate road infrastructure, and resulting inaccessibility. Historically, the Han majority occupied the fertile plains, towns and cities whereas minorities inhabited the mountains. With the exception of a few minorities in the Northeast, the bulk of them are known to live in mountain areas, which tend to be less productive.

The official Chinese policy on poverty and minorities has, until the late 1990s, been largely locational in the sense that poor minority people are assumed to be concentrated in particular areas, which are mostly remote and mountainous. A recent shift in emphasis in targeting poor rural households does not distinguish between minority and non-minority poor. We examine whether poverty is locational or widely dispersed. An answer to this question has important policy implications since the anti-poverty programmes do not cover poor minority households outside the autonomous regions.

We undertook several field trips to China between 1998 and 2001 in connection with this research. During these trips we visited Guizhou, Sichuan and Yunnan in the Southwest region of China. Our trips included visits to poor counties in these provinces in which a large proportion of minority groups are located. We visited the offices of the World Bank-funded Poverty Reduction Project in the three provinces and met staff at the Provincial Foreign Capital Management Centres in charge of the Poverty Reduction Project. We had several useful meetings with the provincial government authorities, local county and municipal government officials, staff of minority institutes, and representatives of poor minority groups. We are grateful to all those who generously gave their time and support to our field research. In particular, we would like to express our debt of gratitude to the following: Dr Guo Shuqing, Deputy Governor, Central Bank of China (formerly Deputy Governor of the Provincial Government of Guizhou); Mr Wang Yuan Hai, Deputy Secretary-General of the Provincial Government of Guizhou; Mr He Wei Xian, Director-General, and Mr Wang Liquan, Vice-President, of the Development Research Centre of the Provincial Government of Guizhou; Professor Zhang Xiao, Institute of Ethnic Culture, Guizhou Academy of Social Sciences, Guiyang; Ms Zhang Chao, Guizhou Institute of Nationalities, Guiyang; Professor Zhao Junchen, Director, Institute of Rural Economy of the Yunnan Academy of Social Sciences, Kunming; Mr Liu Pengnan, Deputy Director, and Mr Yuan Lihui, Division Chief, of the Yunnan Provincial Foreign Capital Poverty Alleviation Project Management Centre, Kunming; Dr Wang Wan Ying and Mr Andreas Wilkes of the Rural Development Research Centre at the Yunnan Institute of Geography, Kunming; Dr Qiao Hengrui of the Sociology Research Institute of the Yunnan Academy of Social Sciences, Kunming; Mr Stephen Tsui, Representative of OXFAM Hong Kong for Southwest China Programme, Kunming; Mr Wang Sitie, Division Chief, Sichuan Provincial Poverty Alleviation Office, Chengdu; Professor Wang Zhenzhong, Deputy

Director, Ms Zhu Ling, Deputy Director, and Dr Liu Xiaoxian, Associate Professor, Institute of Economics, Chinese Academy of Social Sciences (CASS), Beijing; Professor Justin Yifu Lin, Director, China Centre for Economic Research, Peking University, Beijing; Professor Jikun Huang, Professor and Director, Centre for Chinese Agricultural Policy, Chinese Academy of Agricultural Sciences; Professor Zongyi Zhang, Dean, College of Economics and Business Administration, University of Chongqing; Mr Wu Yong Nian, Director, and Ms He Xiao Jun, Deputy Director, Foreign Capital Project Management Centre, State Council Leading Group Office of Poverty Alleviation and Development, Beijing; Mr Toshihiro Tanaka, Assistant Resident Representative, the United Nations Development Programme (UNDP), Beijing; Ms Zhu Zhengxuan, Agricultural Specialist, the World Bank Resident Mission in China, Beijing; Dr Sarah Cook, Programme Officer, Ford Foundation, Beijing; and Ms Fiona McConnon, Head of the Development Section (DFID), and First Secretary, British Embassy, Beijing. Thanks are also due to Professor Lok Sang Ho, Chairman, Economics Department, and Director of the Centre for Public Policy Studies, and Professor Y.Y. Kueh, Dean of the Faculty of Social Sciences, Lingnan University, Hong Kong, for inviting one of the authors (A.S. Bhalla) to give a seminar on poverty alleviation in Southwest China. We are grateful to the participants of the seminar for useful discussions and suggestions.

Professor Xiaming Liu, University of Surrey, UK, and Professor Jinghai Zheng, University of Gothenberg, Sweden, helped us with data processing techniques and statistical analyses. Professor Mark Brenner, University of Massachusetts, Amherst, USA, processed and analysed the CASS household survey data in Chapters 4 and 5.

We are grateful to Sidney Sussex College, General Smuts Travel Fund, University of Cambridge, and the Royal Economic Society Small Grants Scheme for providing research and travel grants which enabled our trips to China as well as data collection and field work.

A.S. Bhalla, Commugny, Switzerland
Shufang Qiu, Cambridge, England

Acknowledgements

In the preparation of this book we have drawn on our following discussion papers and book chapters for which we are grateful to Sidney Sussex College, Cambridge, and Professors Liu and Yao, the editors of the book in which our chapter on Guizhou appeared:

(1) 'Anti-Poverty Policies and Programmes in Southwest China', *Discussion Paper no. 13*, Sino-Indian Research Project, Sidney Sussex College, University of Cambridge, UK, March 2001.
(2) 'Chinese Minorities: Poverty and Socioeconomic Characteristics', *Discussion Paper no. 15*, Sino-Indian Research Project, Sidney Sussex College, University of Cambridge, UK, June 2001.
(3) 'Anti-Poverty Interventions: A Case Study of Guizhou (China)', in Xiaming Liu and Shujie Yao (eds), *Sustaining China's Economic Growth in the Twenty-first Century* (London: RoutledgeCurzon 2003).

List of abbreviations

ADB	Asian Development Bank
BIDS	Bangladesh Institute of Development Studies
CASS	Chinese Academy of Social Sciences
CP	Communist Party
DFID	Department for International Development (UK)
DRC	Development Research Centre (China)
EDRC	Economics and Development Resource Center (ADB)
FGT	Foster–Greer–Thorbecke (Index of Poverty)
FFW	food-for-work programme
GB	Grameen Bank
GOI	Government of India
HDI	Human Development Index
IDRI	International Development Research Institute (Japan)
IDS	Institute of Development Studies (Sussex University, UK)
IFAD	International Fund for Agricultural Development
ILO	International Labour Organization
IMF	International Monetary Fund
IRDP	Integrated Rural Development Programme
JRY	*Jawahar Rozgar Yojana* (Employment Generation Scheme) (India)
LGEDPA	Leading Group for Economic Development of Poor Areas (China)
LGOPAD	Leading Group Office of Poverty Alleviation and Development (China)
LGPR	Leading Group for Poverty Reduction
MACG	Mutual Assistance Credit Group
MP	Madhya Pradesh (India)
NBS	National Bureau of Statistics (China)
NCAER	National Council of Applied Economic Research (India)
NGO	non-governmental organization
NPC	National People's Congress (China)
NSB	National Statistical Bureau (China)
NSS	National Sample Survey (India)
ODC	Overseas Development Council

OECD	Organization for Economic Cooperation and Development
OECF	Overseas Economic Cooperation Fund (Japan)
PADO	Poor Area Development Office
PAF	Poverty Alleviation Fund
PPP	Purchasing Power Parity
PQLI	Physical Quality of Life Indicator
RIDA	Research Institute of Development Assistance (Japan)
SC	scheduled caste (India)
SSB	State Statistical Bureau
ST	scheduled tribe (India)
STICERD	Suntory-Toyota International Centre for Economics and Related Disciplines
TVE	Town and Village Enterprise
UNDP	United Nations Development Programme
UNICEF	United Nations Children's Fund
UP	Uttar Pradesh (India)
WBNS	Wisconsin Basic Needs Study
WFP	World Food Programme
WTO	World Trade Organization

1 Poverty and ethnicity

Studies on poverty are abundant but the term poverty remains a vague and value-loaded term. It means different things to different people, in different cultures, and at different levels of economic development. A good deal of controversy surrounds the poverty concept simply because of people's different perceptions and understanding. The reason lies in the fact that poverty is a multi-dimensional concept: people with different backgrounds and value judgements can have quite different views of it. However, a clear definition of poverty is important for many reasons. First, it is essential for determining the extent of poverty which is often estimated by a poverty line (see below and appendix to this chapter). Second, measurement of the extent of poverty in a country is likely to be fraught with many difficulties even if a definition of poverty is chosen. Third, different definitions of poverty will have different policy implications and different requirements in terms of programmes to alleviate or eliminate it. Finally, economic development and the success of poverty reduction programmes will be judged differently depending on how poverty is defined.

Common approaches to poverty

Poverty refers to a social phenomenon under which the standard of living of individuals and households in a community or a country is persistently below a certain level required physically for sustaining human life according to some accepted social norms. This definition of poverty implies two alternative interpretations. The first is that the resources over which some people enjoy command are not sufficient to enable them to be alive. The second interpretation implies a situation in which means are not sufficient to allow those people to lead a life that is considered normal or 'decent' in a given society. The first interpretation relates to so-called 'absolute' poverty and the second to 'relative' poverty.

Some welfare economists define poverty as a situation in which welfare, derived from command over resources of individuals and households, falls below a certain minimum welfare level, called the poverty threshold (Hagenaars, 1986). Others regard poverty as the lack of resources necessary to participate in activities and to adopt customs and diets commonly approved by society (Townsend, 1979).

Another approach, associated with Sen, defines poverty as a failure of some members of society to enjoy a certain minimum of 'capabilities'. It is not just a matter of being relatively poorer than others but of not having some basic opportunities of material well-being. The minimum set of capabilities is an 'absolute' term in the sense that people's deprivations are judged absolutely, not simply in comparison with deprivations of others in a given society. These capabilities can take several forms: being free from starvation, hunger, undernourishment; being adequately sheltered; being free to travel to see friends, and being able to participate in communal life and so on. According to this approach, it is necessary for a society to set certain absolute standards of minimum material capabilities. Anyone failing to reach that absolute level would then be classified as poor no matter what his or her relative position is *vis-à-vis* others. Therefore, poverty is not ultimately a matter of incomes as such, but of a failure to achieve certain minimum capabilities (Sen, 1985; Bhalla and Lapeyre, 2004).

There seems to be no serious controversy concerning the interpretation of poverty as relative and absolute concepts, although preferences differ. To a large extent, the choice hinges on specific conditions prevailing in a given society and the socioeconomic problems it faces. When a country is at an early stage of economic development with a low general standard of living, there is a tendency to emphasize the absolute nature of poverty, because limited resources have to be allocated to achieve many objectives. On the other hand, talking about poverty only in the absolute sense is not very meaningful when a country becomes developed and average consumption reaches a level well above the requirement of basic survival needs.

Poverty is the state of being poor. If there were no riches, there would be no poor. The rich exist because there are the poor, and *vice versa*. When we say someone is poor, we simply make a statement of judgement about his or her living condition with reference to that of the majority of people in a given society. Explicitly or implicitly some kind of standard is assumed for making a comparison. In the poverty literature this standard is generally called a poverty line. In order to assess the extent of poverty, we need to undertake two exercises: first, to choose a standard of measurement and, second, to find a criterion suitable for making an assessment.

There is always a relative component in the definition of poverty, and the interpretation of absolute factors is always based on some appreciation of the welfare and values of society as a whole, to say nothing of the values and subjective judgement of the researcher. This kind of absolute level may exist but a universal quantity as such can never be established, and this is one of the reasons why people's opinions on poverty are so divided.

In the literature absolute poverty often refers to the poverty based on such concepts as 'basic needs', 'subsistence' and 'minimum calorie intake', whose contents change through time and space. As Adam Smith wrote: 'By necessaries I understand, not only the commodities which are indispensably necessary for the support of life, but whatever the custom of the country renders it indecent for creditable people, even of the lowest order, to be without' (Smith, 1776). He noted that the Greeks and Romans could live comfortably without a linen shirt but it would have been shameful for a decent day labourer to appear in public without one in Europe two hundred years ago. When Marx discussed the determination of wage, he referred to the concept of subsistence within which 'a historical and moral element' should be included (Marx, 1867). Alfred Marshall also made it clear that 'every estimate of necessaries must be relative to place and time' (Marshall, 1946).

Absolute poverty can be understood in four broad senses. First, it is the situation experienced by the much poorer people within the category of the poor. Whatever standard we use, we can identify a group of people who are poor but some of them can be even poorer. Here the adjective 'absolute' is used to stress the severity of poverty. Second, often researchers use some basic physical requirements for human beings to survive as a standard of measurement. The situation of the poor whose living condition is below this standard is described as absolute poverty. There are some critical levels of consumption (mainly food, clothing and shelter) below which persistent suffering will occur and the production and reproduction processes would be threatened.[1] People who have permanently or temporarily failed in the continuous struggle to preserve themselves and their dependants from physical want can be seen as being in absolute poverty or destitution (Iliffe, 1987). In these cases poor people's actual consumption is judged not in relation to the consumption levels of other people in society but to the levels, which are required for human beings to survive and such requirements do not change over time, though they could vary from country to country, region to region or community to community. For example, inhabitants in a tropical country would require less clothing and heating to survive compared with people in a cold country. Third, if people's living standard in a community is so low and pervasive that almost nobody is non-poor, these people can be seen to be in absolute poverty in the eyes of those outside the community.

Generally speaking, there are three dominant characteristics of absolute poverty. The first and pre-eminent is that of starvation and malnutrition. Poorer people rely on starchy foods, mainly simple grains, and thus suffer from a deficiency of protein, vitamins and other nutrients. The second problem is that of health. People in absolute poverty often live in primitive conditions and lack facilities for basic personal hygiene. Lack of public provision of health care facilities is common, age-specific death rates, particularly among infants, are high, and life expectancy is short. The third major problem of absolute poverty is education. When people desperately need food and health services, they cannot afford to send their children to school. Also there is a lack of public facilities for the education of children from poor families. Often it is a kind of vicious circle.

The poorer the people, the higher the illiteracy rate in the next generation and the greater the persistence of poverty (see Chapters 4 and 5). Therefore, special attention in this book is paid to the health and educational access of Chinese minorities.

Indicators of poverty and living standard

As mentioned above, we need to choose from different aspects of the measurement of standard of living to define poverty in operational terms. Efforts to assess economic well-being have been made by economists for a long time.

The commonly used poverty indicators include the following:

(1) *income and consumption-based indicators* such as income and consumption per capita or per household, which enable the poor to enjoy access to goods and services. Income and consumption are necessary but not sufficient: low incomes are only one among many factors, which may include lack of social care and inadequate public resources to provide for the attainment of capabilities. Inadequate levels of consumption (especially of food) may lead to what Dasgupta (1993) calls 'economic disenfranchisement'. The poor may need to raise their consumption of food to a minimum nutritional requirement in order to convert their *potential* labour power into *actual* labour power (see (3) below).

(2) *basic needs indicators*, covering such non-income measures as access to health, nutrition, housing, education and so on, which are essential for the satisfaction of basic human needs. Non-income or social indicators, although too aggregated to indicate the poverty situation directly, can provide some indirect information about the situation of the poor since they indicate whether they have access to social services. Whether the poor actually benefit will, however, depend on the nature and effectiveness of delivery mechanisms. The most frequently used indicators of access to health services, for example doctors and hospital beds per 1,000 population, give an indication of the *availability* of health services but not necessarily about their *utilization*, which will depend on physical access and demand for these services. Neither do they throw any light on the distribution of services among different ethnic and socioeconomic groups. There is also a qualitative dimension which the above quantitative ratios fail to capture (Bhalla, 1995). Without an income dimension, the doctor-to-population ratio does not indicate access; we need information on the share of total population actually treated by doctors to draw any conclusion about the satisfaction of the basic need for health. Information on the utilization of services is hard to find not only for minorities but also for the entire population. But there is ample evidence of regional and rural–urban disparities in health access and services in China (for a recent account, see Knight and Song, 1999: 159-60), which, as we shall note below, extend further into disparities between different ethnic groups. Knight and Song (1999) rightly believe that 'these disparities

might represent either political rank and power or economies of scale in the face of transport costs and difficulties'. The Chinese minorities are unlikely to wield political power even though they enjoy preferential treatment.

(3) *employment-related indicators* refer to employment as a means of reducing poverty. Access to employment may be limited due to lack of skills (low educational levels), inadequate food and nutrition or lack of physical assets (land and capital). Poverty may occur despite employment, due to large household size, high dependency ratios and poor health of workers, by lowering productivity and by restricting the number of hours worked, for example.

Income measures

The use of the term 'poverty' implicitly assumes interpersonal comparability of well-being. To make comparisons one must obtain some indication of individual or household welfare. There are two approaches to the measurement of household welfare: through a consumption-based measure or an income-based indicator. The two may be distinguished as direct and indirect approaches (Sen, 1981).

In industrialized countries measured money income is commonly used as an indicator of economic position or level of economic well-being of an individual or a family. Several reasons can be put forward for using income as a proxy for living standards. First, it can be used to summarize the standard of living in a single indicator and simplify welfare comparison. Second, it is argued that income is closer to a measure of the opportunities open to a family even if it happens to choose a low level of consumption. Third, income may prove to be less sensitive in poverty measurement than some physical consumption level. For example, if poverty measurement is based on calorie intake alone, well-being will be defined as a level below which people are to be identified as poor, because even if people's living level is much improved, the calorie intake will not increase much above a certain level. Finally, in the industrialized countries income data may be easier to obtain than other types of data. One problem associated with the income measure is that a significant part of government expenditure in many countries is devoted to health, education and other social services. For instance, free or heavily subsidized health care, education, training and housing, in some cases universally, in some selectively, are commonly provided. Food stamps, fuel vouchers, free travel are other examples of benefits in kind. To the extent governments choose to combat poverty through non-cash transfers, the effectiveness of their efforts could be seriously underestimated if account is not taken of the value of such transfers.

Another choice needs to be made between current income and *normal* income or *permanent* income. Current income is the income that households receive when an income survey is conducted. Normal income is trend income, which includes income from assets: it takes account of the ability of a family to smooth out temporary variations in income through borrowing or dis-saving. If a family member is temporarily out of work, the current income will be lower than normal income. Friedman's permanent income hypothesis shows that income is a poor proxy for consumption even for households with low income levels (Friedman, 1957).

There can be a big difference between income and consumption, among other things. In some cases, income may understate actual living standards. For instance, in low-income areas peasants receive very little cash income but they consume what they grow (vegetables, grains, meat and poultry products) and wear what they produce. Furthermore, in many countries government provides subsidized transport facilities, public health services and food subsidies. Therefore, people's actual standard of living could be higher than their money income would permit. However, with the same level of income people's actual consumption could vary when they face different market prices for the same product in different areas due to the existence of a segmented market, rationing of commodities, or non-availability of required goods.

It is often believed that even in cases where both income and consumption data are obtained from a common survey and the sample selection and size are the same, the consumption data will be better than the income data for the measurement of poverty. First, people are more likely to understate their incomes in household surveys. For example, they may hide income from the black economy and other illegal income-earning activities. It should also be noted that household surveys exclude the homeless. Second, short-term variations in income are not likely to be matched by equal short-term variations in living standards.

Income suffers from both theoretical and practical difficulties as a welfare indicator in the developing countries. Incomes of a large portion of the population may vary from year to year, especially those of agricultural cultivators. There is a strong tendency for people with variable incomes to save in good years and to dis-save in bad. Thus a given year's income may not match a household's average level of welfare as measured by the consumption of goods and services over time. There are problems of accuracy and availability of income data in developing countries since records of household activities are often not kept.

Non-income measures

Physical units of consumption is an alternative to the income measure of welfare. The two main indicators considered are per capita food consumption and calorie intake, which are described below.

Per capita food consumption: Anand and Harris (1985) argue that per capita food consumption is a suitable indicator of human welfare as it has three advantages. First, data requirements are less stringent. Non-food consumption can be ignored, and associated problems, such as the estimation of the value of owner-occupied housing, are circumvented. Second, food consumption is likely to be more accurately reported in household surveys than non-food consumption.

Third, it is often easier to construct food price indices than to make price comparisons for non-food items (Glewwe and Gaag 1988).

Calorie intake: Several studies are based on calorie intake for fixing a poverty line in the literature on poverty in developing countries. The appeal of this approach lies in its objective foundation in nutritional studies. However, an indicator based on calories or expenditures linked with calories suffers from shortcomings. Some observers argue that, in the long run, indices of poverty based on physical consumption units are one-sided, partial and biased in the direction of exaggerating the poverty situation. When people's income increases, their food consumption does not increase proportionately, as the income elasticity of demand for food has always been less than one even for the poor. People are bound rather rigidly by traditional food habits which do not change very much even when they become more prosperous. Food poverty lingers on a bit longer than other forms of poverty. Thus indices of poverty based on calories or food consumption have a built-in depressing effect; they fail to note improvements in non-food poverty.

Second, several forms of poverty, for example, its non-income aspects such as lack of literacy, education, health (see above), housing and industrial consumer goods, are left out of the calorie and food-based indices. In this book we pay special attention to these non-income aspects, especially literacy, basic education and health.

Third, data on personal expenditure do not reflect massive consumption in the form of heavily subsidized hospital and clinic services. These data grossly understate poverty reduction through public goods (Khusro, 1999)

Households are basic consumption units and data on consumption or expenditure are usually collected on a family basis, but families are not homogeneous and do not have identical needs. The same level of income or expenditure of two households could end up with different welfare levels per capita because of the different size and composition of the households. Total family consumption is likely to overstate the welfare level of persons in a large household, since goods and services consumed must be divided among larger numbers of members. Similarly, even if the number of family members in two households is the same but one household has children and the other consists only of adults, the same level or magnitude of household income will make the household without children worse off because children may consume less. For example, according to some estimates households with a young child aged between 0 and 5 years has a general equivalence scale ranging from 1.16 to 1.24: the range is between 1.30 to 1.82 for households with a child aged between 5 and 16 years at low expenditure.[2] Equivalence scales have been developed to correct this distortion. They are designed to account for economies of scale in the provision of food to individuals in different types of households, and to give lower weights to additional household members when dividing the value of household consumption by household size.[3] Another technique to avoid some of the problems caused by differences in household size and composition is to specify different poverty lines for different types of households.

Determining a poverty line

The most difficult aspect of defining the concept of poverty is the determination of a standard by which the poor and the non-poor can be distinguished, that is, the setting of a poverty line.

In order to identify the poor, the first task is to find a yardstick, that is, a poverty line. Corresponding to the two concepts of poverty discussed above, there can be an absolute poverty line and a relative poverty line. An *absolute poverty line* does not change with a society's standard of living. People are defined as poor when some absolute needs are not adequately satisfied, that is, needs which are not directly related to the consumption pattern of other people in society. A *relative poverty line* is in some way related to the general standard of living in society. This poverty line will increase or decrease by the same percentage point as an increase or decrease in the standard of living. In other words, a completely absolute poverty line has an elasticity of 0 with respect to changes in the general standard of living in society, while a completely relative poverty line has an elasticity of 1 (Kilpatrick, 1973).

Objective and subjective approaches

Many methods have been proposed for determining a poverty line. Generally speaking, there are three approaches: objective approach, subjective approach and a combination of the two.

In an *objective approach*, criteria for a poverty line are based on objective assessment, for example scientific experiment, expert or professional opinions, or a political process. The process of determining a poverty line may be free from the influence of opinions of the potential population under consideration. The approach is objective in the sense that the decision-making process involves no value judgements by members of households in poverty. They have no say in determining consumption priorities and basic needs.

A *subjective approach*, however, allows an individual to state which income level is minimum, in the sense that below that income the individual is not able to make ends meet. The basic idea underlying this approach is that people are poor if they feel poor and that the best way to discover at what income this occurs is to ask them directly. The approach adopted by the Wisconsin Basic Needs Study (WBNS) (Colasanto *et al.*, 1984) is as follows.

Let Y_{min} be individual minimum income, which depends on one's own income Y and family size F_s (the number of family members), then

$$Y_{min} = f(Y, F_s) \qquad (1.1)$$

For a given family size F_s, there exists an income level Y^*_{min} such that

$$Y^*_{min} = f(Y^*_{min}, F_s) \qquad (1.2)$$

If an individual's income is $Y_i p Y^*_{min}$, then he lives in poverty and Y^*_{min} sets a poverty line.

In Hagenaars' (1986) study, the poverty thresholds are estimated on the basis of surveys in which individuals are directly asked the income levels they evaluate as 'good', 'bad', 'insufficient', and so on. The subjectivity of this approach lies in the fact that criteria for determining a poverty line are based on the opinion and feeling of the person concerned. In addition, this procedure is critically dependent on the assumption that individuals attach the same meaning to the words chosen for the survey (for example, 'good', 'bad') and that they can assign monetary values to these words.

In general, the subjective opinion of individuals about whether they consider themselves to be poor will be correlated with objective circumstances like income, family size, and so on. If a poverty line is derived by adopting a subjective approach, it may be biased or it may overestimate the real poverty line when policy intention is to support low-income families.[4] So it is rare that an official poverty line is set only on the basis of opinions of the poor.

Methods of determining a poverty line

Several methods are used in the literature on poverty lines (for technical details, see the appendix to this chapter). These are briefly described below.

(1) *Basic needs method:* This method: (a) defines basic needs, mainly the amount of foodstuffs required for sustaining life; (b) estimates the cost of food chosen; (c) transforms the cost of food into a poverty line. The pioneering studies on poverty lines (Rowntree, 1901) define families whose total earnings are insufficient to obtain the minimum necessities of life. Based on the results of experiments about the effect of diets on the maintenance of prisoners' body weight, Rowntree estimated the average nutritional needs of adults and children, translated these needs into quantities of different foods and into the cash equivalent of these foods. Minimum costs for clothing, fuel and other necessary outlays for a family were added. Rent was treated as an unavoidable addition to the total and was counted in full. The estimation of costs other than food was based on value judgement. Although this procedure poses many questions, it is quite straightforward, which explains why the same procedure in a modified form has been widely studied and used.[5] The main problem with this procedure is a value judgement on what constitutes 'basic needs' and the choice of a bundle of goods as a basis of estimating the poverty line.

The general poverty line measured in this way can be adjusted according to different circumstances and living conditions across regions and between urban and rural areas.

(2) *Food ratio method:* This method is based on the relationship between food expenditure and total income. A certain food–income ratio is taken to be the poverty threshold. The underlying principle on which this poverty line is based is the so-called Engel's Law, which states that the ratio of food expenditure to income declines when income increases. The Engel ratio takes a value between 0 and 1. At the extreme, if all income is spent on food, then the Engel ratio is 1; on the other hand, if no income is spent on food, the ratio is zero. Empirically, one third of this ratio is chosen to define the absolute poverty line. Thus families with an actual food–income ratio higher than this threshold are considered to be poor, and those with a lower food–income ratio are considered to be non-poor (Watts, 1967; Deaton and Muellbauer, 1980).

(3) *Percentage of mean or median income:* This method links the poverty line to some indicator of the standard of living in society. Some authors use the median income, which is the level of income above which 50 per cent of observations lie (Rein, 1971; Lansley, 1980). Others are in favour of using the mean income. They argue that the mean is a more stable point of reference for comparing income inequality in different countries for different years (e.g. Townsend, 1979). Whether the mean or the median is chosen, and whatever percentage is chosen, the resulting poverty line will always be completely relative with respect to the indicator chosen: if the indicator increases by 1 per cent, the poverty line will also increase by 1 per cent. This method is used mainly in the industrialized countries.

(4) *Percentile poverty line:* The percentile method is commonly applied to studies on income distribution. Therefore, it is based entirely on income inequality. Poverty is found in the lowest percentile, e.g. the lowest 10 or 20 per cent. The percentage of the poor according to the percentile poverty line is always fixed, so that attention focuses mainly on the share of aggregate income accruing to the bottom decile or quintile chosen, and to the composition of this lowest percentile. The poverty line measured by this method is completely relative: an increase in the standard of living of all individuals in society by a certain proportion will raise the poverty line by the same proportion.

(5) *Official poverty line*: There are two meanings attached to the so-called official poverty line. The first refers to the poverty line fixed by the government of a country as the official criterion and a basis of government policy towards the poor. The second refers to poverty researchers who adopt the official income support level as a poverty line. The official income support line may be fixed on the basis of scientific studies initially, but it may be adjusted over time in the light of the inflation rate and society's general

standard of living. Often it is an outcome of a political process and is thus sensitive to a government's budgetary situation.

From the above discussion we can see that the perception of poverty is, to a large extent, dependent on the conditions of society in which people live and the resources available to tackle the poverty problem. There is no perfectly satisfactory definition of poverty or method of determining a poverty line.

What explains poverty

Having considered various methods of determining poverty lines, it is now timely to discuss briefly the causal factors underlying poverty.

Thomas Malthus (1798) was the first person to explain the causes of poverty. He argued that overpopulation generates scarcity, and scarcity in turn causes poverty. Malthus delineated his theory by presenting the so-called 'Malthus rations', that is, the population growth outpaces the rate of increase in food supply.

Poverty takes many forms. Some scholars define it in terms of its structural and conjunctural facets (see Iliffe, 1987). The former is the long-term poverty of individuals due to their personal or social circumstances, whereas conjunctural poverty is temporary or 'transient'. There are two kinds of structural poverty. People who are in poverty in a society with rich natural resources (such as land) lack access to the labour needed to exploit them, because they are incapacitated, elderly or young. In a resource-scarce society these people are also poor and include those among the able-bodied who lack access to land and other resources and are unable to sell their labour power at a price sufficient to meet their basic needs.

Marx attributed poverty and misery to exploitative institutions: the capitalist society in which primitive capital accumulation took the form of brutally depriving people's means of production and forcing them to become wage proletarians. Low wages and poor working conditions produce massive poverty.

In his investigation into the causes of poverty in Asia (mainly India) Myrdal finds that one of the main attributes of rural poverty is social and economic inequality. The lower the income per capita in a country, the more severely the poor would suffer as a result of economic and social inequality (Myrdal, 1968). Galbraith (1979) distinguishes between two forms of poverty: minority poverty and mass poverty. The former occurs in a predominantly affluent community, the causes of which vary. However, Galbraith is much more concerned with mass poverty. He disagrees with the common explanations of mass poverty, that is: (1) scarce natural resources and lack of physical endowments (e.g. poor, arid and insufficient land); (2) failures of government policies; (3) lack of capital for development, educated people, experienced technical and administrative talent (these could be the consequences of poverty); (4) deterioration of developing-country terms of trade with industrialized countries. Galbraith argues that the causes of mass poverty in developing countries are linked to the equilibrium of poverty and accommodation to poverty. People who have lived for centuries in poverty have come to terms with this existence. They are satisfied with whatever incomes they can get through the sale of whatever goods and services. Some religious doctrines are responsible for this kind of behaviour. The poor believe that they will pass through the eye of the needle into paradise, whilst the rich with the camels can only remain outside.

One explanation of the causes of poverty is the so-called culture of poverty. Whatever the original causes of poverty, it will generate itself if it develops into a kind of culture. The culture of poverty is both adaptation and reaction of the poor to their marginal position in a class-stratified, highly individualistic capitalist society. It represents an effort to cope with feelings of hopelessness and despair that develop from the realization of the improbability of achieving success in terms of society's values and goals. It is easy to help people in the culture of poverty to get enough food to eat, but it is more difficult to get them out of the vicious circle (Lewis, 1969). In this book we accept that the perception of Chinese minorities about their poverty may in part be cultural and fatalistic. However, this is not to suggest that the economic factors causing poverty are not important. The latter may indeed be crucial.

People's attitudes towards poverty change as time goes on. There was a characteristic prejudice against the poor in the nineteenth century. At that time, the well-established law divided vagrants into three classes: idle and disorderly persons, rogues and vagabonds, and incorrigible rogues. Poverty was described as 'pauperism', 'vagrancy' and 'mendicancy' (Davis, 1979–80). It used to be seen as a condition of life and thus a necessary element in society. It was believed that the labouring poor could only be driven to work hard if they felt the spur of want. 'Fear of want is the only effectual motive to industry with the labouring poor: remove that fear, and they cease to be industrious' (*Encyclopaedia Britannica*, 1929, 4th edition).

It was not until the end of the nineteenth century that the vast increase in general wealth and well-being offered by a modern technological society led to a significant change in people's attitudes towards the poor. Starting from the 1960s, concern about the poor in the Western world has been confined not only to the notion of calorie-based poverty but also to the social and psychological consequences of poverty as 'rediscovered' in the US and the UK.

However, opinions in a society can never be uniform. This is also the case for poverty. It is not difficult to find many people who attribute poor living conditions to the poor themselves. What we can see is that the more some people work or the more property they have, the higher their income. The higher the prices (that is, wages, rents, interest and profits) they receive for each unit of work or of resources, the more their income grows. It follows that low income or poverty is related to the absence or lack of wage or resource income. People below the poverty line often own little or no property, often do not or cannot work, or if they do work, they are paid very low wages. The attitude of many middle-income people towards the poor is that they are poor because they do not want to work, they are lazy and incompetent, or they are profligate and careless with their money. Others say that the poor are poor because they do not save and invest, or they are morally inferior, they breed excessive numbers of children who grow up to add to the poverty population, or they are genetically inferior (see Brinker and Klos 1976). In this book we examine whether Chinese minorities suffer from these poverty characteristics. But before turning to the particular case of minorities, it is necessary to briefly examine overall poverty in China and in its southern and western provinces.

Nature and causes of poverty in China

Against the above background we need to examine the evolution of poverty in China during the transition period since the reforms. Much has been written on the nature, extent and seriousness of poverty and income inequalities in China (see Table 1.1 for a brief review of recent studies). It is not our intention here to present an exhaustive survey of this growing literature. Instead, we present some broad trends of regional variations in poverty over time. Our main concern in this book is with the poverty among minorities. None of the poverty studies examine this issue, partly owing to the lack of disaggregated data.

There are disputes about the level at which a poverty line should be set and how welfare should be measured, whether to use income or consumption data, how to value own consumption and rental income of own housing and so on. Estimates of rural poverty and the number of rural poor vary depending on the assumptions made. These disputes partly explain the apparently conflicting estimates of rural poverty by Khan and Riskin (2001) and Riskin *et al.* (2001). The former estimate a reduction of between 13 and 28 per cent in rural poverty (headcount index) depending on the definition of poverty and the consumer price index used. On the other hand, Riskin *et al.* (2001: 337) find that 'the headcount rate of poverty in 1995 ... is virtually identical with the headcount rate in 1988'. Thus they show that the incidence of rural poverty did not decline between 1988 and 1995, and that the absolute number of rural poor increased because of the growth in rural population. One explanation for the discrepancy between the two sets of estimates is the treatment of the rental value of private housing: while Riskin *et al.* exclude it, Khan and Riskin include it in income.

Poverty in China is generally measured in terms of the head-count ratio, the poverty-gap ratio and the weighted poverty-gap ratio. The latter two measure the intensity of poverty, whereas the first ratio does not (for a technical analysis of these ratios and their measurement, see the appendix in this chapter). Most studies show that the incidence of poverty in China declined significantly in the 1980s and 1990s. The Chinese official estimates show that rural poverty declined from over 30 per cent in 1978 to less than 5 per cent at the end of 1998. Results based on an international poverty line ($1a day) show that while rural poverty has indeed been declining, a larger share of the population, that is, about 11.5 per cent

Table 1.1 Poverty and inequality studies on China

Study/author	Year	Poverty incidence	Causal factors
Bhalla *et al.*	(2003a)	In terms of GDP per capita, convergence occurred during 1952–97 within subregions but not between subregions. Analysis is based on Markovian chains and generalized entropy decomposition. Regional income inequalities widened since the reforms, leading to two income clubs – the rich east and the poor central and west regions. There is no evidence of club formation in the pre-reform period.	Rising inequality in China is explained by (1) nature of the Dengist development strategy, (2) spatial factors, (3) opening up of coastal cities, (4) initial disadvantages of the western region, and lack of human and physical capital.
Bhalla *et al.*	(2003b)	Presents a long-term view of income inequality from 1952 to 1999, examining contribution of intra-regional, interregional, rural, urban and rural–urban inequalities to overall inequality. Both rural–urban and regional inequalities increased in the reform period.	Over 70 per cent of interprovincial inequality in 1999 and all the increase in interprovincial inequality after 1978 is explained by inter-regional inequality.
Riskin and Li	(2001)	Challenges the broad record of recent declines in rural poverty. Using household survey data for 1988 and 1995, the authors show at best 'a constant poverty rate and a growing absolute number of rural poor' (p. 17).	Poverty and growing inequality are caused by market liberalization.
Weiss	(2002)	Regional inequality between urban and rural areas and between rich and poor provinces increased during 1981-99.The western region (southwest and northwest) has a significantly higher incidence of rural poverty compared with the national average.	Locational factors do not have any significant explanatory power. Changes in grain production and prices to farmers are important factors explaining rural poverty.
World Bank	(2001)	Decline in rural poverty but absolute poverty higher than the official SSB estimates suggest.	Poverty is explained mainly by rural–urban and regional inequalities.
Yao and Zhang	(2001a)	Decline in rural poverty in the 1980s due to an increase in agricultural productivity; rise in inequality in the 1990s.	

or about 106 million people, remain in poverty (World Bank, 2001: 1). During the 1990s rural poverty is alleged to have been concentrated mainly in the remote areas of the southwest provinces with substantial minority populations. The severity of poverty as measured by the squared poverty gap index is shown to be highest for the northwest region (Gansu, Inner Mongolia, Ningxia, Qinghai, Shaanxi, Xinjiang) followed by the southwest region (Guangxi, Guizhou, Sichuan, Tibet, Yunnan). In 1996 the severity of poverty is shown to be higher in the northeast (0.52) than in the southwest (0.49) (Table 1.2).

Southwest China is one of the poorest regions of the country. In terms of the head-count ratio, poverty was reduced in Guizhou, Guangxi and Yunnan from 1995 to 1997 (see Table 1.3). However, in Yunnan the poverty incidence increased in 1998 and 1999. The poverty gap and weighted poverty gap ratios suggest that the poorest may not have benefited as much especially in Yunnan. What explains this situation? Could the increase in poverty incidence be attributed to a fall in the price of tobacco, which is the main cash crop of Yunnan? Table 1.3 gives only a general picture of rural poverty, covering the poverty villages under the World Bank-funded project. It is not clear whether the poverty trends among the minorities are similar to the averages shown above. For example, have the preferential policies in favour of the minorities (see Chapter 2) led to a decline in the incidence of poverty? Have the income gaps between the minorities and non-minorities narrowed over time? Anecdotal evidence suggests that, despite preferential policies, income gaps have actually widened (see Sautman, 1999, and Chapter 2).

The southwest region includes provinces in which inequality defined in terms of the Gini coefficients is well above the average based on per capita province-level data on income. For example, in all four provinces (Guangxi, Guizhou, Sichuan and Yunnan) the Gini coefficients are higher than this average (Table 1.4). Overall Gini coefficients as well as rural and urban ones are the highest for Yunnan, suggesting greater income inequalities there than in the other three provinces. This is confirmed by the low rural income shares of the lowest 40 per cent of households. However, the urban income share of the lowest 40 per cent of

Table 1.2 Regional severity of poverty in China: squared gap ratios (1991 and 1996)

	1991	*1996*
National	1.19	0.59
North	1.32	0.27
Northeast	1.36	0.52
East	0.76	0.03
Central	1.05	0.17
Southwest	0.77	0.49
Northwest	1.75	1.45

Source: World Bank (2001).

Table 1.3 Poverty incidence in southwest China (1995–99) (%)

	1995	1996	1997	1998	1999
Guizhou					
Head-count ratio	34.5	31.3	25.4	21.2	20.1
Poverty-gap ratio	5.8	6.9	4.0	4.0	3.5
Weighted poverty-gap ratio	1.2	2.4	0.98	1.05	1.11
Guangxi					
Head-count ratio	26.8	22.1	18.6	11.8	8.7
Poverty-gap ratio	5.1	4.8	3.9	2.8	1.9
Weighted poverty-gap ratio	1.04	1.6	1.28	0.9	0.6
Sichuan					
Head-count ratio	–	–	26.7	19.3	14.2
Poverty-gap ratio	–	–	3.5	2.5	2.3
Weighted poverty-gap ratio	–	–	1.2	0.9	0.7
Yunnan					
Head-count ratio	33.4	27.0	20.0	24.2	27.3
Poverty-gap ratio	6.5	6.2	2.9	4.8	5.9
Weighted poverty-gap ratio	1.5	2.0	0.9	1.4	1.7

– = not available
Source: LGOPAD, 1999.

Table 1.4 Income inequalities in southwest China (1992, 1994)

Province	Gini coefficient	Rural Gini coefficient	Rural income shares (lowest 40% of households)	Urban Gini coefficient	Urban income shares (%) (lowest 40% of house-holds)
	1992	*1992*	*(%)*	*1994*	*1994*
Nation (province-level data)	0.1484	0.1437		0.0910	
Nation (county-level data)	0.3519	0.2003		0.1448	
Guangxi	0.2455	0.1710	–	0.0475	27.7
Guizhou	0.3385	0.1770	26.2	0.0386	26.0
Sichuan	0.3038	0.1752	27.1	0.0445	26.2
Yunnan	0.3886	0.2515	22.2	0.0499	28.3

Source: Lin *et al.* (1998) for Gini coefficients; UNDP (1997a) for income shares.

households in Yunnan is higher than that of the other three provinces, suggesting lower urban inequality.

So far only income aspects of poverty have been discussed. But poverty manifests also in terms of non-income indicators, as we discussed above. Even though the southwest provinces are among the poorest by income indicators, as we shall discuss in Chapter 2, they have made good progress judged by capability indicators, namely, adult literacy rates, gross enrolment ratios and human development index (see Chapter 2).

Studies abound on the analysis of income and consumption inequalities in China (e.g. Jalan and Ravallion, 1998a, 1998b, 1999; Yao and Zhang, 2001a; Khan and Riskin, 2001; Riskin *et al.*, 2001). Most of these studies conclude that income inequalities in China have become worse since the economic reforms in 1978. Interregional inequality across the Chinese provinces has widened over time, whether it is measured by GDP per capita or per capita consumption expenditures. Regional inequality became particularly serious during the 1990s despite rapid economic growth (Zhang and Yao, 2001). The high overall inequality in China is attributed mainly to growing income disparities between rural and urban areas and between coastal and inland areas. The heavy industry development strategy during the pre-reform era, and the policies favouring coastal areas over hinterland, have accounted for regional inequality (Yang, 2002). In addition urban-biased fiscal and monetary policies may have further aggravated inequality (Yang and Cai, 2003).

Some scholars (e.g. Yao and Zhang, 2001a) attribute poverty to geographical factors. This factor underlies the locational thesis of poverty in rural and remote mountainous areas. It challenges the trickledown theory under which growth should benefit all areas. The geographical explanation suggests that the spillover effects of growth centres are lower, the greater is the distance. For example, the western and southern provinces are too far from the coastal growth poles to benefit much. Vast areas here are not suitable for agricultural production and suffer from low land productivity. Their remoteness means that transportation costs are high. This may partly explain why there has not been much income convergence during the reform period, which would be expected under the neoclassical model. In reality, divergent growth clubs have emerged. A recent empirical study by Weiss (2002) attempts to quantify the effect of the geographical factor, which is measured by the proportion of mountainous counties in the total number of counties in each province. It is assumed that inaccessible areas or unfavourable ecological conditions weaken the impact of growth on poverty reduction. Preliminary regression results led Weiss to conclude that 'there is no evidence that the growth–poverty mechanism works differently in the West as compared with elsewhere in the country' (p. 17). However, this conclusion may simply suggest that the proxy used for the geographical factor is not appropriate.

Our concern in this book is to examine whether the above aggregate picture about poverty (mainly rural) applies equally to poverty among Chinese minorities living mainly in the southwest and western parts of China.

Non-income indicators of poverty

So far we have considered only income and consumption indicators of poverty, which alone are not sufficient to explain poverty in China. Non-income indicators also remain relevant. These relate to such factors as access to non-market goods like education and health, child nutritional status and gender disparities. These indicators for China and several Asian countries are presented in Table 1.5. China's position does not compare favourably with other Southeast Asian countries on the basis of all the indicators considered. For example, China's infant mortality rate is much higher than that in Malaysia, Singapore and Sri Lanka. Similarly, the adult illiteracy rate for Chinese females is much higher, except in comparison with India. On the other hand, China's child malnutrition rate is lower than that in other countries for which data are available.

Within China, Table 1.6 compares access indicators including those for health and education in four southwestern provinces (Guangxi, Guizhou, Sichuan and Yunnan) which have significant minority populations (except Sichuan). There are wide variations especially in respect of the proportion of immunized children in 1999. Guizhou, a province with the highest share of minority population among the four provinces, recorded the lowest proportion (56 per cent), compared to Sichuan (98 per cent), which has the lowest share of minority population. There are also interprovincial differences in respect of gender and education indicators, e.g. ratio of female students to total number of students, and enrolment rates for girls compared to those for boys. The non-income indicators improved appreciably between 1997 and 1999 in Guangxi, Guizhou and Yunnan (the 1997 data not reported here as they are not available for Sichuan).

Ethnicity and poverty

Before showing links between ethnicity and poverty, it is essential to consider what ethnicity means. The concept of ethnicity has several connotations: language, culture and religion, and racial affinity. Ethnicity is a complex social phenomenon because it is multi-faceted; it is sometimes equated with social fractionalization (Collier, 1999, 2000). But linguistic and ethnic diversity need not necessarily lead to social fractionalization considering that many ethnic groups may not be very distinct politically and socially. Despite the existence of several ethnic groups, China remains less heterogeneous than a similarly large-sized country like India.

Ethnic homogeneity is considered conducive to growth, as it is assumed to minimize the scope for unrest and civil strife generally associated with ethnic

Table 1.5 Health and education indicators for China and other Asian countries

Country	Indicator								
	Infant mortality rate (per 1,000 live births)		Child malnutrition (% of children under 5)	Life expectancy at birth (years) 1998		Adult illiteracy rate (% of people 15 and above) 1998		Net secondary enrolment (% of relevant age group)	
	1980	1998	1992–98	Male	Female	Male	Female	1980	1997
China	42	31	16	68	72	9	25	63	70
India	115	70	–	62	64	33	57	41	60
Indonesia	90	43	34	64	67	9	20	42	56
Korea, Rep. of	26	9	–	69	76	1	4	76	100
Malaysia	30	8	20	70	75	9	18	48	64
Philippines	52	32	30	67	71	5	5	72	78
Singapore	12	4	–	75	79	4	12	66	76
Sri Lanka	34	16	38	71	76	6	12	59	76
Thailand	49	29	–	70	75	3	7	25	48
Japan	8	4	–	77	84	–	–	93	100

Source: World Bank (2000).

Table 1.6 Non-income indicators of poverty in southwest China (1999)

Indicator	Guizhou	Guangxi	Yunnan	Sichuan
Access indicators				
Villages with electricity (%)	100	95	97	97
Villages linked by highway (%)	95	95	94	86
Villages with primary school (%)	87	100	100	86
Villages with qualified health attendants (%)	76	97	100	94
Children with distance to school 1–2 km (%)	73*	61*	80*	–
Education				
Enrolment rate of children aged 7–15 years	88	91	84	96
Gender and education				
Qualified female teachers (%)	26	35	31	21
Female teachers to total teachers (%)	26	36	33	22
Female students to total students (%)	39	46	43	48
Enrolment rate of girls aged 7–12 years	85	96	89	98
Enrolment rate of girls aged 13–15 years	86	78	70	87
Enrolment rate of boys aged 7–12 years	92	96	88	98
Enrolment rate of boys aged 13–15 years	88	92	75	98
Health				
Number of immunized children	44	51	62	56
Percentage of immunized children	56	82	85	98

Note: Data relate to project villages under the World Bank-funded Poverty Reduction Project in
    southwest China.
Source: LGOPAD, 1999.

diversity. For example, Easterly and Levine (1997) show that slow economic growth is associated with a high degree of ethnic diversity, which is believed to encourage political and social instability, the poor provision of education and other public goods like health and infrastructure and poor economic policies which slow down economic growth. Their argument is presented to explain the dismal economic performance in Africa, one of the most ethnically diverse regions in the world. Easterly and Levine undertake a cross-section study based on data for all countries (excluding the Gulf Oil states) for which the average annual rate of growth of GDP per capita was available for the 1960s, 1970s and 1980s. The empirical results show that ethnic diversity is strongly correlated with low levels of education and infrastructure and a low level of income per worker.

The argument that ethnic diversity leads to slower growth and thereby greater poverty stems from a number of assumptions. First, it assumes that ethnic diversity reduces trust among different groups, which raises transaction costs and lowers incomes. Undoubtedly, social capital in the form of mutual trust and goodwill exists within the ethnic group but it may well be at the expense of other groups in society. The existence of social capital has to be society-wide in order to have a positive impact on growth. Second, ethnic diversity can raise poverty and lower economic and social well-being by reducing the effectiveness of delivery of public services, as is shown by an empirical study using data for US cities (Alesina *et al.,* 1999). Third, ethnic minorities tend to be less mobile than other social groups, which means that they have less access to income-earning opportunities and to goods and services (see Chapters 6 and 7).

Finally, ethnic minority groups may suffer from discriminatory economic and social policies designed by a majority government in power which looks after the interests of its own social groups. This argument further assumes that the government in power represents a dominant group in society, which may not necessarily be the case. In fact, as we discuss in subsequent chapters (particularly Chapter 6), China has introduced positive discrimination (affirmative action) in favour of its ethnic minorities.

It is likely that in a fragmented society no single ethnic group dominates. In such a situation different ethnic groups may more or less neutralize each other's power and prevent dominance of a particular group. Thus discrimination might be minimized (Collier, 2001). But 'dominance' and 'fractionalization' may not be independent, in which case the outcome would become more complex. In China, concentration of ethnic minorities in the southwest region does not lead to their dominance over the Han majority.

Collier (2000) argues that the nature of the political environment determines whether ethnicity adversely affects economic growth. He claims that there are no adverse effects under a democratic regime with plentiful political rights. It is the lack of political rights under a dictatorship that is likely to have an adverse effect on economic growth. Lack of political rights encourages rent-seeking which may benefit an ethnic elite, thus worsening income inequality. As we show in Chapter 3, the above argument does not apply to China, which is a non-democratic regime where political liberalization has not yet gone hand in hand with economic liberalization. Yet China has achieved one of the most impressive economic growth rates in history. Even in southwest China, which is ethnically more diverse, the economic growth rates of many provinces are quite high, though not as high as in coastal provinces (see Chapter 3).

Socioeconomic data on Chinese ethnic minorities are quite sparse. Three sources are available: (1) population censuses, (2) ethnic statistical yearbooks, and (3) household surveys such as the ones undertaken in 1988 and 1995 by the Chinese Academy of Social Sciences (CASS) and foreign scholars. While all these data sources are useful, they are not fully adequate for a proper analysis of poverty and inequality among ethnic minorities of China. Each suffers from some deficiencies. For example, the population censuses do not contain any socioeconomic data; they cover only demographic statistics, and occupational and educational profiles of nationalities and Han Chinese populations. The 2000 Census of Population does not give data on literacy or educational attainment by nationality, thus making it difficult to assess changes over time.

Second, ethnic statistical yearbooks are infrequent and fail to capture the entire poor minority population. Many of the poor ethnic groups live outside the autonomous areas. According to the 1999 Ethnic Statistical Yearbook, only 45 per cent of the ethnic minorities in 1998 lived in the autonomous areas. This ratio remained almost constant between 1990 and 1998. Some estimates suggest that nearly half the poor are outside the designated poor counties (Riskin and Li, 2001). Since the bulk of the poor are from ethnic minorities, they may have been beyond the reach of the anti-poverty policies and measures targeted at the poor counties (see Chapter 6).

Third, the CASS household surveys of 1988 and 1995, though an improvement on earlier household surveys, also suffer from several weaknesses. Despite some adjustments made to the official SSB surveys, they continue to suffer from the basic problems of the official surveys, which use a narrow definition of income and do not estimate the rental value of housing (see Chapter 3).

Appendix to Chapter 1

The measurement of poverty

In this appendix to Chapter 1, we first show how various poverty lines are derived. We then discuss the problem of aggregation and measurement. All poverty line definitions are based on certain assumptions. They reflect the criteria and methods used for judging the welfare level of a population. It is assumed that money income is a good measure of people's welfare. In other words, it amounts to saying that income enables the satisfaction of all basic needs. The method of deriving a poverty line can be different even when the same poverty approach and definition are adopted.

Poverty lines derived following basic-needs approach

Rowntree's poverty line

Rowntree first calculates the minimum cost of food, to which he adds the minimum cost of other expenditure items. The total costs become an income threshold to separate the poor from the rest of the population. Thus we have Rowntree's poverty line as follows.

$$z_1 = c_1 + c_2 = c_1(x_1, p_2) + c_2(x_2, p_2) \qquad \text{(A.1.1)}$$

where c_1 and c_2 represent the minimum spending on food and on other necessities respectively.

Friedman's poverty line

Friedman (1965) proposes another method to derive a poverty line based on minimum food expenditure c_1, in which the Engel coefficient of the poor needs to be known in the first place. The poverty line is obtained by multiplying food expenditure c_1 by the inverse Engel ratio ε_0^{-1}.

.

$$z_2 = c_1 \varepsilon_0^{-1} = c_1 \left(\frac{y}{c_1} \right) \tag{A.1.2}$$

where c_1 is the minimum food expenditure, and y total income.

Conceptually this method has a shortcoming of circular reasoning because in order to obtain the Engel coefficient of the poor it is necessary first to identify who the poor are. However, if the poor can be identified, there is little point in deriving a poverty line.

Poverty line based on the food-ratio method

The poverty line in this case is derived on the basis of the ratio of food expenditure to total income. Let it be r. A maximum value r_0 can be set. If the ratio for an individual or an income unit turns out to be greater than r_0, then the parties concerned can be identified as poor.

The relationship between expenditure on food c_1 and family income y in a community can be expressed by a double log-linear Engel function as follows.

$$\ln c_1 = \alpha_0 + \alpha_1 \ln y \tag{A.1.3}$$

We know that

$$\ln r_0 = \ln \frac{c_1}{y} \tag{A.1.4}$$

and substituting (A.1.3) into (A.1.4) yields

$$\ln r_0 = \alpha_0 + (\alpha_1 - 1)\ln y \tag{A.1.5}$$

Thus the poverty line z_3 corresponding to r_0, which is the solution for y, in terms of an income threshold:[1]

$$z_3 = \exp\left(\frac{\alpha_0 - \ln r_0}{1 - \alpha_1} \right) \tag{A.1.6}$$

Poverty line derived from the percentage of mean or median income

Suppose there are n income units in a society and the income vector in an ascending sequence can be expressed as:

$$y_1, y_2, \cdots, y_n \quad \text{or } y_i \ (i = 1, 2, \ldots, n) \tag{A.1.7}$$

The mean income is

$$\bar{y} = \frac{1}{n}\sum_{i=1}^{n} y_i \tag{A.1.8}$$

A poverty line based on the mean value of income will be

$$z_4 = \delta \, \bar{y} \tag{A.1.9}$$

The focus here should be the determination of the value of coefficient δ, which is also dependent on the income level of $\bar{y}$. It may well be that, on average, all the people are poor if the general standard of living is very low in a society. In practice, in most cases the value of δ is set at a level between 0.50 and 0.80.[2]

Some scholars prefer to use a median value of income than a mean value.[3] A median is the income value in the middle of income units arranged in an ascending or descending order, which divides total income population into two equal parts. A median value of income in a community is obtained when an even number of income units or the numbers in the middle are divided by 2. The advantage of using a median income is that it can avoid some outliers.

The poverty line is derived as follows:

$$z_5 = \varphi \, y_d \tag{A.1.10}$$

where y_d is median income.

Again we face the task of determining the coefficient ϕ.

Percentile poverty line

Let η_0 be the percentile of income distribution at which the poverty line income level is chosen

$$\int_{-\infty}^{\ln z_5} dF(\ln y; \mu_y, \sigma_y) = \eta_0 \tag{A.1.11}$$

where $F(\ln y; \mu_y, \sigma_y)$ is the distribution function of log-incomes, σ_y is the standard deviation of log-incomes and μ_y changes in mean-log-income.

If, for instance, the income distribution is log-normal, the poverty line is derived by

$$z_6 = \exp(N^{-1}(\eta_0)\sigma_y + \mu_y) \tag{A.1.12}$$

This poverty line depends on both average income and income inequality.

Synthesis of a poverty line

Sen (1979) argues that different aspects of poverty could lead to defining two poverty lines. Kakwani (1984), following Sen's line of reasoning, introduces a general poverty line which consists of two components of poverty. One is nutritional poverty, under which the consumption level of an individual or a family is nutritionally inadequate; the second is 'cultural' poverty, which means that the level of income of some people is not adequate to meet the needs defined in terms of the overall living standards of a society.

A general poverty line should reflect both *absolute* and *relative* aspects of poverty. Thus such a poverty line takes the following form:

$$z_7 = z(\beta) = z_0 + \beta\,(\mu_y - z_0) \tag{A.1.13}$$

where z_0 is the nutritional poverty line income and μ_y denotes either the median or the mean income of a society. β lies in the range 0 to 1, which implies that the poverty line can be neither lower than z_0 nor higher than the mean or median income of society. The value of β depends on the society's value judgement about the minimum standard of living which all its members must enjoy.

Measurement of poverty

There is considerable interest in finding an aggregate indicator of poverty, whether poverty is defined as an absolute or a relative concept. The essence of the poverty measurement is how, given a poverty line, the extent of poverty can be summarized at aggregate levels: a country, a province or a community. There is no easy solution; the subject is full of controversy and debates in the poverty literature. In this section, first of all, we review the traditional measurement of poverty. We then discuss new approaches to it.

In order to measure the extent of poverty we first need some notation for income distribution which can be expressed using discrete notation or continuous notation. In the discrete case, if income is arranged in an ascending order and the poverty line is *z*, we have the following expression:

$$y_1 \leq y_2 \leq \cdots \leq y_m \leq z \leq y_{m+1} \leq \cdots \leq y_n \tag{A.2.1}$$

where i ($1, 2, \cdots, n$): income-receiving unit

y_i: the income of unit i

and there are m units below the poverty line.

In the continuous case, let the density and cumulative density functions of income y be given respectively by:

$$f(y); F(y) \qquad\qquad (A.2.2)$$

and let y lie between $\underline{y}$ and $\bar{y}$.

Head-count measurement

The simplest method of measuring the extent of poverty is to count the number of people below a selected poverty line, and then divide this number by the total population. Thus is the poverty index of the so-called head-count ratio derived. This is the conventional measure of poverty commonly used in studies on poverty.

Assuming n is the total number of people in the community in question and m the number of people below the poverty line z, using the notation above the head-count ratio is given as follows:

$$H = \frac{m}{n} \qquad\qquad (A.2.3)$$

or $\quad H = F(z) \qquad\qquad (A.2.4)$

in the continuous case.

A serious flaw of this measure is that it only provides the number of people below the poverty line but fails to reflect the *intensity* of poverty suffered by the poor. This measure does not tell us how far below the poverty line the incomes of the poor will fall (Sen, 1981; Clark *et al.*, 1981). The head-count ratio remains unchanged when a previously poor family becomes even poorer. Furthermore, H could be reduced simply by making some people poorer. For example, policy makers may be tempted to transfer some income from income units far below the poverty line to income units just below the poverty line because some of the poor may live just below the poverty threshold but others could be far below it. This measure can also be misleading for making comparisons of the same community at different times, or across communities at the same time.

Poverty-gap ratio

The United States Social Security Administration proposed the poverty-gap ratio to overcome the problems involved in the head-count ratio (Batchelder, 1971). It assumes that the deviation of a poor man's income from the poverty line is proportional to the degree of misery suffered by him or her (Kakwani, 1980b).

In the literature on poverty different authors use different concepts such as income gap, income-gap ratio, poverty gap, and poverty-gap ratio. Often these concepts are used interchangeably, which causes confusion. Therefore, it would be helpful to explore the meanings of different terms.

The first is the income gap. The income gap I_i of any income unit is defined as the difference between the poverty line z and the income of the unit y_i:

$$I_i = z\text{-}y_i \qquad (\text{i} = 1,2,\cdots, \text{n}) \tag{A.2.5}$$

It is easy to see that the income gap I_i will be positive for the poor and negative for others.

The second term is the poverty gap, which is the shortfall of the income units below the poverty line:

$$P_i = z - y_i \qquad (\text{i} = 1,2,\cdots \text{m}) \tag{A.2.6}$$

The average income gap for a community is often expressed as the average poverty income per capita of the population, whereas the total poverty income gap is borne by every member of the community:

$$I_g = \frac{1}{n}\sum_{i=1}^{m}(z - y_i) \tag{A.2.7}$$

Now we come to the concept of the income-gap ratio[4] which reflects a relationship between the poverty line and the average population-shared income gap in a community.

$$I_r = \frac{I_g}{z} \tag{A.2.8}$$

The value of I_r is not really an indication of the intensity of poverty,[5] but of the degree of difficulty facing the community if all the poor are to be bailed out of poverty. The smaller the I_r, the easier the task of poverty elimination and *vice versa*. Obviously, the value of I_r depends on how the poverty line is defined and how prosperous a society is.

The average poverty gap expressed by (A.2.9) is the income gap between the average income of the population below the poverty line and the poverty threshold income level:

$$P_g = \frac{1}{m}\sum_{i=1}^{m}(z - y_i) \tag{A.2.9}$$

The average poverty gap indicates income difference between the average income of the poor people and the poverty line which distinguishes between the poor and non-poor. P_g is definitely a positive figure, which indicates the amount of income that must be transferred to the poor so that everyone's income below the poverty line could be raised to the threshold z, that is, average income per capita needed to bail the poor out of poverty.

The poverty-gap ratio is an indicator of how poor people are under a certain poverty line. It can be denoted in the discrete and continuous cases respectively as follows:

$$P_r = \frac{P_g}{z} = \frac{1}{zm} \sum_{i=1}^{m} (z - y_i) \tag{A.2.10}$$

$$P_r = \frac{1}{zF(z)} \int_{\underline{y}}^{z} (z - y) f(y) dy \tag{A.2.11}$$

Thus the poverty-gap ratio P_r provides adequate information about the *intensity* of poverty in individual cases. It also gives information on the efforts needed to eliminate poverty in a society.[6] This measure supplements the head-count ratio in various ways. First, it helps us to avoid misleading results, which could be obtained from comparative studies of poverty across countries or over time, or between different family types within a country at any given time.

As we noted above, the use of the head-count measure alone can be quite inadequate. It is possible that the proportion of population below the poverty line is roughly the same in two countries but in one the income of the poor falls much further below the poverty line. Second, the head-count measure could tempt policy makers to allocate available funds not to the poorest but rather to the poor whose income is just below the poverty line (Beckerman, 1979, 1981). On the other hand, the drawback of the poverty-gap measure *vis-à-vis* the head-count measure is that it is insensitive to the number of people in poverty. It does not take account of inequality of income distribution among the poor.

Sen's axiomatic approach

Sen is critical of the head-count ratio and the poverty-gap ratio. He proposes a new index, the so-called ordinalist axiomatic approach (Sen, 1976).

He introduces the following two basic axioms:[7]

Monotonicity axiom: other things remaining the same, a reduction in income of a person below the poverty line must increase the poverty measure;
Transfer axiom: other things remaining the same, a pure transfer of income from a person below the poverty line to anyone who is richer must increase the poverty measure.

There are two general lines of argument underlying these axioms. The first depends on comparisons of utility gains and losses in a world where the marginal utility of income is positive but diminishing. If the utility functions of the poor are identical (or differ by a constant function), any regressive transfer among the poor will lower the utility of the 'giver' by more than the increase in the utility of the 'receiver'. This 'net loss in utility' between the two poor persons might then be interpreted as leading to an increase in poverty. The second is Sen's argument in terms of a notion of relative deprivation, when a regressive transfer takes place from a more deprived to a less deprived person. Sen concludes that 'in a straightforward sense the overall relative deprivation is increased' (Sen, 1981).

It is obvious that the head-count ratio as a measure of poverty violates both axioms and the poverty-gap index satisfies the Monotonicity axiom but violates the Transfer axiom. Neither H nor P_r gives adequate information on the exact income distribution among the poor.

Sen derives his index of poverty by combining the head-count ratio H and the poverty-gap ratio P_r, and at the same time by taking into account income distribution among the poor. At the heart of the Sen measure lies the notion of a ranking of the poor. When there are two persons with the same income, the poorest person has a rank of m, while the poor person closest to the poverty line has a rank of 1.

$$P_s = H \left[P_r + (1 - P_r) G_p \right] \qquad (A.2.12)$$

where G_p is the Gini coefficient of the income distribution among the poor. Note that P_s is initially defined as a normalized weighted sum of the poverty gaps $(z - y_i)$ of all the poor in the community:

$$P_s = A \sum_{i \in S(Y_m)} v_i (z - y_i) \qquad (A.2.13)$$

where A is a constant term for a normalization and v_i are non-negative weights.

The axiom of ordinal rank weights states that the weight v_i on the poverty gap of person i equals the rank order of i in the interpersonal welfare ordering of the poor, that is,

$$v_i = m + 1 - i \qquad (A.2.14)$$

If we assume that all the poor have exactly the same income level, then the poverty index reduces to the following form:

$$P_s = H P_r \qquad (A.2.15)$$

Takayama (1979) points out that Sen's procedure contradicts the argument that poverty is essentially a relative notion, which is Sen's view. The ranking in Sen's index is based on only the truncated distribution, or the poverty distribution, which neglects the existence of people above the poverty line. The normalized poverty value of Sen's index is also somewhat arbitrary. On the other hand, some scholars (e.g. Lewis and Ulph, 1988) fear that such kinds of effort tend to confuse the measurement of poverty with the measurement of inequality. They argue that the distribution of income among the poor should not matter much in measuring poverty.

The Foster–Greer–Thorbecke (FGT) index of poverty

Since Sen (1976), an enormous amount of effort has been devoted to developing poverty measures that move away from the traditional head-count ratio. The various poverty measures proposed fall roughly into three groups. The first includes the more or less direct extension of the Sen measure, obtained, for instance, by adding a constant to, or raising to a power, the weighting system used by Sen.[8] The second group contains measures constructed by using a methodology drawn from the literature on inequality.[9] The third group contains measures whose development was motivated by a practical concern, that is, poverty analysis by population subgroups. Apart from the idea that a poverty measure needs to take into account the distribution of income among the poor, not simply to count how many people are poor, some scholars suggest that it is desirable that the poverty measure be additively decomposable by population subgroups so that aggregate poverty can be represented as an appropriately weighted sum of poverty levels in the component subgroups of a population. This is the motivation behind the development of the FGT index of poverty, which is used to calculate the representative poverty gap.

Foster, Greer and Thorbecke (1984) proposed a class of additively decomposable measure which subsumes both head-count and poverty-gap measures. Their measure is claimed to have three features. First, it is additively decomposable with population-share used as weights; second, this measure satisfies the basic properties proposed by Sen; third, it is justified by a relative deprivation concept of poverty.

The FGT index provides a distributionally sensitive measure by introducing the parameter α. Using our notations introduced above, the FGT class of measures can be expressed as follows:

$$P_\alpha = \frac{1}{n} \sum_{i=1}^{m} \left(\frac{p_i}{z} \right)^\alpha \qquad (A.2.16)$$

or

$$P_\alpha = \int_{\underline{y}}^{z} \left(\frac{p_i}{z} \right)^\alpha f(y) dy \qquad (A.2.17)$$

where $\dfrac{p_i}{z}$ is the poverty-gap ratio for the individual i.

The FGT index uses a different weighting scheme from that used by Sen. As we noticed above, a rank-order weighting scheme is employed in Sen's measurement. The FGT measure takes the weights to be the income shortfalls of the poor themselves. In addition, this measure also satisfies Sen's other arguments, namely, the poorer income units should have higher weights and the weights should be based on a notion of relative deprivation experienced by the poor.

The parameter α can be considered a measure of poverty aversion (Besley, 1990). The value of α represents the weight given to the severity of poverty: the larger is α, the greater is the weight of the severity of poverty in the measure. When α becomes very large, the FGT measurement of poverty approaches a 'Rawlsian' measure which considers only the position of the poorest income unit.[10]

Let us consider three cases:

(1) For $\alpha=0$, the FGT measure reduces to the head-count ratio:

$$[P_\alpha]_{\alpha=0} = P_0 = \frac{m}{n} = H \qquad (A.2.18)$$

(2) For $\alpha=1$, the measure reduces to the poverty-gap ratio, which is expressed as a proportion of the poverty line:

$$[P_\alpha]_{\alpha=1} = P_1 = \frac{1}{n}\sum_{i=1}^{m}\frac{(z-y_i)}{z} \qquad (A.2.19)$$

(3) For $\alpha=2$, the measure takes the following form:

$$[P_\alpha]_{\alpha=2} = P_2 = \frac{1}{nz^2}\sum_{i=1}^{m}(z-y_i)^2 \qquad (A.2.20)$$

P_0 satisfies neither the monotonicity nor the transfer axiom. P_1 satisfies the monotonicity axiom but not the transfer axiom, whereas P_2 satisfies the main axioms of a desirable poverty measure in the literature.

Foster, Greer and Thorbecke (1984) introduce the so-called 'subgroup monotonicity axiom' as a basic requirement for decomposable measurement.

We consider the population divided into k subgroups of income units $j=1, ..., k$ with ordered income vectors $y^{(j)}$ and population sizes n_j .

Let $\hat{y}$ be a vector of incomes obtained from y by changing the incomes in subgroup j from $y^{(j)}$ to $\hat{y}^{(j)}$, where n_j is unchanged. If $\hat{y}^{(j)}$ has more poverty than $y^{(j)}$, then $\hat{y}$ must have a higher level of poverty than y.

This axiom requires that, other things being equal, a change in incomes in a subgroup leads this subgroup and total poverty to move in the same direction. The following index has a stronger decomposability property:

$$P_a(y;z) = \sum_{j=1}^{k} \frac{n_j}{n} P_a(y^{(j)};z)$$

(A.2.21)

Thus overall poverty index can be written as a weighted sum of the subgroup poverty indices.

The physical quality of life indicator (PQLI)

Poverty is the counterpart of well-being. Therefore, an indicator of well-being can also be used as an indicator of poverty. The focus of a poverty measure is, of course, the lowest welfare encountered by a part of a population group. For example, poverty and low income are often taken to be synonymous.

There are two ways of measuring human well-being. One is to measure the constituents of well-being such as utility and freedom, and the other is to value the commodity determinants of well-being such as goods and services which are inputs in the production of well-being. The former procedure measures 'output' and the latter aggregates and evaluates 'inputs' (Dasgupta, 1993). We may call these procedures 'outcome measurement' and 'means assessment' respectively.

The money income measure belongs to the means assessment of well-being. It has its limitations, although it is currently the most commonly employed single index because it is very convenient, readily available and easily understandable. Alternative methodologies for welfare analysis and poverty estimation pay more attention to the total quality of life rather than to income in money terms or to calories or food consumption. They include consumption of public goods rather than personal expenditures alone. The motivation behind the development of alternative measures came from the limitations of the income measure. First, income does not and cannot capture all the features of social behaviour. It is not a measure of total welfare but of goods and services which are valued in money terms. Many productive activities are excluded: the work of housewives and 'do-it-yourself' activities around the home are standard examples. Second, the income measure encompasses some activities that many scholars believe should not be included (for example, police protection in urban areas), because they can be viewed as a cost of urban life, a 'regrettable necessity'. Third, a single per capita income figure does not convey information about the distribution of income within countries, and about their development potential when we use it to make international comparisons. Fourth, income does not measure a society's physical qualities of life, for example life expectancy, birth, death and mobility characteristics of a society and its literacy rate. Finally, money income is not even an adequate measure of the performance of a single country; therefore problems become compounded when we attempt to compare the performance of two or more countries.

The construction of the PQLI is based on the following assumptions. First, people generally prefer to have few deaths among the infants born to them. Second, under almost all circumstances people prefer to live longer rather than shorter lives. Third, desire for literacy could at least serve as a surrogate for the individual capacity for effective social participation.

Three indicators are used in estimating the PQLI: infant mortality at birth, life expectancy at the age of 1 year, and basic literacy.

The infant mortality rate is the number of children dying before their first birthday out of every thousand born. This indicator is important because infants are more vulnerable than adults to the physical handicaps associated with poverty. It is also significant because parents and societies typically place a high value on the survival of their children. Much of the difference in the life span between low-income societies and more affluent societies is attributable to differences in the infant death rates. Although the infant mortality rate is related to life expectancy at birth, it focuses on nutrition and hygiene at the earliest stage of life. It is also related to the mother's health and her educational attainments.

Life expectancy at age 1 is the number of years a 1-year-old infant would live, if prevailing patterns of mortality at the time were to stay the same throughout its life. It is perhaps the most comprehensive of the different measures of mortality.

Literacy is defined as the capacity to read and write. Compared with the enrolment rate or number of students at school, a basic literacy indicator provides information about the potential for human development and the capability of the poor to take advantage of opportunities offered by new technology developments. It reflects literacy gains not only through formal educational establishments but also through informal channels.

Unlike calculating the GDP, in estimating PQLI various goods and services are combined via market price as a common element. However, the three indicators have no common *numeraire* that values them all. A simple indexing system is used. For each indicator, the performance of individual communities is placed on a scale of 0 to 100, where 0 represents an absolutely defined 'worst' performance and 100 represents an absolutely defined 'best' performance. A composite PQLI index is calculated by averaging the three indicators, giving equal weight to each of them. The PQLI thus ranges from 0 to 100.

There is no problem with a literacy rate which is reported as a percentage ranging from 0 to 100. However, with the other two indicators some scaling is necessary simply because the original indicators can never stretch fully on the normal 100 per cent range. This scaling makes it possible for a country to show a negative number, should a big social catastrophe occur.

Suppose the reported infant mortality rate is I_i: the formula to convert I_i into the mortality rate index used in the PQLI is as follows:

$$I_d = \frac{229 - I_i}{2.22} \qquad \text{(A.2.22)}$$

Following the same logic, the reported life expectancy at one L_i is also converted into L_d used in calculating PQLI. The upper limit of life expectancy is set at 77 years, two years above the then best 75 years of Sweden's record achieved in the late 1970s.[11] The lower limit of life expectancy at age 1 is set at 38 years, recorded by Vietnam in 1950. Therefore, the life expectancy at age one index in the PQLI ranges from 38 to 77 years and is assigned a value of 0 to 100. Therefore, we have the following conversion formula:

$$L_d = \frac{L_i - 38}{0.39} \qquad \text{(A.2.23)}$$

Let the literacy rate used by the PQLI be K_d, equal to the reported literacy rate L_i. The PQLI gives equal weight to the three indices; it is thus derived for a country by the following formula:

$$\text{PQLI} = \frac{I_d + L_d + K_d}{3} \qquad \text{(A.2.24)}$$

The PQLI has several advantages: it is simple and permits calculations for a wide range of countries, facilitating an examination of changes in the index over time. It is claimed to measure the results of social process rather than inputs and is sensitive to the distribution effect (Morris, 1979)

However, there are some disadvantages associated with the PQLI. First, the two components of the PQLI, life expectancy and infant mortality, are interdependent. Second, it is difficult to raise life expectancy above a certain level. Third, the weighting system of the PQLI is arbitrary; there is no rationale for giving equal weights to literacy, infant mortality and life expectancy at age one. Finally, data relating to infant mortality are relatively easy to process but difficult to collect. So it is not possible to prove that the PQLI portrays an adequate picture of human progress.

Human development index (HDI)[12]

The latest attempt to develop a comprehensive and systematic measure of the economic well-being of people in both developing and industrialized countries was made by the United Nations Development Programme (UNDP). In its annual Human Development Report, initiated in 1990, the UNDP constructs and develops the so-called Human Development Index (HDI).

The motivation behind the development of the HDI is much the same as for the development of the PQLI. The perception of the authors of the UNDP reports is that income is a means to a better life, and a higher income indicates less binding material constraints than a lower income. Income is considered an essential ingredient in human development, but it is not the sole or even a principal measure of that process. GDP growth is absolutely necessary to meet all essential human objectives, but it does not automatically improve people's lives. Countries differ in the way they translate growth into human development. Thus income level and GDP growth alone are not the best indicators of human development.

The HDI includes three key components: longevity, knowledge and income. It is an unweighted average of the relative distances measured in longevity, education and resources. Longevity is measured by life expectancy at birth as the sole unadjusted indicator; knowledge is measured by two educational stock variables: adult literacy and mean years of schooling. The measure of educational achievement is adjusted by assigning a weight of two-thirds to literacy and one-third to mean years of schooling. Income is measured by adjusted real per capita income on the basis of the purchasing power of each country's currency.

The breakthrough in the HDI methodology was to choose distance as the common denominator. All components in the HDI are expressed in different units so that there does not appear to be a common denominator. This poses a question about combining the three components. As a common denominator, the use of distance gives the index a dynamic quality, that is, it measures the movement towards a desired objective.

The HDI is developed as follows. First, a deprivation index is constructed for each of the three variables – life expectancy at birth L_a, adult literacy E_a, and the adjusted real per capita income Y_a. The deprivation index is measured as the difference between the desirable (maximum) value of the index minus the actual value of the index divided by the difference between the desirable (maximum) and minimum values of the index (those actually observed across countries). Suppose life expectancy currently is L_a in a country, the global maximum life expectancy is L_{max}, and the global minimum life expectancy is L_{min}. Instead of entering the L_a directly into its HDI, the required index L_d, that is, the life expectancy deprivation index, for calculating the country's HDI is obtained by the following formula:

$$L_d = \frac{L_a - L_{min}}{L_{max} - L_{min}} \qquad\qquad (A.2.25)$$

Similar normalization is pursued for the adjusted GDP[13] per capita deprivation index Y_d.

$$Y_d = \frac{Y_a - Y_{min}}{Y_{max} - Y_{min}} \qquad\qquad (A.2.26)$$

E_d takes two-third adult literacy rate and one-third mean years of schooling:

$$E_d = \frac{2}{3}\left(\frac{T_a - T_{min}}{T_{max} - T_{min}}\right) + \frac{1}{3}\left(\frac{S_a - S_{min}}{S_{max} - S_{min}}\right) \qquad \text{(A.2.27)}$$

The second step is to combine the three deprivation indicators to obtain an average deprivation index for a country; it is a simple average of the three indices.

$$H_d = \frac{1}{3}\left(L_d + E_d + Y_d\right) \qquad \text{(A.2.28)}$$

Finally, HDI is obtained simply by subtracting H_d from 1.

$$\text{HDI} = 1 - H_d \qquad \text{(A.2.29)}$$

Like the PQLI, the HDI attempts to rank all countries on a scale of 0 to 1, representing lowest and highest human development. The HDI has opened up new perspectives on measuring and analysing poverty and development. The index is best seen as a measure of people's ability to live a long and healthy life, to communicate, to participate in the life of the community and to have sufficient resources to obtain a decent living.

The HDI is particularly suitable for ranking low-income developing countries. The index uses the real GDP per head as an indicator of both development and deprivation. If a country's PPP income per capita is at or above $4,829, the index rates it 1 for development and, on the other hand, it rates it 0 for deprivation. The HDI is useful for poverty comparisons because what we first get is the *human deprivation index* before obtaining HDI. It is also true that when a country yields a literacy rate of 99 per cent and life expectancy beyond 76 years, it would be very difficult for this country to raise the index by making further achievements on these fronts.

Both the PQLI and HDI are closely related to the 'basic-needs approach', which assesses the evolution of human capital. The difference between the two indices is that instead of using the infant mortality figure, the HDI includes the income per capita component and the PQLI sticks to the principle of 'basic needs', that is, measuring results not expenditure, whereas the HDI takes both means and ends into consideration.

The drawbacks associated with the HDI indicator are that the concept of human development is much broader. Thus, like any other measure, it cannot perfectly capture all its elements. Some elements such as human rights, insecurity and discrimination for human development were initially omitted due to the paucity of data. Furthermore, the index suffers from other inherent weaknesses. For example, it is difficult to use the HDI as a base for a time series because in many countries the literacy rate and life expectancy data are not available annually. Third, both literacy and life expectancy change only slowly and usually in an upward direction, which might give real GDP the leading part in fluctuations and diminish the significance of the index as a distinctly separate indicator.

2 Socioeconomic characteristics of Chinese minorities

It is essential to provide some background information and socioeconomic characteristics of the principal Chinese minority groups before analysing their poverty situation. In China there are 55 recognized ethnic minority groups with a total population of 91 million in 1990 and 105 million in 2000 (a little over 8 per cent of the total population) (see Table 2.9), of which about three quarters live in autonomous counties, prefectures or regions. Besides these regions at the provincial level there are autonomous districts or autonomous counties. The minorities live in the autonomous regions as well as outside these regions. By the end of 1998, 155 minority autonomous local administrations were established, of which five are autonomous regions (provinces), 30 prefectures, 120 counties and 1,256 townships (Government of China, SSB, *China's Ethnic Statistical Yearbook*, 2000: 47).

Generally the population and economic data on the minorities are reported mainly for the national autonomous regions. One of the key requirements, therefore, is to disentangle the total minority population in each province and the population of those living in autonomous areas. Information on the socioeconomic characteristics of the Chinese ethnic minorities is sparse. Much of the basic data reported in the Chinese statistical yearbooks pertains to locational characteristics, that is, with minorities in autonomous regions rather than with the ethnic minority population. The census of population and the CASS household surveys for 1988 and 1995 are the two other sources of data on ethnic minorities.

Although minorities are spread throughout China, a substantial proportion is concentrated in southwest China. Information on the areas of concentration of key ethnic minorities and their distribution in southwestern provinces are presented in Table 2.1. It shows the relative importance of three ethnic minorities, namely, Zhuang, Miao and Yi, which represent the largest proportion of total minority population. Such ethnic minorities as Bai, Miao and Yi are located in at least three out of four southwestern provinces. The minorities are less significant in Sichuan than in the other three provinces.

Table 2.1 Areas of concentration of minority nationalities in southwest China

Minority nationality	Main provinces of concentration
Zhuang	Guangxi, Yunnan, Guangdong
Miao	Guangxi, Guizhou, Sichuan, Yunnan
Yi	Guizhou, Sichuan, Yunnan
Tibetans	Sichuan, Yunnan,
Dong	Guangxi, Guizhou, Hunan
Buyi	Guizhou
Yao	Guangxi, Hunnan, Yunnan, Guangdong
Bai	Guizhou, Hunnan, Yunnan
Naxi	Yunnan
Jingpo	Yunnan
Shui	Guangxi, Guizhou

Source: Government of China, SSB, *China's Ethnic Statistical Yearbook*, 1999.

The autonomous units at different levels of administration were created to give recognition and autonomy to the ethnic minorities and to allow them to manage their own affairs. The main changes in policy towards minorities occurred in the 1980s. A positive discrimination in their favour was probably a consequence of social unrest in Tibet and other areas. Subsequently the Chinese authorities gave a high priority to national unity (Mackerras, 1994). The principle of the minorities' autonomy was enshrined into law in the 1982 State Constitution, which recognized their equality rights and freedom to preserve and promote their language, religion and customs. The Chinese constitution provided for the heads of autonomous units at different levels to be from the relevant minority in order to improve relations between Han and minority people. The constitution introduced a new clause prohibiting any secession, fearing that some minority nationalities might like to secede (see Mackerras, 1985, 1994). Special policies regarding economic development, family planning and education favoured the autonomous regions, which also receive substantial financial grants and subsidies from the central government. We explore whether these preferential policies had the desired result in terms of better standards of living, higher education and better health services for the minorities (see Chapters 3 to 5).

Controversy exists over whether the minorities enjoy self–determination (see Cannon, 1989). In 1982 a well–known Chinese anthropologist, Fei Xiaotong, noted (in a speech to the Second Enlarged Conference of the Sichuan Provincial Nationalities Affairs Commission) that equality of minorities with one another and with the Han majority was not being achieved and that minority areas and populations continued to remain economically backward (cited in Mackerras, 1985). Mackerras (1994: 134) concludes that 'the overall record among China's minorities in the first half of the twentieth century reveals a general failure to integrate the minorities either with the Han or into a unified China'.

It is somewhat paradoxical that the autonomous regions are often quite rich in natural resources but their populations remain quite poor. Over 39 per cent of China's forest areas are located in the autonomous regions, which produce substantial quantities of minerals, notably iron, manganese, copper and lead. Despite natural richness, most of these areas are poor because of low land fertility, mountainous terrain and inadequate road infrastructure. Historically, the Han majority occupied the fertile plains, towns and cities, whereas the minorities inhabited the mountains. With the exception of a few minorities in the northeast, the majority are known to live in mountain areas which tend to be less productive.

In this chapter we analyse such minority characteristics as gender, age distribution, occupational profiles and educational attainment, which affect the level and intensity of their poverty. We examine three main sources of information: the minority autonomous areas, the minority counties (whether they are officially classified as 'autonomous' or not – we assume that any county with a minority population of over 50 per cent is a minority county), and the minority households based on the CASS 1988 and 1995 household surveys. As most of the minority population is concentrated in the Chinese southwest and west regions, we pay special attention to the situation of minorities in these regions relative to that of the Chinese population as a whole.

We discuss the economic and demographic characteristics of the minorities, their occupational and educational profile, and their access to such public-good type services as education. All these factors influence the poverty situation of individual minority groups and households. For example, the demographic factor affects the household size, influences the dependency ratio and puts a strain on household resources and assets. Similarly, the educational level affects poverty so that generally an increase in levels/years of education lowers the probability and extent of poverty (McKay and Lawson, 2003).

Economic characteristics

Table 2.2 gives such basic economic characteristics as per capita income, agriculture's share in GDP and ratio of investment to GDP in the provinces in the southern and western parts of China inhabited by minority ethnic populations. While both these regions are poorer relative to the coastal areas, there are wide interprovincial variations between provinces in these regions. For example, the regional per capita income of the west in 1997 was much higher than that of the south, which consists of the poorest provinces like Guizhou whose per capita income was much below the average for the south. In Guizhou the share of agriculture in GDP is much higher and the ratio of investment to GDP is much lower than other provinces in the region, which may partly explain its relative backwardness.

Table 2.2 Economic characteristics of China's south and west provinces
with predominance of ethnic minorities

Region/ province	Per capita income (1997 at 1992 yuan)	Annual per capita income growth (1993–97) (%)	Share of regional GDP in total GDP (1995–97) (%)	Agriculture's share in GDP (1993–97) (%)	Ratio of total investment to GDP (1993–97) (%)	Share of population in total population (%)
South	1,974	10.3	12.0	28.3	39.4	19.3
Guangxi	2,723	12.8	2.7	30.3	36.1	3.8
Guizhou	1,458	7.1	1.1	34.8	35.8	2.9
Sichuan	2,443	10.3	6.1	27.5	40.2	9.3
Yunnan	2,522	9.2	2.1	24.5	43.4	3.3
West	2,557	8.2	4.8	24.2	50.6	7.5
Gansu	2,089	8.6	1.0	23.4	40.2	2.0
Ningxia	2,618	8.8	0.3	21.4	51.8	0.4
Qinghai	2,670	7.2	0.3	21.5	48.7	0.4
Shaanxi	2,356	8.2	1.7	22.1	46.7	3.0
Tibet	2,571	11.6*	0.1*	43.3*	47.1**	0.2*
Xinjiang	3,562	7.5	1.4	27.2	63.5	1.5
China	3,586	9.4	100.0	19.9	40.6	100.0

* Data cover 1984–97
** Data cover 1992–97.
Source: Dayal-Gulati and Husain (2002).

In the west, Gansu's per capita income (2,089 yuan) is the lowest among all the provinces in the region, and even lower than that of Tibet. However, it is interesting to note that its agriculture's share in GDP is much lower and the ratio of investment to GDP quite significant at over 40 per cent during 1993–97, compared to 47 per cent in Tibet.

The aggregate ratios in Table 2.2 conceal the intercounty and intracounty incidence of poverty among minority groups. Available information on 12 autonomous counties in Guangxi suggests that counties with smaller proportions of ethnic minority population are generally more prosperous in terms of (1) per capita GDP, (2) per capita grain output and (3) rural net per capita income. For example, the two counties with the lowest proportions of minority population, namely Fuchuan Yao and Gongcheng Yao respectively, enjoy the highest per capita GDP, net per capita rural income and per capita grain output (Table 2.3). Comparative data for the minority and Han nationalities for Guangxi and Guizhou indicate that both per capita income and the expenditure of minority rural households surveyed are lower than those of the Han majority. Expenditures on clothing and medical services are particularly low, at 80 per cent and 70 per cent of Han figures respectively. Yet these items constitute important components of a basic needs bundle of goods and services (Table 2.4).

Table 2.3 Guangxi: socioeconomic and povery characteristics of
             autonomous counties (1994, 1998)

County	Minority population in total county population (%)		Per capita GDP (yuan)	Rural per capita net income (yuan)		Per capita grain output (kg)
	1994	*1998*	*1998*	*1994*	*1998*	*1998*
Huanjiang Maonan	91.6	92	3,850	1,048	1,806	408
Shujiang Dong	–	83	1,730	–	1,456	227
Longlin Gezu	79.5	79	1,489	553	1,519	438
Jinxiu Yao	77.4	78	2,690	780	1,572	417
Longsheng Gezu	75.6	77	4,133	947	2,016	357
Luocheng Mulao	–	73	2,891	–	1,877	396
Rong Shui Miao	71	72	1,758	–	–	291
Gongcheng	–	55	5,342	–	2,865	468
Fuchuan Yao	48	47	4,876	–	2,108	438

Note: The counties are listed in the descending order of the proportion of minority
        population for 1998.
Source: Government of China, SSB, *China's Ethnic Statistical Yearbook*, 1995, 1999.

Table 2.4 Guangxi and Guizhou: relative income and expenditure of rural
             minority households (1997)

	Guangxi			Guizhou		
	Minority	*Han*	*Minority to Han ratio*	*Minority*	*Han*	*Minority to Han ratio*
	(yuan)		*(%)*	*(yuan)*		*(%)*
Total gross annual per capita income	2,307	2,960	78	1,630	1,966	83
Agricultural income	953	1,146	83			
Forestry income	42	57	74			
Livestock income	707	793	89			
Income from fishery	12	44	27			
Annual net income per capita	1,575	2,102	75	1,402	1,740	82
Annual gross per capita expenditure	1,986	2,374	84			
Food expenditure	736	848	87			
Clothing expenditure	48	60	80			
Housing expenditure	185	213	87			

Source: *Statistical Yearbook of Guangxi*, 1998; *Statistical Yearbook of Guizhou*, 1998.

In Sichuan, economic and social indicators for minority localities have been improving (see Table 2.5). However, the minority populations in mountainous and autonomous regions of Liangshan, Ganzi and Aba districts remain quite poor. They account for the bulk of four million poor people in the province. A comparison of poverty for three ethnic minority districts in terms of income per head and grain consumption per head is given in Table 2.6. In 1997, these districts accounted for nearly 40 per cent of the poor with income per capita below 400 yuan per annum.

Table 2.5 Basic economic and social indicators of minority localities in Sichuan (1995–97)

Economic indicator	1995	1996	1997
GDP (million yuan)	13.8	16.0	17.8
GDP per capita (yuan)	2, 414	2,782	3,057
Gross agricultural output (million yuan)	7.7	9.3	10.3
Gross industrial output (million yuan)	8.0	8.2	9.3
Cultivated land area (10,000ha)	50.9	51.4	51.6
Total wage bill (million yuan)	2.1	2.2	2.4
Total number of students (000)	720	755	786
Students in primary schools (000)	578	606	632
Students in ordinary middle schools (000)	121	127	129
Students in professional middle schools (000)	14	15	17
Students in institutions of higher learning (000)	6	6	7

Source: *Statistical Yearbook of Sichuan*, 1998.

Table 2.6 A comparison of three ethnic minority districts of Sichuan relative to the provincial and national situation (1997)

	Net income (yuan per head)	Grain consumption (kg per head)	Poor below income of 400 yuan (000)
National average	2,901	–	–
Sichuan province	1,660	453	1,170
Registered poor	1,032	408	–
Aba prefecture	864	358	199
Ganzi prefecture	738	300	951
Liangshan prefecture	727	451	348

Source: Data supplied by the Provincial Statistical Bureau of Sichuan, Chengdu.

The county–level economic situation of ethnic minorities in Sichuan is presented in Table 2.7. Of the three counties, Ebian Yi, with the lowest proportion of ethnic minorities, has the highest per capita GDP and rural per capita income, and the second highest per capita grain output. This suggests that the minorities are relatively poorer in the light of the three criteria.

The socioeconomic and poverty characteristics of autonomous counties of Yunnan are presented in Table 2.8, which shows that in general counties with a smaller proportion of minorities have higher per capita GDP and per capita rural income. For example, Shilin Yi county, with only 34 per cent minority population, has among the highest per capita GDP (3,588 yuan which is the fourth highest level), rural per capita income (1,508 yuan, the third highest level) and per capita grain output (490 kg, the highest level).

Demographic characteristics

The shares of minority populations across provinces differ a great deal (see Table 2.9). According to the 1990 Population Census these shares ranged from 0.2 per cent in Jiangsu to 62 per cent in Xinjiang and 96 per cent in Tibet. Although in the 2000 Population Census the minority shares in both Tibet and Xinjiang declined (due to in–migration of Han populations and out–migration of minorities to other provinces), the spread across provinces remained quite significant. Between 1990 and 2000, the minority population increased exceptionally significantly in Guangdong, a rapidly growing province which has obvious attraction for minorities in search of jobs. The increase in minority populations was also significant in Beijing, Shanghai, Jiangsu and Zhejiang. In two provinces, namely, Jilin and Heilongjiang, minority populations actually declined.

Table 2.10 presents the population growth of specific minorities of the three southwest provinces, namely, Guangxi, Guizhou and Yunnan for 1953 to 2000. It shows a significant increase in the population of most minority groups. Table 2.11 presents growth of the Chinese total population and total minority populations for

Table 2.7 Sichuan: socioeconomic and poverty characteristics of autonomous counties

County	Minority population in total county population (%)		Per capita GDP (yuan)	Rural per capita net income (yuan)		Per capita grain output (kg)
	1994	*1998*	*1998*	*1994*	*1998*	*1998*
Muli Tibetan	–	76	2,745	–	705	294
Mabian Yi	36.4	37	1,958	530	1,302	434
Ebian Yi	26	29	3,823	827	1,711	347

Source: Government of China, SSB, *China's Ethnic Statistical Yearbook*, 1995, 1999.

Table 2.8 Yunnan: socioeconomic and poverty characteristics of autonomous counties (1994, 1998)

County	Minority population in total county population (%)		Per capita GDP (yuan)	Rural per capita net income (yuan)		Per capita grain output (kg)
	1994	1998	1998	1994	1998	1998
Ximeng Va	94.6	95	1,069	363	450	374
Gongshang Dulong and Nu	95.8	94.1	2,860	–	669	298
Lanping Bai and Pumi	94	94	2,059	735	707	352
Cangyuan Va	93	93	2,064	–	490	358
Menglian Dai, Lahu and Va	88	88	1,799	472	705	416
Jimping Miao, Yao and Dai	85	85	963	–	588	309
Lijiang Naxi	83	83	3,503	–	888	392
Weixi Lisu	82.5	82.5	1,873	–	524	361
Jiangcheng Hani	79	82	2,175	604	589	352
Ninglang Yi	79	79	1,335	416	396	222
Yuangjiang Hani, Yi and Dai	78.2	78.7	3,869	1,088	1,613	394
Lancang Lahu	77	77	1,127	448	605	312
Mojiang Hani	73	73	1,154	590	753	289
Xinping Yi and Dai	70	70	2,417	988	1,294	393
Hekou Yao	63	64	3,972	619	1,120	196
Eshan Yi	61.6	63	4,664	1, 010	1,773	402
Yangbi Yi	62.8	62.8	1,633	729	1,044	406
Pingbian Miao	60	61	1,739	578	612	373
Zhenyuan, Yi, Hani and Lahu	51.1	52	1,655	574	962	357
Gengma, Dai and Va	51	51	3,268	765	824	340
Nanjian Yi	49	49	2,129	605	1,235	373
Puer Hani and Yi	49	49	3,015	704	1,114	386
Jingdong Yi	46	47	2,142	608	1,044	378
Jinggu Dai and Yi	46	46	2,649	719	1,118	378
Shuangjiang Lahu, Va, Blang and Dai	44	44	1,576	591	539	356
Weishan Yi and Hui	43	43	2,414	452	1,308	385
Shilin Yi	–	34	3,588	–	1,508	490
Luquan Yi and Miao	30	30	1,874	528	1,201	354
Xundian Hui and Yi	21	21	1,841	738	1,030	345

Source: Government of China, SSB, *China's Ethnic Statistical Yearbook*, 1995, 1999.

Guangxi, Guizhou, Yunnan and Sichuan from 1953 to 1990. Although the census population data are not strictly comparable owing to variations in definitions and coverage, there is an indication of significant population growth of minorities during 1964–82. This is also the period of high total population growth in three out of the four provinces.

The data for the 1953 and 1964 population censuses for minorities may not be comparable with the data for later years because ethnic identification during these two years was more arbitrary. Also minorities were more easily re-classified and

Table 2.9 Minority population by province (1990, 2000)

Province	1990			2000			Increase of minority population
	Total population (000)	Minority population (000)	Minority population as % of total	Total population (000)	Minority population (000)	Minority population as % of total	1990–2000 (%)
Total for China	1,130,511	91,323	8.1	1,242,612	105,226	8.5	15.2
Beijing	10,819	414	3.8	13,569	585	4.3	41.4
Tianjin	8,785	203	2.3	9,849	267	2.7	31.7
Hebei	61,083	2,409	3.9	66,684	2,903	4.3	20.5
Shanxi	28,759	82	0.3	32,471	103	0.3	25.3
Inner Mongolia	21,456	4,166	19.4	23,323	4,858	20.8	16.6
Liaoning	39,460	6,166	15.6	41,824	6,718	16.1	9.0
Jilin	24,660	2,525	10.2	26,802	2,453	9.1	−2.8
Heilongjiang	35,216	1,999	5.7	36,237	1,772	4.9	−11.3
Shanghai	13,342	62	0.5	16,408	104	0.6	66.9
Jiangsu	67,057	153	0.2	73,043	260	0.4	69.5
Zhejiang	41,446	213	0.5	45,931	395	0.9	85.8
Anhui	56,181	324	0.6	59,000	398	0.7	22.7
Fujian	30,048	467	1.5	34,098	584	1.7	25.1
Jiangxi	37,710	101	0.3	40,397	126	0.3	24.1
Shandong	84,392	506	0.6	89,972	633	0.7	25.1
Henan	85,534	1,009	1.2	91,237	1,144	1.2	13.3
Hubei	53,970	2,141	4.0	59,509	2,597	4.4	21.3
Hunan	60,658	4,824	8.0	63,274	6,411	10.1	32.9
Guangdong	62,830	355	0.6	85,225	1,269	1.5	257.2
Guangxi	42,245	16,578	39.2	43,854	16,830	38.4	1.5
Hainan	6,558	1,117	17.0	7,559	1,314	17.4	17.6
Sichuan	107,218	4,890	4.6	112,861	6,093	5.4	24.6
Guizhou	32,391	11,242	34.7	35,248	13,336	37.8	18.6
Yunnan	36,973	12,358	33.4	42,360	14,159	33.4	14.6
Tibet	2,196	2,115	96.3	2,616	2,458	93.9	16.2
Shaanxi	32,882	156	0.5	35,365	176	0.5	12.8
Gansu	22,371	1,857	8.3	25,124	2,199	8.7	18.4
Qinghai	4,457	1,878	42.1	4,823	2,217	46.0	18.0
Ningxia	4,655	1,549	33.3	5,486	1,896	34.6	22.4
Xinjiang	15,157	9,461	62.4	18,459	10,969	59.4	15.9

Note: The Sichuan figure includes Chongqing to enable comparison with 1990 data.
Source: China Population Census, 1990, 2000.

re–registered among different ethnic groups.[1] It is reported that in the border areas of Yunnan minority populations were estimated somewhat arbitrarily on the basis of interviews (Mackerras, 1994: 237).

In some cases the minority population declined between 1953 and 1964 due to the following factors: the impact of the famine in 1960 following the disastrous strategy of the Great Leap Forward, emigration of Tibetans to India and exodus of such minorities as Kazaks, Kirgiz and Uzbeks to the former Soviet Union. The faster growth of the minority population in 1982 and 1990 may be due to more rapid health improvements, decline in mortality rates and poor implementation of the population control policies among the minorities.

Table 2.10 Population growth of key minority groups in selected southwest provinces (1953–2000)

	Population (000)					Period population growth (%)			
	1953	*1964*	*1982*	*1990*	*2000*	*1953– 64*	*1964– 82*	*1982– 90*	*1990– 2000*
Guangxi									
Zhuang	6,496	7,567	12,324	14,215	14,207	16.5	62.8	15.3	−0.06
Yao	471	532	864	1,327	1,472	13.0	62.2	53.7	10.9
Miao	203	217	337	426	463	6.6	55.4	26.4	8.7
Dong	150	139	229	287	303	−6.9	64.6	25.2	5.6
Guizhou									
Miao	1,425	1,579	2,582	3,667	4,300	10.8	63.5	42.0	17.3
Buyi	1,222	1,347	2,099	2,481	2,798	10.2	55.8	18.2	12.8
Dong	439	476	851	1,399	1,628	8.3	78.8	64.5	16.4
Yi	274	345	564	707	843	25.6	63.7	25.3	14.5
Shui	132	153	276	323	370	15.5	80.1	17.2	19.3
Yunnan									
Yi	1,825	2,145	3,352	4,060	4,706	17.5	56.3	21.1	15.9
Bai	567	704	1,121	1,341	1,506	24.1	59.3	19.6	12.3
Hani	481	628	1,058	1,249	1,425	30.6	68.3	18.0	14.1
Tai	479	534	836	1,014	1,142	11.6	56.4	21.4	12.6
Zhuang	325	564	894	1,011	1,144	73.8	58.4	13.0	13.2
Miao	360	428	752	896	1,043	18.9	75.7	19.0	16.5
Hui	217	267	438	521	643	22.8	64.2	19.1	23.5
Lagu	139	191	304	408	448	37.5	59.0	34.2	9.7
Wa	286	200	298	348	383	−30.0	49.0	16.4	10.1
Lili	310	262	468	283	610	−15.0	78.0	−39.5	115.5
Naxi	143	154	236	265	295	7.2	53.7	12.3	11.5

Sources: Data for 1953, 1964 and 1982 are from the *Population Statistical Materials Collection 1949–1982* (1988, Beijing: China Financial and Economic Publishing House).
Data for 1990 are from the *Tabulations on the 1990 Population Census of the People's Republic of China* (1993, Beijing: China Statistical Publishing House).
Data for 2000 are from Government of China, SSB (2003).

Table 2.11 Population growth and geographical distribution of minorities in
        southwest China (1953–90)

	1953	1964	1982	1990	Period pop. growth (1953– 64)	Period pop. growth (1964– 82	Period pop. growth (1982– 90
Guangxi							
Total population (million)	19.5	20.8	36.4	42.2	6.5	74.7	16.0
Total minority population (million)	7.4	8.5	13.9	16.6	15.3	62.9	19.0
Minority population as % of total population	37.9	41.0	38.2	39.2	–	–	–
Guizhou							
Total population (million)	15.0	17.1	28.5	32.4	13.9	66.6	13.4
Total minority population (million)	3.9	4.0	7.4	11.2	1.8	85.1	51.4
Total minority population as % of total population	26.2	23.3	26.0	34.7	–	–	–
Sichuan							
Total population (million)	61.6	67.9	99.7	107.0	10.1	46.7	7.5
Total minority population (million)	0.5	1.7	3.7	5.0	244.9	111.7	33.5
Total minority population as % of total population	0.8	2.5	3.7	4.6	–	–	–
Yunnan							
Total population (million)	17.1	20.5	32.5	36.9	19.7	58.6	13.6
Total minority population (million)	5.6	6.4	10.3	12.3	13.6	61.3	19.7
Total minority population as % of total population	32.9	31.2	31.7	33.4	–	–	–

Sources: Data for 1953, 1964 and 1982 are from the *Population Statistical Materials Collection
        1949–1982* (1988, Beijing: China Financial and Economic Publishing House).
        Data for 1990 are from the *Tabulations on the 1990 Population Census of the People's
        Republic of China* (1993, Beijing: China Statistical Publishing House).

The population of ethnic minorities in the autonomous areas has been rising in
both absolute and proportional terms since 1980, from 4.7 million (40.7 per cent)
in 1980 to 7.6 million (or 45.6 per cent) in 1998 (see Table 2.12)

Table 2.13 gives rural and non–rural population of the Han majority and five
minority groups, namely, Buyi, Miao, Yao, Yi and Zhuang. It shows that the
Zhuang minority, concentrated mainly in Guangxi, lived in rural households.
Miao were concentrated in Guizhou, accounting for over 12 per cent of non-rural
households and only 4.5 per cent of rural households. The picture is similar for
Buyi, Yao and Yi.

Table 2.12 Ethnic minorities in the autonomous areas (1980–98)

Year	Total population in the autonomous areas (million)	Agricultural population (million)	Population of minority nationalities (million)	Minority nationalities as proportion of total population (3 as % of 1)
	1	2	3	4
1980	11,586	9,717	4.7	40.7
1981	11,767	9,864	–	–
1982	12,127	10,161	5.0	41.3
1983	12,659	10,601	5.3	42.2
1984	12,900	10,769	5.5	42.6
1985	13,548	11,263	5.8	43.2
1986	13,927	11,567	6.1	43.6
1987	14,246	11,794	6.2	43.9
1988	14,580	12,038	6.4	44.2
1989	15,060	12,382	6.7	44.4
1990	15,296	12,580	6.9	45.0
1991	15,463	12,660	7.0	45.6
1992	15,630	12,769	7.1	45.6
1993	15,776	12,808	7.2	45.5
1994	15,974	12,890	7.2	45.6
1995	16,044	12,878	7.2	45.1
1996	16,230	12,942	7.4	45.6
1997	16,408	13,054	7.4	45.4
1998	16,616	13,155	7.6	45.6

Source: Government of China, SSB, *China's Ethnic Statistical Yearbook*, 1999.

Educational, occupational and gender profiles

The poverty situation of minorities will be affected by their location (rural or non–rural), occupational and sectoral background (engaged in rural or non–farm activities) and educational profile (whether they are literate, semi–literate or school and university graduates). We discuss in detail the literacy and basic education among minorities in Chapter 4. However, in Tables 2.14 and 2.15 we examine the situation of the Chinese minority population with respect to sectoral, occupational and educational backgrounds and profiles. The total minority population with university education amounted to only 0.4 per cent of the total Chinese population aged 6 years and above. This ratio is also low for the four southwest provinces (namely, Guangxi, Guizhou, Sichuan and Yunnan), although the situation in Sichuan province is slightly better than that in the other three provinces. Even when the minority population with college and secondary technical education is added, the proportion for the minorities is no higher than 2.6 per cent for China as a whole. The proportion of minority population with secondary education and above is below 2 per cent in all four provinces. The share of illiterate and semi–literate population in these provinces ranges between

Table 2.13 Population of rural and urban households: the Han and selected minorities (000) (1990)

Province/household	Total population	Han	Zhuang	Miao	Yi	Buyi	Yao
Guangxi	42,244	25,667 (60.7)	14,215 (33.6)	426.4 (1.0)	7.2 (0.02)	11.6 (0.03)	1,327 (3.1)
Rural	36,543	21,390 (58.5)	13,024 (35.6)	404.0 (1.1)	6.1 (0.02)	9.6 (0.03)	1,220 (3.3)
Non-rural	5,484	4,105 (74.8)	1,152 (21.0)	21.7 (0.4)	1.1 (0.02)	1.9 (0.04)	103.6 (1.9)
Sichuan	107,218	102,328 (95.4)	4.6 (0.05)	533.9 (0.5)	1,787 (1.7)	7.3 (0.006)	0.4 (–)
Rural	91,508	86,972 (95.0)	1.7 (0.002)	502.6 (0.5)	1,717 (1.9)	5.9 (0.006)	0.15 (–)
Non-rural	15,249	14,921 (97.8)	2.9 (0.02)	29.4 (0.2)	53.3 (0.3)	1.3 (0.006)	0.26 (–)
Guizhou	32,391	21,149 (65.3)	38.2 (0.1)	3,667 (11.3)	707.2 (2.2)	2,480 (7.6)	30.4 (0.09)
Rural	28,339	17,803 (62.8)	26.4 (0.1)	3,474 (12.2)	672.3 (2.4)	2,335 (8.2)	28.6 (0.1)
Non-rural	3,857	3,200 (83.0)	11.4 (0.3)	174.9 (4.5)	32.6 (0.8)	129 (3.3)	1.7 (0.05)
Yunnan	36,972	24,614 (66.6)	1,011 (2.7)	896 (2.4)	4,060 (11.0)	34 (0.09)	173 (0.5)
Rural	32,405	20,891 (64.5)	960 (2.9)	876 (2.7)	3,832 (11.8)	30 (0.09)	168 (0.5)
Non-rural	4,508	3,678 (81.6)	51 (1.1)	18 (0.4)	225 (5.0)	3 (0.07)	4 (0.09)

– = insignificant.

Note: Figures in brackets are percentages of the total.

Source: Government of China, SSB, tabulation on China's Nationality (data of 1990 Population Census) (1994).

21 per cent in Guangxi and 51 per cent in Sichuan, which is well above the average of 31 per cent for China as a whole. As is to be expected, a much larger proportion of females than males are illiterate or semi–literate. With the exception of Guangxi, over 60 per cent of females are illiterate or semi–literate (Table 2.14).

The bulk of the minority populations in all four southwest provinces is engaged in agriculture, forestry and fisheries, activities which generate very low and unstable income. Those engaged in manufacturing form only 3.4 per cent of the population in Guangxi, 1.9 per cent in Sichuan, 2 per cent in Guizhou and 2.4 per cent in Yunnan. Many minority people are engaged in state bureaucracy (cadres, for example) and social organizations in all four provinces. A higher

Table 2.14 Educational attainment of minority populations in southwest China (1990)

Educational attainment/sex	Total (China)	Guangxi	Sichuan	Guizhou	Yunnan
Population 6 years and over (million)					
Total	**78.25 (100)**	**14.35**	**4.24**	**9.66**	**10.60**
Male	40.07 (100)	7.35	2.16	5.03	5.39
Female	38.18 (100)	7.00	2.08	4.63	5.21
Population with university education (000)					
Total	**335.2 (0.4)**	**27.6 (0.2)**	**11.7 (0.3)**	**16.1 (0.2)**	**18.7 (0.2)**
Male	231.7 (0.6)	21.8 (0.3)	8.1 (0.4)	12.5 (0.2)	13.4 (0.2)
Female	103.5 (0.3)	5.8 (0.1)	3.6 (0.2)	3.6 (0.1)	5.3 (0.1)
Population with college education (000)					
Total	**504.4 (0.6)**	**61.2 (0.4)**	**14.6 (0.3)**	**30.6 (0.3)**	**28.4 (0.3)**
Male	344.5 (0.8)	47.2 (0.6)	10.6 (0.5)	23.6 (0.5)	21.2 (0.4)
Female	159.9 (0.4)	14.0 (0.2)	4.0 (0.2)	7.0 (0.1)	7.2 (0.1)
Population with technical (secondary school) education (000)					
Total	**1,270.8 (1.6)**	**193.7 (1.3)**	**54.5 (1.3)**	**106.9(1.1)**	**109.4 (1.0)**
Male	768.0 (1.9)	128.2 (1.7)	36.0 (1.7)	75.5(0.8)	72.8(1.3)
Female	502.8 (1.3)	65.5 (0.9)	18.5 (0.9)	31.4(0.7)	36.6(0.7)
Illiterate and semi– illiterate population (15 years and over) (%)					
Total	**30.8**	**20.99**	**50.97**	**43.1**	**45.5**
Male	20.5	9.7	38.9	25.4	31.1
Female	41.6	32.7	63.5	62.3	60.3

Note: Figures in brackets are percentages of the total population 6 years and over. Figures may not add up to 100 due to rounding.

Source: State Statistical Bureau (SSB), tabulation on China's Nationality (Data of 1990 Population Census) (1994).

proportion of females than males are engaged in agriculture and a smaller proportion in manufacturing. Only in such occupations as commerce, real estate, public utilities, public health and social welfare are the shares of females and males evenly matched or slightly in favour of females (see Table 2.15).

The CASS household surveys

We use the CASS household survey data for 1988 and 1995 in this book to analyse the socioeconomic characteristics of minorities versus those of the Han majority. The basic household data for 1988 and 1995 are presented in Tables 2.16 and 2.17.

The CASS household surveys asked questions of rural and urban households concerning occupation and sector of economic activity (farming or non-farming, town and village enterprises). Information on educational variables at middle-school level and above for minorities and non-minorities is presented in Table 2.17 by way of illustration.

There is some evidence of a growing gap between minorities and non-minorities in terms of educational attainment between 1988 and 1995. However, the differences are not large, especially given the small sample size. In the case of rural population there are significant differences between the educational attainment of adult minorities and adult non-minorities. We do not have data on years of schooling for 1988, but in 1995 adult minorities had, on average, a year less of schooling (the average number of years of schooling at middle level in China is six years). The proportion of young people (under 18 years old) who are students does not differ substantially between minorities and non-minorities in either 1988 or 1995, although the absolute difference between the two is enormous between the two years.

The data in Table 2.18 are presented separately for poor and non-poor regions. Minorities live in both these regions: in 1995 minorities accounted for 14 per cent of the population of the non-poor regions compared to 25 per cent in the poor regions. In 1988 the share of minority population in the non-poor regions was much smaller (only 3 per cent). In 1995 the level of total medical expenses by the households was similar in the poor and non-poor regions, whereas it was higher for the latter in 1988.

Table 2.15 Occupational/sectoral profiles of minorities in southwest China (000) (1990)

	Guangxi	*Sichuan*	*Guizhou*	*Yunnan*
Grand total	8,982 (100)	2,832	6,186	6,897
Male	4,671 (100)	1,462	3,244	3,544
Female	4,310 (100)	1,370	2,942	3,353
Agriculture, forestry and fisheries	8,011 (89.2)	2,587 (91.3)	5,734 (92.7)	6,316 (91.6)
Male	4,023 (86.1)	1,288 (88.1)	2,923 (90.1)	3,134 (88.4)
Female	3,987 (92.5)	1,299 (94.8)	2,810 (95.5)	3,182 (94.9)
Manufacturing	304 (3.4)	55 (1.9)	122 (2.0)	165 (2.4)
Male	194 (4.1)	37 (2.5)	85 (2.6)	112 (3.2)
Female	110 (2.5)	18 (1.3)	38 (1.3)	53 (1.6)
Construction	37 (0.4)	5 (0.2)	17 (0.3)	38 (0.6)
Male	30 (0.6)	4 (0.3)	14 (0.4)	33 (0.9)
Female	7 (0.2)	1 (0.1)	3 (0.1)	5 (0.1)
Transport, postal and telecommunication services	65 (0.7)	14 (0.5)	26 (0.4)	51 (0.7)
Male	55 (1.2)	12 (0.8)	22 (0.7)	45 (1.3)
Female	10 (0.2)	2 (0.1)	4 (0.1)	6 (0.2)
Commerce, supply and marketing services	168 (1.9)	33 (1.2)	66 (1.1)	84 (1.2)
Male	84 (1.8)	18 (1.2)	35 (1.1)	46 (1.2)
Female	84 (1.9)	15 (1.1)	31 (1.0)	38 (1.1)
Real estate and public utilities	28 (0.3)	5 (0.2)	10 (0.2)	11 (0.2)
Male	15 (0.3)	2 (0.1)	5 (0.1)	5 (0.1)
Female	13 (0.3)	3 (0.2)	5 (0.2)	6 (0.2)
Public health and social welfare	39 (0.4)	10 (0.3)	20 (0.3)	23 (0.3)
Male	19 (0.4)	5 (0.3)	11 (0.4)	11 (0.3)
Female	20 (0.5)	5 (0.4)	9 (0.3)	12 (0.4)
Education, culture and art	183 (2.0)	63 (2.2)	96 (1.5)	105 (1.5)
Male	132 (2.8)	50 (3.4)	72 (2.2)	75 (2.1)
Female	51 (1.2)	13 (0.9)	24 (0.8)	30 (0.9)
Scientific research and polytechnics	6 (0.1)	2 (0.1)	2 (0.03)	3 (0.04)
Male	4 (0.1)	1 (0.1)	1 (0.03)	2 (0.06)
Female	2 (0.04)	1 (0.1)	1 (0.03)	1 (0.03)
Finance and insurance	19 (0.2)	6 (0.2)	10 (0.2)	13 (0.2)
Male	13 (0.3)	4 (0.3)	7 (0.2)	10 (0.3)
Female	6 (0.1)	2 (0.1)	3 (0.1)	3 (0.1)
State organs and social organizations	116 (1.3)	51 (1.8)	81 (1.3)	84 (1.2)
Male	96 (2.0)	40 (2.7)	66 (2.0)	69 (1.9)
Female	20 (0.5)	11 (0.8)	15 (0.5)	15 (0.4)

Notes: (1) Figures in brackets are percentages of the total.
        (2) Figures may not add up to 100 due to rounding.
Source: SSB, Tabulation on China's Nationality (data of 1990 Population Census) (1994).

Table 2.16 Total number and proportion of minorities in each province (1988, 1995)

The MEANS Procedure: Analysis (Variable: minority)			
Province of household residence	*No of observations*	*Sum*	*Mean*
(1988)			
Beijing	1,580	73.0000000	0.0462025
Shanxi	3,569	25.0000000	0.0070048
Liaoning	3,068	93.0000000	0.0303129
Jiangsu	3,995	40.0000000	0.0100125
Anhui	3,040	54.0000000	0.0177632
Henan	3,721	125.0000000	0.0335931
Hubei	3,430	26.0000000	0.0075802
Guangdong	3,743	16.0000000	0.0042746
Yunnan	3,399	260.0000000	0.0764931
Gansu	2,230	82.0000000	0.0367713
(1995)			
Beijing	1,529	95.0000000	0.0621321
Shanxi	2,110	16.0000000	0.0075829
Liaoning	2,212	86.0000000	0.0388788
Jiangsu	2,450	19.0000000	0.0077551
Anhui	1,527	20.0000000	0.0130976
Henan	1,939	86.0000000	0.0443528
Hubei	2,310	33.0000000	0.0142857
Guangdong	1,821	79.0000000	0.0433828
Sichuan	2,486	26.0000000	0.0104586
Yunnan	2,010	455.0000000	0.2263682
Gansu	1,304	52.0000000	0.0398773

Table 2.17 Educational characteristics of minorities and non-minorities (1988, 1995) (%)

	Minorities		*Non–minorities*	
	1988	*1995*	*1988*	*1995*
Urban households				
College graduate or above	5.9	4.54	6.1	7.82
Community college graduate, professional school graduate, or middle–level professional, technical or vocational graduate	18.1	26.2	15.9	28.0
Upper middle school graduate	18.0	18.7	21.6	21.2
Lower middle school graduate	40.3	32.9	37.8	30.2
Rural households				
College graduate or above	0.2	0.5	0.6	0.1
Community college graduate, professional school graduate, or middle–level professional, technical or vocational graduate	0.8	1.2	0.83	1.7
Upper middle school graduate	5.9	5.4	8.9	9.2
Lower middle school graduate	24.6	28.7	31.7	36.7

Note: Average middle-level schooling in China lasts for six years, three years for the lower level and three for the upper.

Source: Based on the CASS household survey data.

Table 2.18 Socioeconomic characteristics of rural populations of poor and non-poor regions (1988, 1995)

	1988					*1995*
	Non-poor regions (a)	*Poor regions (b)*	*Ratio a/b*	*Non-poor regions (a)*	*Poor regions (b)*	*Ratio a/b*
Individual						
Income (yuan)	206	222	0.93	543	495	1.10
Minority nationality (%)	3	21	0.14	14	25	0.56
Completed five years of education (%)	68	54	1.26	53	42	1.26
Illiterate (self–reported) (%)	25	38	0.65	27	37	0.73
Primary occupation: farming (%)	95	98	0.97	92	93	0.99
Self–employed (%)	91	95	0.96	93	93	1.00
Household						
Total medical expenses (yuan)	14	11	1.23	125	124	1.01
Went to hospital/clinic at least once (%)	48	57	0.86	–	–	–
Fixed productive assets (yuan)	506	618	0.82	2,228	2,081	1.07
Financial assets (including savings) (yuan)	65	26	2.45	2,648	1,020	2.60
Annual productive expenses (yuan)	961	744	1.29	2,784	1,789	1.56
Have electricity (%)	83	61	1.36	96	91	1.05

Source: Riskin and Li (2001:338).

3 Poverty and inequality among Chinese minorities

Much has been written on poverty alleviation in developing countries. The bulk of the poverty literature assumes that rapid economic growth will more or less automatically create a real dent in the poverty problem. There are those who believe that high and rapid growth is a necessary but not a sufficient condition for poverty alleviation (Drèze and Sen, 1990). China is a classic example of a high rate of growth for sustained periods. Even though this rate has slackened somewhat due partly to the 1997 Asian financial crisis[1], it still remains quite impressive and higher than that of most other countries, developed or developing. In this chapter we show that rapid economic growth has not coincided with poverty alleviation in the Chinese economy, particularly among minorities in southwest China. The existing literature attempts to measure poverty in the aggregate without measuring its incidence among the minorities, which are concentrated in this region. The neglect of the minorities' poverty situation is not surprising considering the political sensitivity surrounding the subject (especially in Tibet and Xinjiang), the relatively small proportion of the minority population, and lack of adequate information and statistics on the ethnic minorities. Nevertheless, the issue of poverty among minorities is important, as no study of poverty in China can be complete without disaggregating its incidence among different ethnic and social groups of the population. Furthermore, although the minorities form only a small proportion of the total population, over 60 per cent of the land area is occupied by them. Although minority people constitute only 10 per cent of the population, they represent between 40 and 50 per cent of the number of absolute poor in China (World Bank, 1995).

The State Planning Commission divides China into eastern and western regions, the latter including Guizhou, Yunnan, Tibet, Shaanxi, Gansu, Qinghai and Ningxia, and the eastern region including Hebei, Liaoning, Shandong, Tianjin, Jiangsu, Fujian, Zhejiang, Guangdong, Hainan and Guangxi (Chai, 1996: 46). For our analysis of poverty reduction among the minorities, we concentrate on the provinces in the southwest region of China in which the minority populations are mainly concentrated. This region is the poorest in China and ethnic minorities account for nearly 50 per cent of the total population. The region accounts for one fifth of China's total population, that is, 240 million. Guangxi is included in the southwest region even though it has a small coastline. The rationale for doing this is that it is less open than many coastal provinces.

Evidence from the autonomous areas and counties

Of the 592 poverty counties in China, 257 are minority autonomous counties. In Guangxi, Guizhou and Yunnan, such minority groups as Miao, Yao, Buyi and Zhuang constitute over one-third of the population. Isolation, remote living in mountainous areas, poor-quality land, rapid deforestation and population growth are some of the reasons for the high incidence of poverty among the minorities. Mountainous terrain makes the provision of low-cost transportation and services difficult. But other socioeconomic factors such as lack of education, which limits the expansion of social capabilities and opportunities, must also play a role in explaining why the poor among minorities remain poor (see Chapter 4).

Information on the minorities is rather sparse; it is therefore difficult to assess their poverty in a systematic fashion.[2] However, indicators of income, health and educational access throw some light on their poverty situation, which we discuss below. As we noted in Chapter 1, aggregative indicators may not reveal the true picture of poverty. However, to the extent that poverty is widespread, especially in very poor provinces and regions, averages for minority areas relative to the average for China as a whole, or for a province as a whole, give some useful indications of the development of these areas.

Autonomous administrations represent the basic political arrangements in dealing with minority issues. There are three levels of autonomous administrations: five provincial-level autonomous regions, namely, Tibet, Xinjiang, Ningxia, Guangxi, Inner Mogolia; 30 autonomous prefectures or cities at the administration level between province and county; and 120 autonomous counties. These minority entities are a combination of geographical and minority factors. Thus, the names of all the autonomous entities consist of a geographical name and the name(s) of one or two minority(ies) for example, Guangxi Zhuang Autonomous Region is a combination of Guangxi (geographical area) and Zhuang (Zhuang ethnic minority), Zhenning Buyi and Tujia Autonomous County (Zhenning is a county name within Anshun District of Guizhou province and Buyi and Tujia are two main ethnic minorities within Zhenning county).

Minorities live in the 'autonomous areas' as well as outside. It could therefore be argued that looking at these areas may not give a representative picture. However, since a large proportion of the minorities (over 40 to 50 per cent) live in the autonomous areas, their economic and social situation relative to the total should give a fairly good picture. As Table 3.1 indicates, the minority areas are largely agricultural (both in terms of output and employment); they account for a very small and stagnant share of the total industrial output of China.

Table 3.1 Economic indicators for the autonomous areas relative to the total
economy (1980–98) (%)

	1980	1985	1990	1996	1998
Annual rural net per capita income	39.8	68.3	58.6	67.5	75.5
Gross agricultural output	10.5	12.1	14.3	12.6	12.7
Grain output	10.4	10.6	12.0	13.5	14.0
Cultivated area	16.7	18.0	18.5	26.9	19.7
Gross industrial output	4.6	4.9	5.4	4.9	4.5

Source: Government of China, SSB, *China's Ethnic Statistical Yearbook.*

Income and consumption indicators

Annual rural net per capita income in the minority areas as a proportion of the
average for the whole economy increased significantly between 1980 and 1998
(see Table 3.2). However, the gap between average rural per capita income for
China and its minority regions has been widening (see Figure 3.1). This may be
due to the widening gaps between the coastal and non-coastal areas. But income
gaps also exist within the non-coastal areas. Sautman (1999) cites a 1995 study
on Hainan showing that GDP in minority counties and two cities declined from
nearly 26 per cent of the provincial total in 1987 to about 18 per cent in 1994. He
further notes that, in Yunnan in 1996, 'the richest Han area had income level 20
times that of the poorest minority area; the income level of Han peasants near the

Table 3.2 Average rural net annual per capita income in the autonomous areas
(1994, 1998)

Province/ indicator	1994							1998
	Total (1) (yuan)	Minority areas (2) (yuan)	(2) as % of (1)	(2) as % of the national average	Total (3) (yuan)	Minority areas (4) (yuan)	(4) as % of (3)	(4) as % of the national average
National	1,221	820	67.1	67.1	2,162	1,633	75.5	75.5
Autonomous areas								
Inner Mongolia	1,062	920	86.6	75.3	1,982	1,577	79.6	72.9
Guangxi	1,107	1,083	97.8	88.7	1,972	1,972	100	91.2
Tibet	976	–	–	–	1,231	1,231	100	56.9
Ningxia	911	911	100	74.6	1,756	1,721	98	79.6
Xinjiang	936	936	100	76.6	1,600	1,600	100	74
West								
Guizhou	787	495	62.9	40.5	1,334	1,259	94.4	58.2
Sichuan	946	555	58.7	45.4	1,754	1,181*	67.3	54.6
Yunnan	803	472	58.8	38.6	1,387	1,164	83.9	53.8
Gansu	724	664	91.7	54.4	1,393	989	71	45.7
Qinghai	869	664	76.4	54.4	1,426	1,139	79.9	52.7

* Average of Sichuan and Chongqing.
Source: Government of China, *China's Ethnic Statistical Yearbook* 1995, 1999; *Comprehensive
Statistical Data and Materials on 50 Years of New China.*

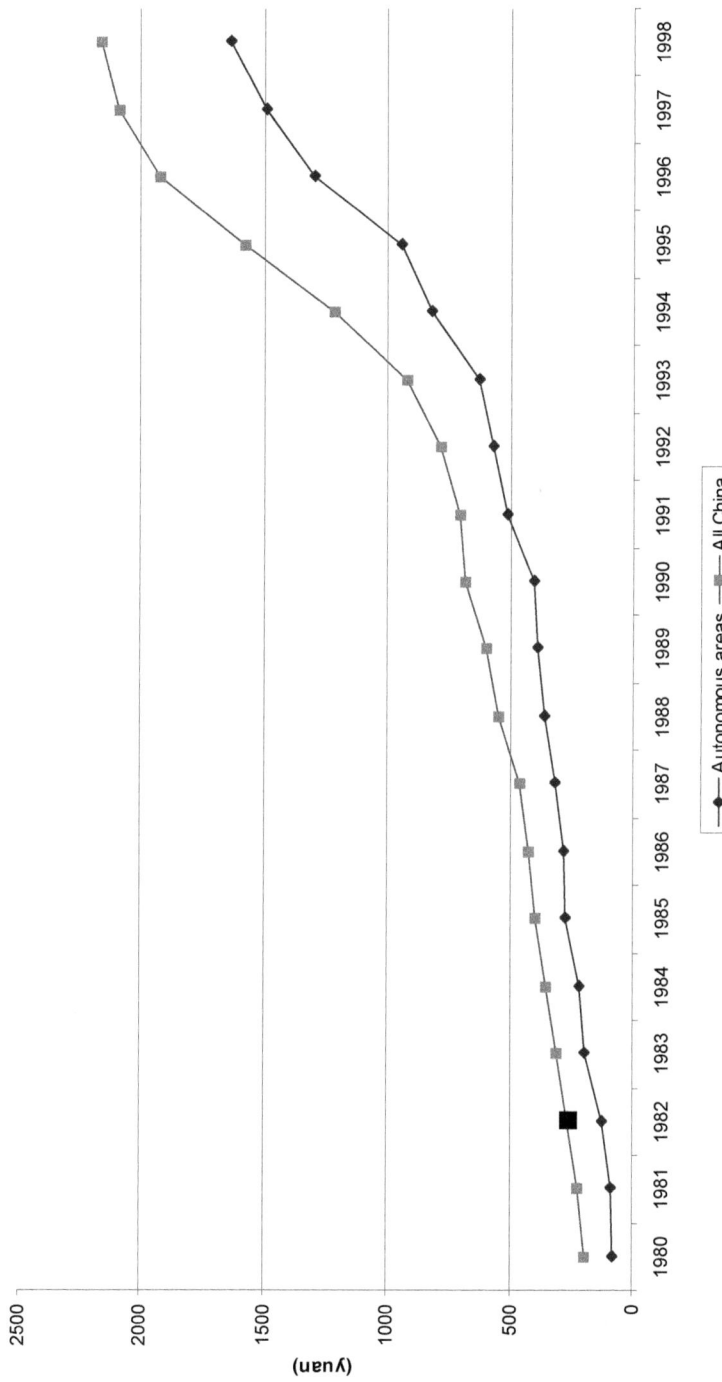

Figure 3.1 Annual net per capita income of rural households in China and its autonomous areas

Sources: Based on data from *China's Ethnic Statistical Yearbook; Comprehensive Statistical Data and Materials on 50 Years of New China.*

capital, Kunming, was 4 to 5 times the income level of minority peasants in impoverished Guangnan county' (p. 174). With the exception of Guangxi and Ningxia, in all the other minority areas rural income per capita was below 75 per cent of the national average in 1998. Between 1994 and 1998, minority areas made substantial progress in Guizhou, Guangxi and Yunnan, in which substantial proportions of minority groups are located. But this was not the case for the minority areas in the west. The income gap would have been even wider if the hinterland states had not shared the fruits of rapid economic growth.

Information on annual rural household per capita expenditure for the minorities is not available for the same years. So changes over time cannot be measured. However, data for 1998 show that overall rural per capita expenditure is only 63 per cent of the total, and that for food, 65 per cent. The corresponding ratios for Sichuan are 52 per cent and 59 per cent, and for Qinghai, they are 63 per cent and 79 per cent respectively (*China's Ethnic Statistical Yearbook,* 1999).

Non- income (educational) indicators

We noted in Chapter 1 that income indicators by themselves are not sufficient. They need to be supplemented by such non-income indicators as educational and health access (see Chapters 4 and 5 for a detailed analysis). Here we discuss some general educational indicators. Information is available on some educational indicators for minority areas, namely, schools and graduates by level of education (see Figures. 3.2 and 3.3). The number of minority-area schools in the total at primary and higher levels of education remained almost constant throughout 1979–98. However, the number of minority-area secondary schools showed a steady increase. The share of graduates at secondary level was also quite stable. However, there was a gradually rising trend of graduates from primary schools.

A regional picture of education in minority areas is obtained by looking at the number of teachers at primary, secondary and higher levels of education. Between 1994 and 1998, the share of primary teachers in minority areas increased from 42 per cent to 45 per cent. However, there are inter-provincial and inter-area variations. In some cases (e.g. Guangxi and Tibet) the share of primary teachers declined; in others (e.g. Inner Mongolia) they increased. The share of primary teachers also increased in the west region (see Table 3.3).

Health indicators

Indicators of access to health services in the autonomous areas show even less improvement than the educational indicators. As we note in Chapter 5, the share of doctors in the autonomous areas and the west region declined between 1980 and 1992. Between 1992 and 1998, while the autonomous area share of hospitals started increasing that of hospital beds, doctors and medical personnel gradually started declining up to 1996, before starting to rise again.

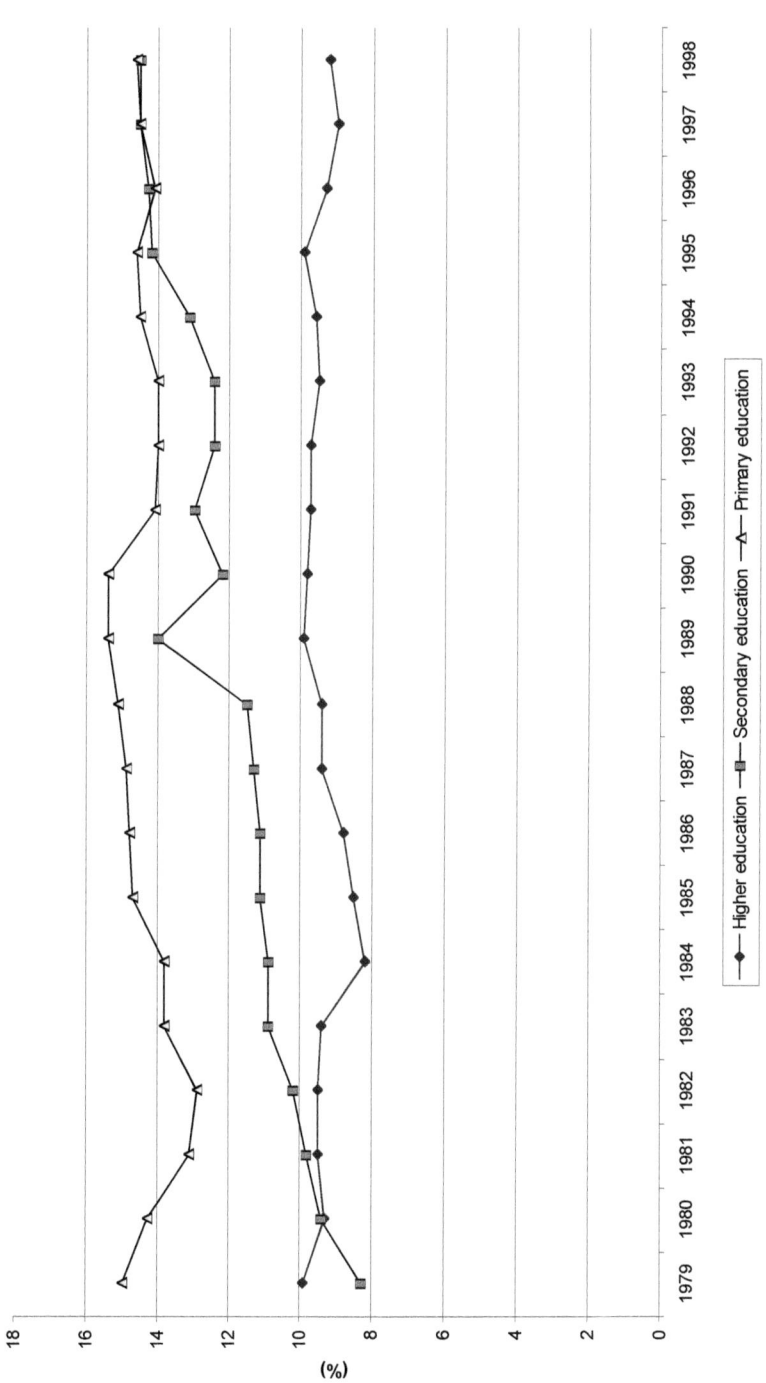

Figure 3.2 Shares of minority schools by type of education

Sources: Based on data from *China's Ethnic Statistical Yearbook; Comprehensive Statistical Data and Materials on 50 Years of New China.*

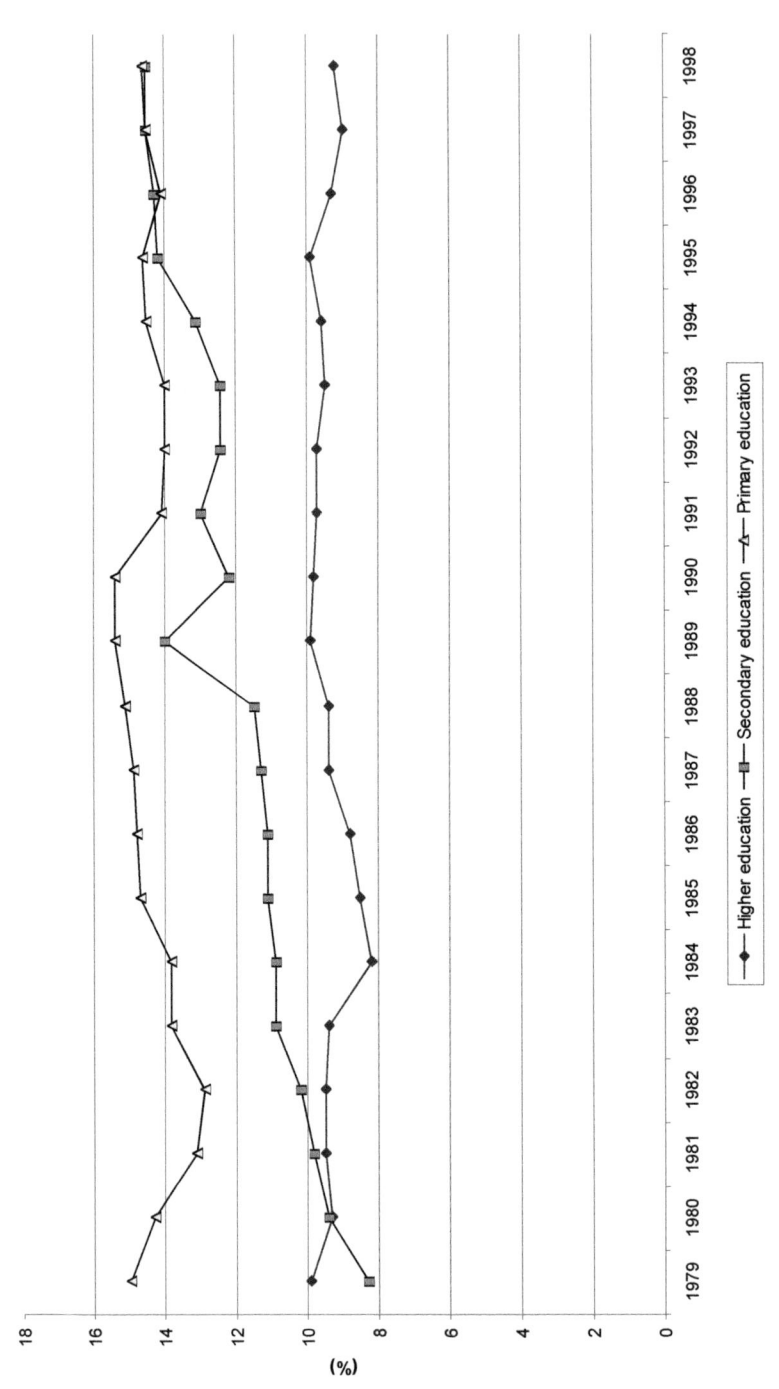

Figure 3.3 Graduates in minority areas by level of education (% of the total)

Sources: Based on data from *China's Ethnic Statistical Yearbook*; *Comprehensive Statistical Data and Materials on 50 Years of New China*.

Table 3.3 Educational indicators for the autonomous areas: teachers by level of education (1994, 1998)

Province/ indicator	1994			1998		
	Total (000)	Minority (000)	Ratio (%)	Total (000)	Minority (000)	Ratio
National total						
Primary	5,611	478.8	8.5	5,819	536.9	9.2
Secondary	3,757	207.6	5.5	4,312	260.3	6
Higher	396	21.1	5.3	407	23.2	5.7
Autonomous areas						
Primary	461	195.2	42.3	470.2	210.8	44.8
Secondary	311.6	–	–	343.6	115.2	33.5
Higher	24.4	–	–	25.5	7.5	29.4
Tibet						
Primary	11.5	11	95.7	13.9	13.2	95
Secondary	3.4	–	–	4.4	3	68.2
Higher	0.8	–	–	0.8	0.4	50
Guangxi						
Primary	194.1	75.9	39.1	196	74	37.8
Secondary	112.1	–	–	135.9	43.5	32
Higher	7.4	–	–	8	1.6	20
Inner Mongolia						
Primary	153.5	35.5	23.1	137	35.4	25.8
Secondary	101.3	–	–	99.1	21.7	21.9
Higher	6.9	–	–	7.3	2.2	30.1
Ningxia						
Primary	–	6.7	–	–	8.5	–
Secondary	19.2	–	–	20.7	3.8	18.4
Higher	1.7	–	–	1.7	0.3	17.6
Xinjiang						
Primary	101.9	66	64.8	123.3	79.7	64.6
Secondary	75.5	–	–	83.6	43.2	51.7
Higher	7.6	–	–	7.6	3	39.5
West Region						
Primary	1,121	233.7	20.8	1,168	267.4	22.9
Secondary	612.9	–	–	679.3	110.8	16.3
Higher	66.9	–	–	68.9	11.1	16.1

Autonomous areas include Guangxi, Tibet, Inner Mongolia, Ningxia and Xinjiang. West region includes Guizhou, Sichuan, Gansu, Ningxia, Qinghai, Tibet, Yunnan and Xinjiang.

Sources: Government of China, SSB, *China's Ethnic Statistical Yearbook*; *Comprehensive Statistical Data and Materials on 50 Years of New China*.

Autonomous counties

The above information relating to the autonomous areas is too aggregative to reveal intra-area and inter- and intra-county variations in the poverty situation of minorities. It is therefore useful to examine data relating to counties in southwestern provinces with predominant minority populations. Guizhou is a case in point, as we noted earlier. Among the southwestern provinces/areas considered, it has the second largest proportion of minority population (nearly 38 per cent (see Chapter 2, Table 2.9).

In 1998 there were 12 autonomous counties in Guangxi, 11 in Guizhou, 3 in Sichuan and 29 in Yunnan. As there are no exclusively minority counties, some idea of the relative poverty situation of minorities can be obtained by comparing the predominantly ethnic minority counties with those with relatively less dominant minority populations (see below). In order to analyse the relative position of minority populations, we use the minority counties in Guizhou as an example. We group the 11 minority autonomous counties into three subgroups: (1) autonomous minority counties with the highest shares of minority population, (2) those with the middle-level shares of population, and (3) those with the lowest shares of minority population. Invariably all the autonomous counties are designated as either central or provincial poverty counties. The relative economic situation of autonomous poor counties is compared and contrasted with that of the provincial, regional (south, west) and national averages. There are striking similarities among all three subgroups of counties, suggesting that the predominance of minority populations in the counties has no influence on the level of real rural per capita income. Furthermore, the increase in rural real income per capita can be characterized by three distinct phases for the three groups of counties:

(1) *the first phase (1978–85)* in which rural real net income per capita rose rather slowly in all 11 autonomous counties, although it rose slightly faster in three counties, namely, Daozheng, Guanling and Ziyun, with middle shares of minority population.

(2) *the second phase (1985–90)* in which rural real net income per capita hardly rose in the four counties with the lowest shares of minority population and the three counties with middle shares of minority population. However, rural real net income per capita rose, though slowly, in the four counties with the highest shares of minority population.

(3) *the third and final phase (1991–98)* in which rural real net income per capita rose remarkably fast in all 11 autonomous counties, especially after 1993 or 1994. This exceptional growth in rural per capita incomes coincides with the introduction of the 8–7 Poverty Reduction Programme under which the centrally and provincially designated poor counties received special financial and other support. Could this be policy-driven growth because especially favourable conditions were created for the development of the relatively poor autonomous counties in which the bulk of the minority populations lived? It

was also a period of overall rapid economic growth, which must have given a special boost to growth in rural real per capita incomes.

There may be another explanation for differences between the different phases. Rural consumer prices fell considerably during 1995–98, which may partly account for high real income per capita during this period. Consumer prices peaked during 1988–90, which may account for low rural real per capita income during the second phase. Rural consumer prices also peaked during 1994–96, but this price hike had only a limited dampening effect on rural real per capita income because of a rapid overall growth of the economy.

A comparison of the average rural net per capita income of (1) autonomous poor counties, (2) other poor counties, (3) all counties in the province and (4) the national economy of China for 1978–98 shows some interesting results. First, there is hardly any difference between the average rural net per capita income of (1) and (2). Second, the gap between the poor counties (1 and 2) and the provincial average for Guizhou started widening in 1993 and continued until 1996 when the catching-up process started. The poor counties started narrowing the gap after that. Third, the gap between the provincial average and the national average real rural per capita income started widening in 1994 and continued to do so in 1998. This growing inequality accompanies a reduction in absolute poverty because elsewhere the rural net per capita income is growing faster and the rich are becoming richer. Thus a decline in absolute poverty does not conflict with an increase in income inequality.

Evidence from the CASS household surveys

Household surveys in China are conducted annually by the National Bureau of Statistics (NBS, formerly SSB). The two CASS surveys undertaken by the Institute of Economics in collaboration with foreign scholars (e.g. Griffin, Khan and Riskin) incorporate modifications and improvements on the regular SSB surveys. For example, improvements made to the official surveys in the CASS surveys of 1988 and 1995 consist of the following: inclusion of the rental value of housing in income estimates, valuing of self-consumed farm produce at market prices and widening of the range of subsidies included in income. However, although the CASS household surveys are undoubtedly an improvement on the earlier household surveys, they suffer from several weaknesses. Adjustments made to the official SSB surveys do not remove some of the basic problems of the official surveys, which use a narrow definition of income and do not estimate the rental value of housing. Furthermore, the rural household surveys of the 1980s did not adequately cover non-agricultural or rural activities. Bramall (2001: 698) notes: 'revised estimates remain seriously deficient, largely because they are still based on the data collected by the SSB. Some of the deficiencies produce a continuing underestimation of true income inequality.' Several factors account for this continuing underestimation: exclusion from the urban sample of illiterate and remote households and of the 'floating population' of migrants. A further difficulty arises from estimating personal income on the basis of current prices and from regional price differences. The very rich (estimated at over a million) are also likely to be excluded from the urban sample. Even those rich who might be included would under-report their true incomes. On the other hand, exclusion of the 'floating population' would tend to exaggerate income inequality. Thus, while Bramall's above conclusion of underestimation may well be correct, when there are offsetting forces at work it is difficult to determine the net effect (underestimating or overestimating) on the degree of inequality (Riskin *et al.*, 2001: 7).

In comparing the 1988 and 1995 results of the household surveys concerning minorities (see Chapters 2 to 5), one needs to bear in mind the following limitations of the CASS household surveys:

(1) The size of the sample in 1988 was much larger than that in 1995. The sample size had to be reduced in 1995 owing to cost considerations.
(2) In 1988 the rural sample included all the provinces except Tibet and Xinjiang, which have large minority populations. In 1995 the following nine provinces were excluded in addition to the above two: Fujian, Guangxi, Hainan, Heilongjiang, Inner Mongolia, Ningxia, Qinghai, Shanghai and Tianjin. As Guangxi, Inner Mongolia, Ningxia and Qinghai have substantial minority populations, our analysis based on household surveys is unable to provide a comprehensive coverage of ethnic minorities.
(3) Both the *Ethnical Statistical Yearbooks* and the 1988 and 1995 CASS household surveys give data only for two years, which is not fully satisfactory. Ideally one would need income and other data for several years to eliminate any biases due to transitory or special factors. Unfortunately we do not have such overall data, let alone those on ethnic minorities. It is not possible to distinguish between different ethnic minorities on the basis of the CASS surveys.

We believe that despite the above problems the 1988 and 1995 CASS household surveys are the best source for a study of poverty among the Chinese minorities. The problems considered above should apply equally to minorities and the Han majority populations. Therefore, a comparative analysis of the two groups should, by and large, remain unaffected.

The samples for the CASS surveys were drawn from the SSB samples used for its annual household surveys. The size of the sample differed between 1988 and 1995. The 1988 rural household survey consisted of 10,258 rural households and 51,352 persons. In the 1995 survey the sample was reduced to 7,998 rural households and 34,739 persons. As we noted above, this survey excluded several provinces included in the 1988 survey. Therefore, for the following analysis we concentrate on those provinces which were included in both surveys. Thus our analysis excludes the following provinces/autonomous regions not covered in

1995: Fujian, Guangxi, Hainan, Heilongjiang, Inner Mongolia, Ningxia, Qinghai, Shanghai and Tianjin.

Income differences between the Han and the minorities

Between 1988 and 1995 the average incomes of the Han and various minorities has diverged, thus widening the gap, due partly to lack of education among minorities and their location in remote areas (Riskin *et al.*, 2001). Gustafsson and Li (2003) show that the average income was not the same for the minorities and Han majority either in 1988 or in 1995 (see Table 3.4). They note (pp. 809–10): 'Average household income grew from 1988 to 1995, although the increase for minorities was marginal and household size decreased for both categories. The growth in average income per capita for the majority population was an impressive 52.4 per cent. In contrast the mean income per capita of the minority population increased by 21.8 per cent. From this it follows that the minority–majority income gap thus almost doubled – certainly a dramatic increase. If the minority–majority income gap continued to deteriorate at the same pace, by the year 2000 the income level of Chinese minorities would be less than half that of the majority.'

On the inequality of incomes between minorities and the Han majority, Gustafsson and Li reach the following conclusions:

(1) In 1988 the minority and majority populations in rural China did not differ in income inequality.
(2) In 1995 there was less income inequality among the minority population of rural China than among the majority population.

They note that in Guizhou and Yunnan in 1988 'there was scarcely any minority–majority income gap'. During the following seven years to 1995 income grew much faster among minorities in the two provinces (33 per cent) than among the Han majority (only 9 per cent). The situation for rural China is different from that for Guizhou and Yunnan. In rural China as a whole the majority income grew much faster than that of the minority, and the per capita income of the majority was higher in 1988 as well as 1995. This is not the case for Guizhou and Yunnan, where the minority per capita income in 1995 overtook the level of the majority per capita income (Table 3.4).

Why do we get the unusual result that minority populations in Guizhou and Yunnan have done better than the Han majority in improving their incomes between 1988 and 1995? Gustafsson and Li (2003) offer several explanations. First, the Han majority and the minorities live separately and not close to each other: minorities are concentrated in the autonomous areas. Therefore, the income growth of minorities in the two provinces may be spatial in nature. Second, tourism is concentrated in some minority areas, e.g. Buyi in Yunnan. Third, the policy of the opening up of border trade may have helped economic growth in

Table 3.4 Per capita income and its growth among minority and majority
households in rural China, Guizhou and Yunnan (1988, 1995)

Household type	1988		1995		Growth rate of per capita income (%)
	Household size (persons)	Per capita income (yuan)	Household size (persons)	Per capita income (yuan)	
Rural China					
Minority	5.6	632	4.7	767	21.8
Majority	5.0	782	4.3	1,196	52.4
Guizhou					
Minority	5.8	475	5.1	622	30.9
Majority	5.6	547	4.7	603	10.2
Yunnan					
Minority	5.9	621	5.0	830	33.7
Majority	5.7	649	4.7	699	7.8
Both provinces					
Minority	5.9	572	5.1	622	32.9
Majority	5.7	592	4.7	603	9.0

Note: The figures are estimated using the same weights in the two provinces in both 1988 and
1995. Income is expressed in 1988 prices.

Source: Gustafsson and Li (2003).

border areas inhabited by minorities. Fourth, between 1988 and 1995 the
educational gap between minorities and the Han majority disappeared, which
may be of greater positive benefit to the growth of incomes among minorities.
Fifthly, the proportion of rural people in non-farm activities grew more rapidly
among minorities than among the majority in the two provinces.

Does ethnicity explain poverty?

In Chapter 1 we briefly discussed the relationships between ethnic diversity,
economic growth and poverty. We noted the Easterly–Levine (1997) argument
that greater ethnic diversity retards economic growth and raises poverty.
Ethnically China is much less heterogeneous than Africa, but its ethnic diversity
(as we discussed above) varies a great deal across the country. The degree of
ethnic diversity in China is much higher in the southwest region than in the rest
of the country. Therefore, in principle one can extend the Easterly–Levine
arguments to test whether policies in this region are growth-retarding and thus
poverty-enhancing compared to those in the other regions which are ethnically

more homogeneous. In other words, does ethnicity lie at the root of the backwardness of Chinese minorities and their low per capita incomes? Although evidence is not conclusive, available information suggests that poverty is more acute among minorities. The Han areas enjoy much higher per capita income than the minority areas. However, as we showed earlier, the average annual rural income per capita has grown over time in such ethnically diverse provinces as Guangxi, Guizhou and Yunnan. This suggests that economic growth has occurred in these provinces despite ethnic diversity.

If the Easterly–Levine argument about the growth-retarding influence of ethnic diversity were to apply to the Chinese southwest region, one would expect very low growth rates in its provinces. However, the facts do not show this. Bramall (2000: 35–6) notes that per capita income growth at 1990 prices between 1978 and 1996 was rapid in every province in China; it was over 7 per cent in all four southwest provinces, Guizhou, Guangxi, Sichuan and Yunnan. Even Qinghai, one of the poorest provinces, grew by over 5 per cent per annum, and Xinjiang, with over 62 per cent minority population, at nearly 9 per cent. These facts certainly run counter to the Easterly–Levine thesis that a high degree of ethnicity is growth-retarding. While it is true that the southwest provinces did not grow as fast as the coastal provinces (Table 3.5), their per capita income growth rates appear far more impressive than anywhere else in the developing or industrial countries. Periodization of these growth rates in the post-reform period does not change the picture. With the exception of the 1978–82 period, per capita income growth of the west region ranged between 7 and 11 per cent, and that in

Table 3.5 Regional per capita income growth rates in China (annual average) (%)

Region	1978–82	1983–87	1988–92	1993–97	1978–97
North (Beijing, Hebei, Inner Mongolia, Shanxi, Tianjin)	5.2	9.6	6.7	11.7	8.4
Northeast (Heilongjiang, Jilin, Liaoning)	3.9	10.2	5.6	9.3	7.4
Coastal (Fujian, Guangdong, Hainan, Jiangsu, Shandong, Shanghai, Zhejiang)	8.4	11.3	9.7	14.4	11.1
Southeast (Anhui, Henan, Hubei, Hunan, Jiangxi)	7.4	10.0	5.6	12.7	9.0
South (Guangxi, Guizhou, Sichuan, Yunnan)	6.7	9.1	6.6	10.3	8.3
West (Gansu, Ningxia, Qinghai, Shaanxi, Tibet, Xinjiang)	4.8	10.7	6.7	8.2	7.7
China	6.0	10.3	7.0	9.4	8.3

Source: Dayal-Gulati and Husain (2002). Estimates are based on SSB data from Government of China, SSB, *China Statistical Yearbook* (various years) and *Gross Domestic Product of China 1992–95*.

the south region, between 7 and 10 per cent. In fact, these growth rates were nearly as high as the average growth rates for China as a whole.

An alternative explanation for the backwardness of minorities is simply their extreme poverty and location in remote mountainous areas (Riskin, 1994). This locational model sees poverty as confined to certain pockets rather than being widespread. A socioeconomic explanation of poverty among ethnic groups, to which we subscribe, sees it as dispersed, not localized. It is however, not due to the growth-retarding influence of ethnic divisions as Easterly and Levine argue. Do ethnic divisions in China lead to a low provision of such public goods and services as infrastructure, education and health? Let us take the case of education. The ethnicity view of low schooling is based on the assumption that different preferences among minority groups for language instruction and curriculum, for example, lead to a lower provision of education (Alesina and Spolaore, 1997). Does this argument apply to the Chinese provinces with a predominance of different ethnic groups? Although the issue is complex, we argue that it does not necessarily do so. It is true that some minorities are known to attach less importance to children's schooling. Many minorities (e.g. Tai Buddhists) are noted for 'failing to see any significant economic and social advantage in spending money on school education' (see Hansen, 1999: xv). The low education level of the Tai minority is known to have been due partly to the language barrier. This situation seems similar to that in rural India. The caste-based fatalism among the Indian rural poor hinders growth by reinforcing parents' preference for child labour instead of education, which is perceived as futile when job opportunities are limited (see Bhagwati, 1993; Bhalla, 2002; Weiner, 1991). Thus, the failure of some minorities to provide adequate education for their children may simply be a reflection of poor job prospects and extreme poverty than of purely cultural factors. Poverty is linked to the lack of basic education and high illiteracy, which may again be explained by low incomes and poor job prospects (see Chapter 4).

Cultural factors are difficult to define, and their effect on poverty equally difficult to determine, much less measure. Yet Chinese authorities continue to attribute poverty among Chinese minorities to their different culture and social values. Similar arguments have been made in the American literature on poverty among African-Americans. Oscar Lewis (1969), one of the main proponents of the thesis of culture of poverty, believed that several behavioural and social values distinguished the poor from the non-poor (see Chapter 1). He argued that the poor were largely responsible for their own impoverishment, a view very similar to that of the 'undeserving poor' prevalent in the nineteenth century. Many American scholars believed that African-Americans were genetically inferior (see Cherry, 1995 for a review of different opinions on this minority). The culture-of-poverty thesis enumerates such factors as large welfare benefits and dependence on other government programmes, a poor work ethic and laziness, and a lack of interest in education contributing to poverty among ethnic minorities. However, there may be nothing inherent about a minority's poor work ethic. Low incomes may prevent their access to higher education, which will limit their employment prospects in the regular job market. Thus they may be forced into casual and precarious employment, which does not promote habits of punctuality and dedication. Iceland (2003: 96) notes: 'Overall, studies examining cultural differences do not provide overwhelming evidence that most of the poor people adhere to very different value systems than non-poor people.'

We argue that the ethnic minority culture in China is mistakenly considered inferior to the Han culture. The Chinese authorities explain the backwardness of the minorities in terms of lack of culture and its adverse effect on economic development. For example, it is believed that the minorities are risk averse and fail to adopt technological modernization due to religious beliefs and superstitions. Furthermore, it is also assumed that they indulge in conspicuous consumption in festivals and customs rather than saving and investing for capital accumulation. Thus, minority culture is regarded as a drag on economic development (Harrell, 1995). Lal (1988) elaborates on low 'Hindu equilibrium' due to the caste system, which accounts for fatalism, inertia and lack of motivation on the part of the lowest castes.

If cultural factors hindered growth, as is claimed by Lal in the context of India, how would one explain the very high (and at least quite reasonable) growth rates in China not only in coastal areas but also in provinces dominated by minorities or which are ethnically very diverse as discussed above? One can argue that at least in the case of China there is no adverse cultural influence on economic growth. On the contrary, the Confucian philosophy may indeed facilitate growth by promoting higher savings (the savings rate in China is the highest in the world), capital accumulation and motivation. One can equally argue that the ethnic minorities save and invest just as much as the Han majority. In fact, there are indications that remittances by Chinese ethnic migrants are productively invested for agricultural improvements and non-farm activities (see Chapters 6 and 7). There is empirical evidence from other regions of the world (e.g. Africa which is ethnically most diverse) that ethnic groups contribute to economic modernization and growth by promoting private investment and mobilizing resources for public purposes. Bates and Yackovlev (2002: 319) conclude that 'ethnic groups strengthen incentives to educate and train the young. ... They promote the flow of people from rural areas to towns and from agriculture to industry. By helping shift people from sectors in which diminishing returns constrain the possibilities for higher incomes into sectors in which increasing returns are possible, ethnic groups have promoted the modernization of societies and the development of economies throughout the globe.'

Concluding remarks

In this chapter we have examined the poverty situation among Chinese minorities in terms of income and basic needs indicators. We have discussed, for the autonomous areas and the west region, minorities' access to income and to such public services as health and education. The gap between the average rural per capita income for China as a whole and that for its minority regions has been widening over time but it would have been worse but for the impressive growth in the regions dominated by minority groups.

For the non-income aspects of poverty, a regional picture of minority education is obtained by looking at the minority enrolments and teachers by different levels of education. While there is an increase in these indicators, it is not always very significant. The health indicators (e.g. hospitals, hospital beds, and doctors and medical personnel) show even less improvement in the minority autonomous areas than the educational indicators (see Chapter 5). Data on access to urban and rural health facilities show that the share of villages without health care stations in the minority areas has been gradually declining. While the share of rural doctors has been rising, that of rural medical personnel steadily declined. The ratio of doctors to population shows wide variations, with a rather high ratio for Tibet, which is surprising. It is not clear whether this unusually high ratio is due to a large number of low-quality barefoot doctors, or simply due to statistical inaccuracies. Health data in China and other developing countries are known to be of a rather poor quality.

Finally, we argue that the reasons for the backwardness of the Chinese minorities are largely economic rather than cultural. The non-economic or cultural explanation of poverty among minority groups is difficult to sustain considering that average rural per capita incomes in ethnically heterogeneous provinces has been rising and that their economic growth rates have been quite impressive by any standards.

4 Literacy and basic education

A.S. Bhalla and Mark Brenner

The poverty situation of minorities will be affected by their location, occupational backgrounds and educational profile. In Chapter 3 we discussed these factors and reviewed data from the autonomous areas to assess non-income (educational) disparities by ethnicity. In this chapter we discuss the educational aspects with special reference to literacy and basic education.

Minority literacy and basic education

Minority literacy rates in many poor provinces in the southwest and west of China are indeed quite low, much lower than the national average. Illiteracy is concentrated mainly among the minorities, which may partly explain their poverty and backwardness. Generally, minorities in rural areas have lower levels of education and schooling than the majority Han people, as we show below using CASS household survey data for 1988 and 1995. Their rural and ethnic features put the minority at a double disadvantage. But in the more advanced urbanized regions (e.g. Beijing, Hebei and Tianjin), contrary to expectations, minority literacy rates are actually higher than those for the Han Chinese (see Figure 4.1). This may be because the better-educated minority people move to the urban areas. On the basis of the 1988 CASS household survey, Knight and Song (1999) also found that in urban areas the minorities have a higher level of education than the Han majority. This finding is confirmed by Sautman (1999), who notes a higher level of education among Huizu (Muslim Chinese) minority people in Jiangsu province. This suggests that urban areas are inhabited by minority groups which are more successful and put greater value on education. An economic factor may better explain the higher level of education of minority people in urban areas; they might have originated in less poor families and with educated parents. Some minority groups (e.g. Miao) may attach greater importance to education than others. Knight and Song (1999: 132) argue that one reason for urban minority people to have more education 'could be a process of self-selection whereby successful minority people have spread to cities throughout China'. Another plausible reason they give is the affirmative action in favour of the minorities. If this indeed was the case, why do the rural

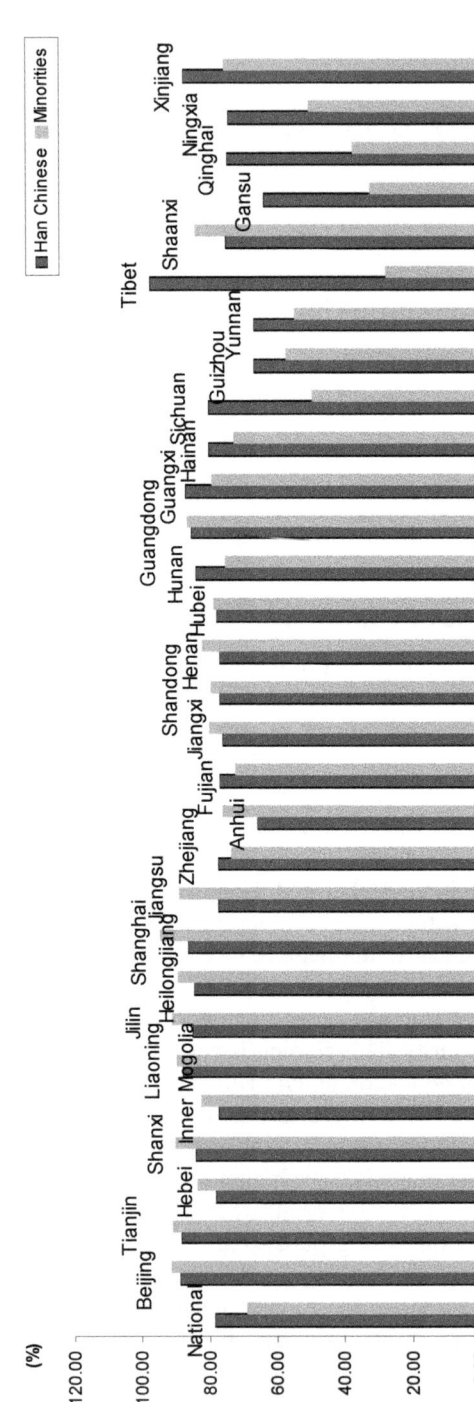

Figure 4.1 Literacy rates for minorities and Han Chinese by province (1990)

Source: 1990 population census data, based on data of population of 15 years old and over.

minorities (who are also covered by preferential policies) have less education than Han people? The explanation seems to lie in the overall urban bias of the Chinese authorities (see Chapter 6).

Of course, we should not ignore the fact that although the minority literacy rate in urban or advanced areas was higher than that for the Han Chinese, the share of minorities in the total population of these areas was quite small, except for Inner Mongolia and Liaoning. The share of minority population in the 17 provinces where minority literacy rates were higher than those of Han Chinese was only 3 per cent among those aged 15 and older. The population share was 15 per cent in the other 13 provinces, where these rates were lower than those of Han Chinese. The better-educated minority population in the 17 provinces accounted for only 26 per cent of the total minority population of 15 years and above; the share of minority population in the other 13 provinces was 74 per cent (see Table 4.1).[1]

To show gender disparity across provinces, we estimate female to male literacy ratios in Table 4.2. The higher the ratio, the lower the disparity and *vice versa*. The ratio of 1 will imply the absence of any disparity. Several features of the table are worth noting. First, in both China as a whole and the seven provinces, female literacy rates among minorities improve for the population age group 6 years and above compared to 15 years and above, suggesting greater attention to the education of very young girls. Second, in contrast to the female rates, the male minority rates decline for China as a whole and for Guangxi and Tibet; they remain unchanged for Qinghai, and improve for Guizhou, Yunnan, Ningxia and Xinjiang. What do the lower literacy rates for very young male children suggest? Are they due to child labour or lack of preference for basic male education because young boys are needed on the farms? Thirdly, gender disparity is extremely low in Xinjiang (one of the five autonomous regions) for both the age groups considered. Generally the F/M ratio is lower for poorer provinces, suggesting neglect of female education.

A China–India comparison

Drèze and Sen (1995: 65) discuss the importance of basic education in China and India and note that China has done much better than India in literacy and basic education. They compare India's literacy rates for the population 7+ years, and China's for 15+ years.[2] We would like to determine whether their point about China's superior performance still holds when the Chinese literacy rates are estimated separately for minorities and Han majority population.

The Chinese minority literacy rates are extremely low in poor provinces. For example, in Tibet the minority literacy rate is only 27 per cent compared to 31 per cent for the combined minority and Han population. The minority literacy rates for China for poor provinces are much closer to minority (SCs and STs) literacy rates in the poor Indian states. This is the case, for example, in poor provinces such as Gansu, Tibet and Qinghai. Minority literacy rates for Tibet and Gansu are

Table 4.1 Minority and Han Chinese literacy rates by gender (%) (population 15+) (1990)

	Minority			Han Chinese			Share of minority population		
	Total	*Male*	*Female*	*Total*	*Male*	*Female*	*Total*	*Male*	*Female*
National	69.17	79.50	58.35	78.47	87.62	68.85	7.37	7.36	7.38
Beijing	91.70	95.23	87.87	88.98	94.61	82.96	3.74	3.77	3.72
Tianjin	91.14	95.77	86.58	88.34	94.63	81.87	2.28	2.24	2.32
Hebei	83.63	89.76	77.07	78.17	87.06	69.01	3.79	3.86	3.72
Shanxi	90.21	95.24	85.42	84.17	89.46	78.00	0.29	0.27	0.31
Inner Mongola	82.46	87.71	77.07	77.48	85.20	68.95	16.97	16.49	17.50
Liaoning	89.85	93.86	85.54	88.26	93.35	83.02	14.48	14.72	14.23
Jilin	90.87	94.57	87.07	85.14	90.09	79.96	9.83	9.73	9.93
Heilongjiang	89.52	93.22	85.38	84.81	90.37	78.99	5.48	5.64	5.30
Shanghai	94.33	98.24	90.32	86.45	94.02	78.58	0.44	0.44	0.44
Jiangsu	88.72	95.40	83.44	77.24	87.94	66.31	0.23	0.20	0.26
Zhejiang	73.51	83.50	64.19	77.06	86.73	66.89	0.49	0.46	0.52
Anhui	75.82	84.93	67.29	65.60	78.81	51.61	0.56	0.53	0.60
Fujian	71.96	83.78	58.17	76.92	89.49	63.80	1.52	1.60	1.43
Jiangxi	80.01	90.08	68.18	75.90	87.65	63.40	0.27	0.28	0.26
Shandong	79.51	87.90	71.86	76.97	86.69	67.12	0.58	0.55	0.61
Henan	82.00	88.24	75.76	76.86	85.84	67.62	1.16	1.14	1.18
Hubei	78.35	86.89	68.70	77.66	87.49	67.25	3.93	4.05	3.80
Hunan	75.08	85.81	63.16	83.66	91.25	75.46	7.58	7.67	7.48
Guangdong	86.16	92.25	82.23	84.93	94.20	75.40	0.60	0.46	0.74
Guangxi	79.01	90.27	67.33	86.74	93.83	78.82	38.70	37.85	39.62
Hainan	72.68	82.64	62.66	79.98	91.40	67.60	15.60	15.13	16.12

Table 4.1 continues

Table 4.1 continued

	Minority			Han Chinese			Share of minority population		
	Total	Male	Female	Total	Male	Female	Total	Male	Female
Sichuan	49.03	61.13	36.48	79.98	88.09	71.28	3.97	3.90	4.03
Guizhou	56.90	74.56	37.72	66.49	80.59	51.41	33.54	33.70	33.37
Yunnan	54.50	68.88	39.68	66.29	78.59	53.19	31.88	31.53	32.25
Tibet	27.18	40.54	14.45	96.91	97.80	94.92	95.01	93.07	96.93
Shaanxi	83.94	88.38	79.38	74.83	83.59	65.42	0.50	0.49	0.51
Gansu	31.76	44.56	18.52	63.31	76.17	49.41	7.83	7.68	8.00
Qinghai	37.26	53.52	20.70	74.22	84.73	62.22	38.60	37.30	40.02
Ningxia	50.29	64.81	35.12	73.64	83.07	63.62	30.48	30.30	30.67
Xinjiang	75.32	77.99	72.50	87.14	92.00	81.72	56.37	55.66	57.14

Source: Based on the 1990 Population Census of China.

even lower than those for SCs and STs in Orissa, one of the poorest Indian states. Thus China's record looks less impressive if one considers high illiteracy among minorities and among females (see Tables 4.1 to 4.3).

One can argue that the very low minority literacy rates in China affect a much smaller population (only 8–9 per cent) than in India, where scheduled castes and tribes (SCs and STs) form nearly 25 per cent of the population. While this is true, it is fair to note that the low rates among minorities in China persist despite affirmative action, suggesting a general urban bias, which adversely affects minorities living mainly in rural areas.

In India the overall literacy rates for the sizeable Muslim minority are fairly close to those for the majority Hindu population. However, there are wide inter-provincial variations (see Table 4.4). For example, in Rajasthan and Uttar Pradesh (UP) the Muslim literacy rates are much lower than the Hindu rates, but in Orissa and Bihar they are the same and in Madhya Pradesh (MP), even a little higher. Gender disparity among the minorities is high in both China and India, but it is more serious in India if one compares the literacy rates for 6+ years. The female to male ratios (F/M) for minorities are much lower than those in China. Within India, for Muslims the average F/M ratio is slightly higher than that for Hindus. But the F/M gap is quite wide in Rajasthan (in favour of Hindus) and UP (in favour of Muslims) (see Table 4.5).

The survey data for India in Tables 4.3 and 4.4 refer to the rural population of minorities (scheduled castes and tribes), whereas those for China refer to averages for rural and urban population, which may vitiate comparison. However, in China minorities live mainly in rural areas; therefore, the rates for the two countries may be reasonably comparable.

Literacy and basic education in Tibet

Literacy rates in Tibet, inhabited by an ethnic minority, are extremely low for both males and females. Drèze and Sen (1995: 66) note Tibet's extremely low literacy rate and state: 'there is a strong possibility of comprehensive neglect of Tibet in the promotion of elementary education. There is an issue here of some importance in linking political freedom with economic and social achievements.' This neglect, however, does not apply to Tibet alone; literacy rates, particularly those of females, are also very low in Gansu and Qinghai. Raising literacy rates in Tibet is particularly difficult because of the difficulty in recruiting teachers locally, and in attracting Han teachers who may have no knowledge of the Tibetan language, or who may be unwilling to stay in Tibet given the severe climate and high altitude.

The low literacy rate in Tibet has a historical origin. Before China took control of Tibet in 1951, the educational situation was much worse than that of the rest of China. There were only 20 schools run by Tibetan local authorities and 96 small private educational institutions. The total number of students was about 3,200 (Zhang, 1989). The first new school (Changduo Primary School) was

Table 4.2 Literacy rates of Chinese minorities by gender and selected provinces (1990)

| | 6 years and above | | | | 15 years and above | | | |
	Total	Male	Female	F/M ratio	Total	Male	Female	F/M ratio
National	70.14	79.03	60.80	0.77	69.17	79.50	58.35	0.73
Guangxi	79.59	88.78	69.97	0.79	79.01	90.27	67.33	0.75
Guizhou	59.44	75.35	42.17	0.56	56.90	74.56	37.72	0.51
Yunnan	57.36	69.79	44.51	0.64	54.50	68.88	39.68	0.58
Tibet	26.73	38.03	15.78	0.41	27.18	40.54	14.45	0.36
Qinghai	39.08	53.28	24.60	0.46	37.26	53.52	20.70	0.39
Ningxia	52.25	65.34	38.60	0.59	50.29	64.81	35.12	0.54
Xinjiang	76.44	78.43	74.35	0.95	75.32	77.99	72.50	0.93

Source: Based on the 1990 Population Census of China.

Table 4.3 Minority literacy rates by gender in India and China (1990–91)

	All	Male	Female	F/M ratio
China				
National	70	79	61	0.77
Poor provinces				
Tibet	27	38	16	0.42
Gansu	33	45	21	0.47
Qinghai	39	53	25	0.47
Ningxia	52	65	39	0.60
Sichuan	49	60	37	0.62
Yunnan	57	70	44	0.63
India				
National	37 (41)	50 (54)	24 (28)	0.48 (0.52)
	30 (39)	41 (51)	18 (26)	0.44 (0.51)
Poor states				
Rajasthan	30			0.36 (0.18)
Bihar	28			0.42 (0.40)
Madhya Pradesh	32			0.39 (0.38)
Uttar Pradesh	32			0.54 (0.29)
Orissa	35			0.60 (0.44)

Sources: Censuses of population of China and India. The Chinese rates are based on population age 6+, whereas the Indian rates are for population 7+. The Indian rates in brackets are based on a 1994 survey of 33,000 rural households. So are the rates for minorities (scheduled castes and tribes; see Shariff, 1999).

established in 1951 and at the end of 1959 the number of primary schools in Tibet increased to 462, with 16,300 pupils. There were also three secondary schools with 1,732 students. By 1984 three universities had been established with 1,732 students and the number of secondary schools increased to 89 with 20,713

Table 4.4 Minority literacy rates in India by province, ethnicity and gender
(7 years and above) (1991)

State	Muslims		Hindus		Scheduled castes/tribes	
	Total	F/M	Total	F/M	Total	F/M
All India	49	0.64	53	0.60	52	0.52
Rajasthan	28	0.17	42	0.32	30	0.18
Bihar	43	0.53	44	0.50	28	0.40
Madhya Pradesh	49	0.45	44	0.46	32	0.38
Uttar Pradesh	35	0.43	48	0.29	32	0.29
Haryana	30	0.15	56	0.56	46	0.48
Himachal Pradesh	58	0.74	68	0.72	63	0.68
Punjab	33	0.38	62	0.71	46	0.60
West Bengal	52	0.75	61	0.75	54	0.73
Gujarat	59	0.56	59	0.66	47	0.61
Maharashtra	64	0.69	58	0.64	43	0.52
Andhra Pradesh	60	0.56	49	0.65	38	0.56
Karnataka	59	0.74	54	0.66	44	0.63
Kerala	87	0.93	88	0.91	77	0.89
Tamil Nadu	80	0.68	63	0.70	48	0.65
Orissa	54	0.60	54	0.60	35	0.44

F/M: Female-to-male ratio.

Source: Shariff (1999). Based on 1994 rural household survey.

Table 4.5 Muslim vs Hindu literacy rates in India (1991)

State	Muslim			F/M	Hindu			F/M
	All	Male	Female		All	Male	Female	
All India	49	59	38	0.64	53	66	39	0.60
Rajasthan	28			0.17	42			0.32
Bihar	43			0.53	44			0.50
Madhya Pradesh	49			0.45	44			0.46
Uttar Pradesh	35			0.43	48			0.29
Orissa	54			0.60	54			0.60

Source: Shariff (1999). Based on 1994 rural household survey.

students, and the number of primary schools to 2,526 with 125,469 pupils (Zhang, 1989). Since 1985 various educational indicators have shown a rising trend (see Table 4.6). The number of primary school teachers rose from 7,931 in 1985 to nearly 14,000 in 1999, and primary school enrolments nearly tripled during the same period. The enrolment rate of primary school-age children rose from 46 per cent in 1985 to 82 per cent in 1999. This rate is still below the goal of universal primary education. Furthermore, it may conceal high drop-out rates, reflecting the low quality of education, difficulty in passing Chinese language examination, and the poverty situation of Tibetan parents which forces children out of schools. In 1999 only 45 per cent of primary-school graduates entered secondary schools compared to 68 per cent in 1995 (Table 4.6).

The low starting point and poor natural conditions were partly to blame for the government's failure to raise educational profiles quickly in Tibet. In 1951 Tibet's total area was more than 1.2 million square kilometres, equivalent to that of three Japans and 39 Switzerlands, but it had a population of only 957,000, that is, 0.8 persons per square km. The population doubled between 1950 and 1980, but the population density of 1.6 persons per square km in 1982 was still only 1/60th of the national average. It was difficult to provide adequate schooling facilities and educational infrastructure with such a low population density. Second, Tibet is 4,000 metres above sea level, with an annual average temperature of below zero. Low pressure and thin oxygen make it very difficult for people from outside Tibet to stay there for long periods, which reduces the possibility of attracting externally the large number of teachers required. Thirdly, the central government not only made efforts to establish a modern education system in Tibet by sending teachers from other provinces, but it also mobilized educational resources and facilities in other parts of China for the benefit of Tibetans. In 1974 the central government issued written instructions to other provinces to select teachers for secondary schools and colleges to work in Tibet. These teachers were to stay in Tibet for two years, after which they were to be replaced by others. By the end of 1987, 2,969 teachers were sent to Tibet to overcome the teacher shortage. Of these, 2,544 were secondary school teachers and 425 were university and college teachers (Editorial Board of Modern China, 1991). Recognizing the difficult

Table 4.6 Tibet: educational indicators over time (1985–99)

	1985	*1990*	*1995*	*1999*
No. of primary school teachers (000)	7.93	8.5	13.3	13.7
Primary student enrolment (000)	119.9	157.4	258.6	310.4
No. of primary school graduates (000)	11.38	9.3	14.4	30.7
Enrolment of school-age children (%)	46	67.4	70.4	81.7
Graduates of primary schools entering senior secondary schools (%)	44.9	62.1	67.7	45.2

Source: Government of China, SSB, *Tibet Statistical Yearbook*, 2000.

climatic and socioeconomic conditions in Tibet noted above, in the mid-1980s the government decided to ask 19 other provinces to set up Tibetan schools and classes in Tibetan in their territories for Tibetan students. Three Tibetan schools were set up in Beijing, Chongqing and Lanzhou; Tibetan classes were also introduced in other provinces. There were 1,301 students from Tibet studying in these special schools and classes; the figures for 1986, 1987 and 1988 were 1,227, 1,400 and 1,150 respectively. In 1997, 7,000 Tibetan pupils were sent to other provinces to study (Iredale *et al.*, 2001: 161). While some returned to Tibet, others went on to study further or to take up jobs in other provinces. The number of Tibetan-language schools also increased from the late 1980s onwards (Upton, 1999). On the basis of fieldwork in 1996, Upton (1999: 307) notes that, 'contrary to Western and Tibetan exile rhetoric', the textbooks in schools 'do contain a fair amount of material drawn from Tibetan sources and relevant to Tibetan cultural life in the broad sense'.

The government operating expenditure in Tibet for culture, education and health care rose from 21.7 per cent in 1990 to 23 per cent in 1999. Although government subsidies declined during the 1990s, they still represented 70 per cent of Tibet's total expenditure in 1999 (see *Tibet Statistical Yearbook* 2000).

Drèze and Sen (1995: 66) state that 'literacy rates in Tibet are not only abysmally low (even lower than in the educationally backward states of North India), they also show little sign of significant improvement over time'. This claim is not fully justified. Between 1990 and 1997, Tibet's literacy rate rose from 31 per cent (combined rate for Han and minority population) to 46 per cent, an increase of nearly 48 per cent, which is quite significant. As the ethnic minority of Tibetans form over 95 per cent of the total population of Tibet, we can assume that its average literacy rate is close to that for the Tibetan ethnic minority. Therefore, it would be appropriate to compare this rate to the Indian minority literacy rates for different states. The average literacy rate for Tibet (31 per cent) is close to SC literacy rates in poor Indian states. Literacy rates in other western provinces with sizeable minorities also increased during the period: from 64 per cent to 74 per cent in Guizhou and from 67 per cent to 74 per cent in Ningxia.

A comparison of Tibet with the other four autonomous regions is also instructive. Figures 4.2 and 4.3 show respectively primary-school enrolments per 1,000 population and the number of primary school teachers per 1,000 population in the autonomous regions and for China as a whole. Figure 4.2 on primary-school enrolment shows that since the early 1990s the autonomous regions (with the exception of Inner Mongolia) had a higher ratio than the average for China as a whole. Although Tibet's ratio until 1994 was lower than those for the other four autonomous regions, it exceeded that of Inner Mongolia and China since then. The pattern is somewhat similar for the ratio of primary teachers (see Figure 4.3). Though lower until the early 1990s, Tibet's ratio exceeded that of Guangxi and China. This suggests that the autonomous regions with predominant minority populations have been performing well in terms of the basic educational indicators.

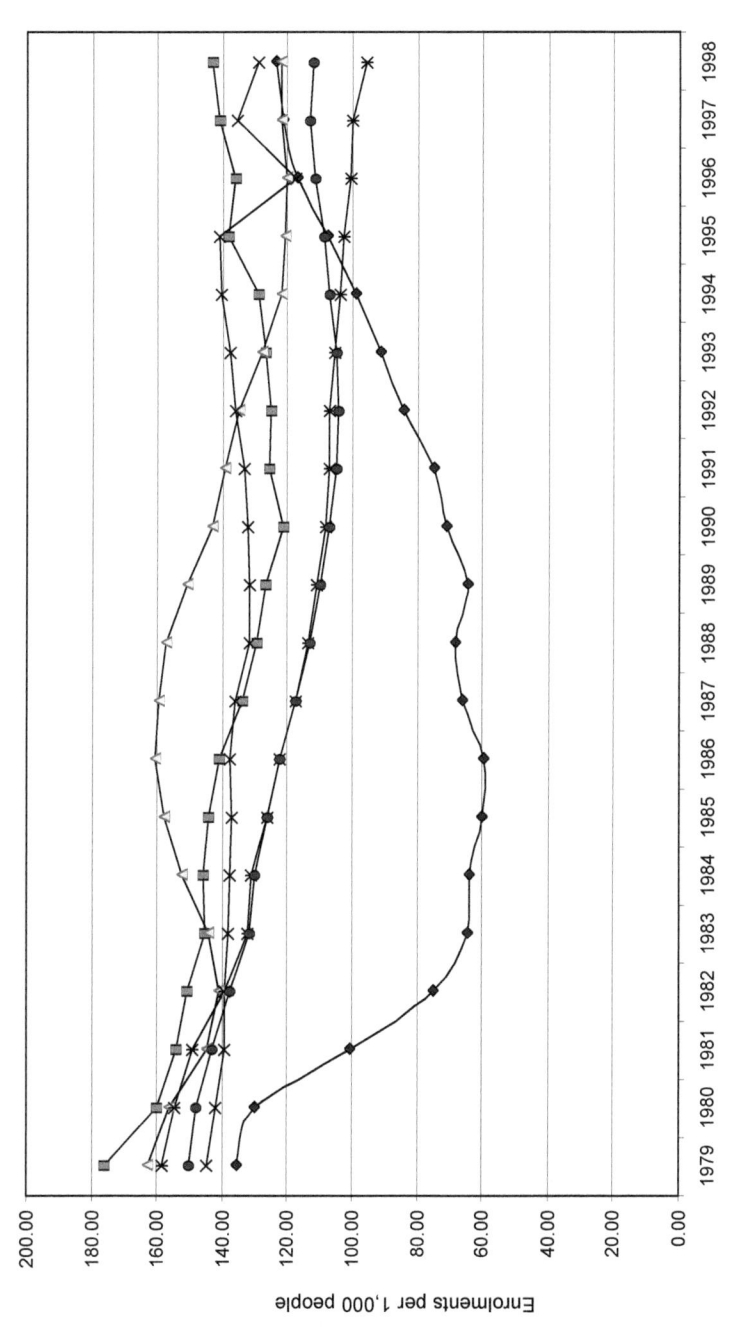

Figure 4.2 Primary school enrolments per 1,000 population in the autonomous areas (1979–98)

Sources: Based on data from *China's Ethnic Statistical Yearbook*; *Comprehensive Statistical Data and Materials on 50 Years of New China*, 1999

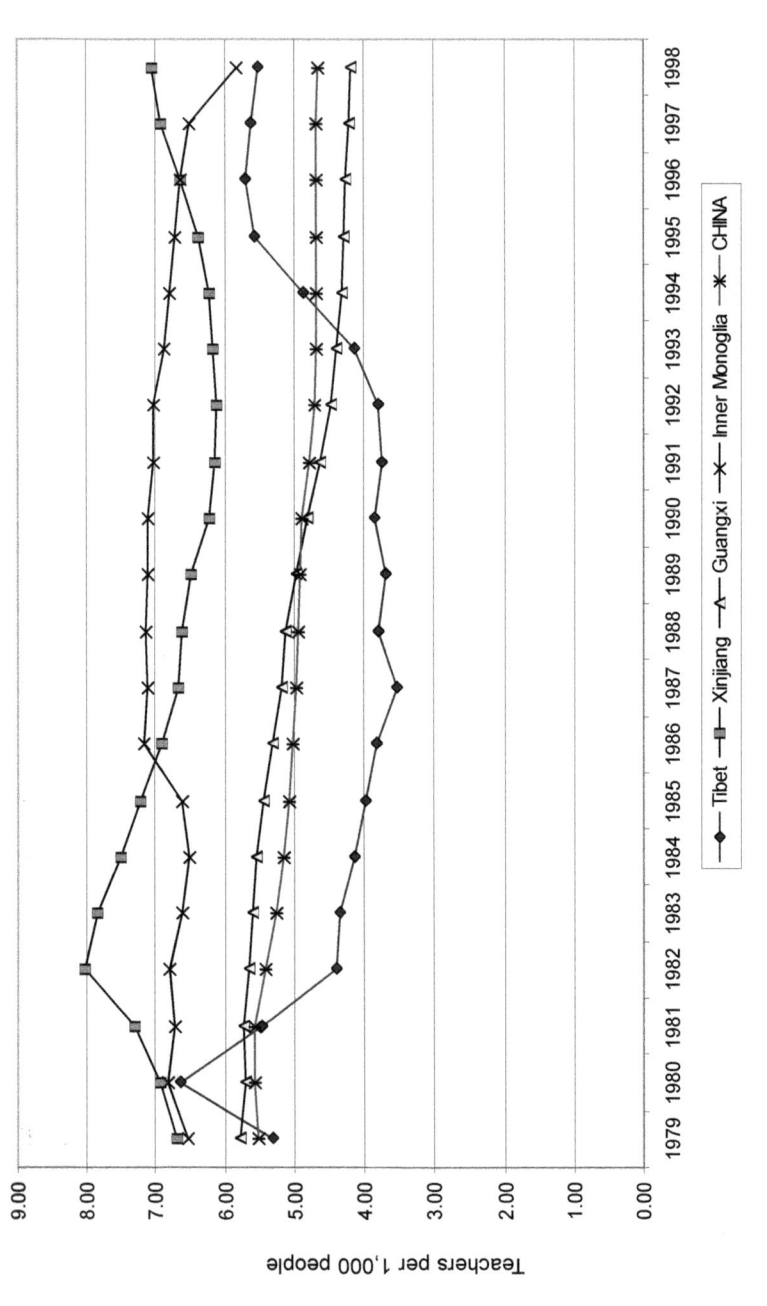

Figure 4.3 Number of primary school teachers per 1,000 population in Tibet and other autonomous areas (1979–98)

Sources: Based on data from *China's Ethnic Statistical Yearbook*; *Comprehensive Statistical Data and Materials on 50 Years of New China*, 1999.

Minority enrolments and teachers

Between 1994 and 1998 shares of primary-school enrolment remained constant in the autonomous areas, although they increased slightly for primary teachers. The share of primary teachers also increased in the west region (see Table 4.7). Primary-school enrolments for minority students rose much faster during the 1980s than the 1990s, when they actually flattened out. Minority enrolments for institutions of higher education and technical schools also grew extremely slowly during the 1990s (see Figure 4.4). Stagnation in minority enrolments may be linked to a change in educational policy for minorities. In the 1970s and early

Table 4.7 Primary education: minority enrolments and teachers by selected regions (1994, 1998)

Province/indicator	1994					1998
	Total (000) (1)	Minority (000) (2)	(2) as % of (1)	Total (000) (3)	Minority (000) (4)	(4) as % of (3)
National total						
Enrolment	128,226	11,492	9	139,538	12,402	8.9
Teachers	5,611	478.8	8.5	5,819	536.9	9.2
Autonomous areas						
Enrolment	11,622	4,876	42	11,750	4,931	42
Teachers	461	195.2	42.3	470.2	210.7	43
Guangxi						
Enrolment	6,316	2,408	38.1	6,036	2,179	36.1
Teachers	194.1	75.9	39.1	196	74	37.8
Inner Mongolia						
Enrolment	2,352	515.2	21.9	2,248	480	21.4
Teachers	153.5	35.5	23.1	137	35.4	25.8
Tibet						
Enrolment	233	226.3	97.1	310.2	303.5	97.8
Teachers	11.5	11	95.7	13.9	13.2	95
Ningxia						
Enrolment	614.8	208.9	34	652.5	224.4	34.4
Teachers	–	6.7	–	–	8.5	–
Xinjiang						
Enrolment	2,106	1,518	72.1	2,503	1,744	69.7
Teachers	101.9	66	64.8	123.3	79.7	64.6
West region						
Enrolment	26,344	5,981	22.7	30,357	6,713	22.1
Teachers	1,121	233.7	20.8	1,168	267.6	22.5

Sources: Government of China, SSB, *China's Ethnic Statistical Yearbook*, 1995, 1999; *China Statistical Yearbook*.

1980s, measures were adopted to educate minority people in non-formal educational schools and 'nationalities institutes', which have since been de-emphasized. While minorities continue to receive special treatment (see below), a shift in policy towards formal instead of non-formal education, under which the minorities have to compete with the Han students, places them at a disadvantage.

The number of minority teachers as a proportion of all teachers is illustrated in Table 4.7. The situation regarding minority teachers is somewhat different from that of minority enrolments discussed above. In primary schools they represented a greater and growing proportion of all teachers than in other educational categories. The proportion of those in higher education hardly increased in the 1990s, and actually underwent a sharp decline in 1998.

One reason for this may be a preference of minority people for cadre jobs rather than academic work. Both supply and demand responses may be at work here; the government may be keen to show greater representation of minority people among the cadres since their share is at present rather low.

The regional picture of minority teachers shows wide variations across provinces and autonomous regions. As is to be expected, in most provinces it is the share of minority primary teachers that is highest, except in Gansu and Inner Mongolia. It is rather odd that in Inner Mongolia the minority teachers' share is higher at the higher educational level than at primary and secondary levels.

Evidence from the CASS household surveys

Our next concern is to obtain a more comprehensive picture of literacy and basic education among minorities by analysing the CASS household survey data for 1988 and 1995.

We would like to attempt to answer the following questions:

(1) Do ethnic minorities in rural areas have lower literacy rates and basic education than the Han majority?
(2) Do females among minorities suffer particularly badly from lack of literacy compared to male members?
(3) What factors determine the low literacy rates among minorities? Are economic factors more or less important than the cultural or value factors in explaining educational discrepancies between minorities and Han populations? Cross-country analyses (see Stewart, 1985) show a positive correlation between average per capita income and literacy rate because incomes provide the resources with which private expenditure is likely to be financed. But does this also hold for an economy like China, where such basic needs as education for the minorities may be financed/subsidized heavily by the state for social and political reasons?

A positive correlation between education and income may work in several ways. First, a higher level of education enables an increase in incomes through

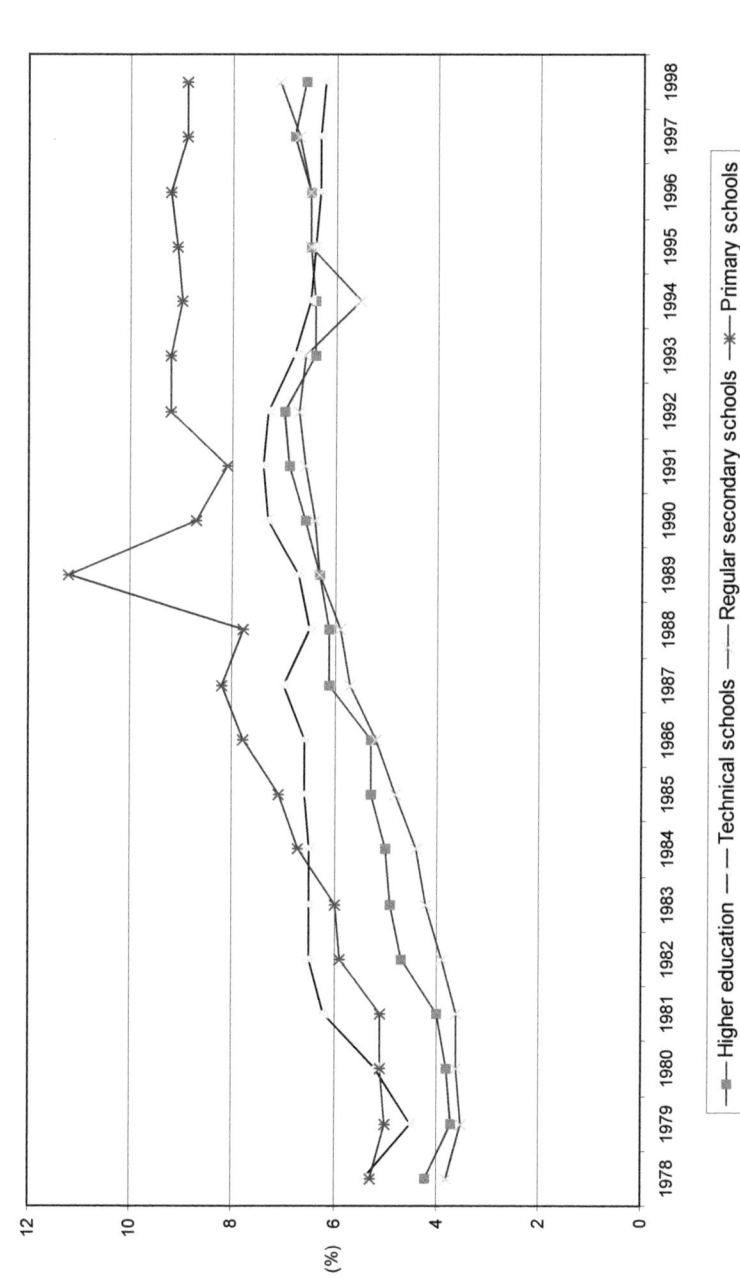

Figure 4.4 Minority enrolments as a proportion of all enrolments

Sources: Based on data from *China's Ethnic Statistical Yearbook; Comprehensive Statistical Data and Materials on 50 Years of New China*, 1999.

higher wages and earnings. There is an abundant literature showing high economic returns to primary education (see Alderman *et al.*, 1993; Psacharapoulos, 1988).

Second, a rise in per capita income should, in principle, lead to greater demand for education by raising affordability.

Third, there is the human development aspect of basic education; it enables a better quality of life, improved family planning and child nutrition.

Educational improvements should be reflected in higher standards of living among the minorities to the extent to which education and income are positively correlated. Of course, one can argue that in a socialist country like China such a correlation may not hold since primary and secondary education are considered a social and political goal. A cross-section regression between per capita income and educational attainment showed no statistically significant correlation for primary education, although it did for secondary education and college graduates (see Bhalla, 1995: 263). However, under market reforms, Chinese education is being gradually privatized, with students having to pay tuition fees, which will put poorer minority students at a disadvantage. Private education and market mechanisms are inadequate tools for providing basic education to the poor and disadvantaged groups. China's pre-reform experience shows that public action (literacy campaigns, for example) and services were responsible for significant achievements in education and health (see Drèze and Sen, 1995).

Several economic and non-economic factors may explain differences between minorities and non-minority populations. The determinants of levels of and access to education are a complex interaction of economic, political, institutional and cultural variables. Furthermore, public and private resources for education as well as incentives may also have important roles to play. Economists generally believe that inequalities in education and health are largely income determined. But the causation may work both ways. While low incomes may deny poor minorities access to education, low access to education and low levels of schooling may also be the cause of low incomes. We noted in Chapter 3 that minorities in rural areas have much lower per capita income than the Han population. The ability of an individual or a household to pay for education determines access to it in most market-oriented developing countries. As China has become increasingly market-oriented in education, with private fee-paying schools, the private costs of education to parents of children have been increasing. *A priori* in China, where the majority of schools are state-owned and education is heavily subsidized, the cost of education to individuals should be low or negligible. But in practice there is growing evidence of the rising costs of education. Drèze and Saran (1995) note that in She Tan village in Zhejiang province in eastern China, the school fees rose from 4 yuan per child per year in the early 1980s to 100 yuan in 1993. In Xinjiang in 1995 tuition fees at the higher education level were 2,000 yuan per annum (and in Sichuan, at the Southwest Nationalities University in Chengdu, 1,700 yuan for most subjects), too high for the rural minority families with grant of subsidies (Sautman, 1999).

Public expenditure on education at the local level in many counties and villages in China has also declined since the introduction of the rural household responsibility system in the 1970s. There are several sources of expenditure: the central and county governments, local bodies (rural townships), and private households. In the case of primary education the state bears most of the expenses of urban schools but not of rural schools. The latter are funded mainly by rural townships (formerly communes). At the local level, rural primary schools are financed mainly by tax revenues and educational fees paid by farmers, although the existing Education Law stipulates that this expenditure should be charged to the fiscal budgets of the county governments. A recent report by the Development Research Centre (DRC) of the State Council notes that this situation reflects 'more like the Chinese traditional family-based education instead of the so-called public or compulsory education' (cited in *People's Daily*, 21 December 2002). In May 2002 reforms to reduce farmers' financial burden declared illegal the education surtax and other types of fees levied on them in the name of rural education. However, it is not clear whether the poor local governments with a low tax base can afford to finance primary education without central subsidies.

The Chinese government underinvests in education compared to many other Asian countries. For example, in 1997 China spent 2.3 per cent of GNP on education compared to 3.2 per cent by India, 3.7 per cent by the Republic of Korea, 4.9 per cent by Malaysia, and 4.8 per cent by Thailand (World Bank, 2000). We do not have separate data on public expenditure on the education of minorities.

A distinction has been made between the literacy rate (or *nominal* rate) and an *effective* literacy rate. While the nominal literacy rate is the number of literate adults as a proportion of the total number of adults, an effective rate 'takes into account the intra-household externality arising from the presence of a literate member' (Basu and Foster, 1998: 1733). The distribution of literate persons across households is likely to be very uneven, so that some households may have no literate members whereas others (particularly large ones have several literate members). A more even distribution pattern of literacy would ensure more effective literacy. In the case of Chinese minorities, we noted above that rural literacy rates are generally much lower for both males and females. Their effective literacy rates are also likely to be lower. The probability of *isolated illiterates* (without any literate member in a household) is likely to be much greater among minorities living in remote mountainous areas with very low incomes than among the majority population living in more dense and prosperous rural areas. Thus minorities may be denied access to a positive externality, that is, access to a literate person who can offer information on farm prices, for example. Even if there is some positive externality enjoyed by minorities, it might be depleted by rural-to-urban migration of literate members of minority households. Another leakage could be through any fees charged by literate members from illiterate household members. The policy implications of the effective literacy measure is that government policies should target female illiteracy within households and ensure that each rural household has at least one literate member.

Market incentives can have an adverse effect on minority education in many ways. Payment of tuition fees will mean that minority people, being much poorer, will not be able to afford private education. Public education facilities in remote mountainous areas where these people generally live are of low quantity and quality because of the limited revenue-generating capacity of the local governments. The private rate of return to education in these areas is likely to be low. Furthermore, minority perceptions about a lack of job opportunities may lead to their placing a low value on education of children, especially when the opportunity cost is not that low. These adverse effects would occur despite positive discrimination in favour of minorities.

Empirical evidence

Turning to the evidence from the CASS surveys, we first address the educational attainment of minorities *vis-à-vis* non-minorities in rural China in both 1988 and 1995. Table 4.8 provides a detailed comparison for all adults in provinces with a sizeable minority population. We restrict our analysis to provinces surveyed in both years, specifically Hebei, Liaoning, Jilin, Hunan, Guizhou and Yunnan.

Consistent with the results from Table 4.1, our survey data reveal a much lower level of literacy for minorities in rural China *vis-à-vis* the Han majority. We find that in 1988 only 67 per cent of minority adults were literate versus 82 per cent of adults in the Han majority. These educational gaps between the majority and minority populations persist at higher levels of educational attainment as well. From Table 4.8 we see that only 65 per cent of the minority population has completed four or more years of schooling, as compared with 80 per cent for the Han majority, with similar gaps for both lower middle school and above (32 per

Table 4.8 Adult educational attainment in Chinese provinces with a sizeable rural minority population (1988, 1995) (percentages)

	1988 Minority	1988 Non-minority	1995 Minority	1995 Non-minority
Illiterate or semi-illiterate	33.0	18.0	22.6	15.0
1–3 years of primary school	2.1	2.3	8.4	6.3
4+ years of primary school	33.4	37.7	33.4	31.0
Lower middle school graduate	24.6	31.7	28.7	36.7
Upper middle school graduate	5.9	8.9	5.4	9.2
More than upper middle school	1.0	1.4	1.7	1.9
Number of observations	1,373	5,326	1,639	4,884

Note: These results are calculated from the CASS survey data for Hebei, Liaoning, Jilin, Hunan, Guizhou, and Yunnan. We define as adult anyone 18 years or older.

cent versus 42 per cent) and upper middle school and above (7 per cent versus 10 per cent).

In 1995, by contrast, the literacy rates for both groups had increased substantially, rising to 77 per cent for minorities and 85 per cent for the Han population. The data reveal that the biggest shift is an increase in educational attainment at the lowest levels (that is, at least one to three years of primary schooling) with little or no change at higher levels of educational attainment.

Focusing our attention on the minority population, what differences, if any, do we observe between men and women in the two years of our survey data? Table 4.9 sheds light on this question, reporting rates of educational attainment for both male and female adult minorities.

What we find, consistent with the national data presented in Table 4.2, is a much higher rate of educational attainment for male minorities as opposed to females. In 1988, for example, nearly half of all female minorities were illiterate (47.4 per cent), whereas men registered an illiteracy rate of less than half that figure (20.2 per cent). The gap remains wide for higher levels of education. For example, drawing on the data in Table 4.9, we can see that only 21.6 per cent of female minorities report completing lower middle school, compared to 40.4 per cent of men. The picture is similar for upper middle school completion (4.4 per cent versus 9.2 per cent).

Mirroring the trends in the general population, we observe a sharp decline in the reported rate of illiteracy for both male and female minorities between 1988 and 1995, dropping to 34 per cent for women and nearly 11 per cent for men. As before, these trends are broadly explained by a much larger proportion of the minority population achieving at least one to three years of schooling, rather than a general upward trend in minority educational attainment. These trends also illustrate the continued gender disparities between male and female minorities, as the male illiteracy rate fell much more sharply than did the female rate over the period. Indeed, the ratio of female to male illiteracy rose from 2.3 to 3.2 between

Table 4.9 Female vs male minority educational attainment in rural China (1988, 1995) (percentages)

	1988 Female	1988 Male	1995 Female	1995 Male
Illiterate or semi-illiterate	47.4	20.2	34.1	10.7
1–3 years of primary school	1.7	2.5	8.7	8.0
4+ years of primary school	29.3	37.0	30.8	36.1
Lower middle school graduate	17.2	31.2	21.7	35.8
Upper middle school graduate	3.6	8.0	3.6	7.2
More than upper middle school	0.8	1.2	1.1	2.2
Number of observations	645	728	829	810

Note: These results are calculated from the CASS survey data for Hebei, Liaoning, Jilin, Hunan, Guizhou, and Yunnan. We define as adult anyone 18 years or older.

the two years. At higher levels of education wide gaps persist between male and female minorities, but by contrast women's performance improved slightly *vis-à-vis* men.

As noted earlier, individual educational attainment does not tell the complete story about the social isolation and economic marginalization that can occur when multiple members of a household are illiterate. Table 4.10 gives us a picture of this problem.

Table 4.10 illustrates the wide gaps between minorities and non-minorities along the dimension of effective illiteracy. In 1988, for example, 7.4 per cent of minorities reported living in a household where all members were illiterate, as compared with 3.1 per cent for non-minorities. These figures rise slightly if we only consider all adults (9.1 per cent versus 3.9 per cent). In that same year we find that roughly a quarter of minorities reported living in a household where the household head was illiterate, compared with approximately 12.5 per cent of non-minorities, with the figure dropping only slightly if we consider whether both the head of household and spouse are illiterate (23.8 per cent versus 10.8 per cent).

As with our earlier survey results, Table 4.10 also reflects the dramatic improvements in educational attainment between 1988 and 1995. For both minorities and non-minorities we find that by 1995 virtually all survey respondents report at least one household member having some formal education. Only 1.5 per cent of minorities report living in a household where all adult members are illiterate compared to 0.6 per cent for non-minorities. The proportion of individuals living in households where the head is illiterate is significantly higher for minorities than non-minorities (10.6 per cent versus 5 per cent). As before, these figures drop slightly when we consider households where both the head of household and spouse are illiterate (8.4 per cent versus 4.2 per cent).

Regression analysis

Our discussion of literacy and educational attainment thus far has made use of summary statistics, both from the Chinese government as well as from the CASS household survey data. We are now in a position to more formally examine the determinants of educational attainment using regression analysis. Specifically, we will explore the factors influencing the completion of at least four or more years of schooling using logistic regression techniques. We will restrict our analysis to children aged 13 to 18, living with their parents. In this manner, we will be able to examine the influence of important household factors such as per capita income, minority status (or ethnicity and culture), location and geography (households in plains, hilly areas or poverty regions), as well as parental characteristics such as educational attainment and occupation. Our selection of independent variables closely follows Gustafsson and Li (2003), who examined the determinants of income gaps between minority and non-minority households.

Table 4.10 Different measures of effective illiteracy in rural China (1988, 1995)
(percentages)

	1988 Minority	1988 Non-minority	1995 Minority	1995 Non-minority
All household members are illiterate	7.4	3.1	**	**
All adults in household are illiterate	9.1	3.9	1.5	0.6
Household head is illiterate	24.9	12.5	10.6	5.0
Head and spouse are illiterate*	23.8	10.8	8.4	4.2
Number of observations	1,574	9,787	2,444	7,129

Note: These results are calculated from the CASS survey data for Hebei, Liaoning, Jilin, Hunan, Guizhou, and Yunnan. We define as adult anyone 18 years or older. * Where spouse is present. ** For both groups less than 0.5 per cent of the sample reports all household members as being illiterate.

Table 4.11 reports the results of our model for both 1988 and 1995. In the first column for each year we report the results from the logistic regression, while in the second we estimate the marginal effects. These marginal effects capture an increased (or decreased) probability that a child will complete four or more years of schooling, given a one unit increase in the independent variable. For locational factors, we assume that one unit increase measures the effect as if an individual moved from not being in a particular location (say a hilly area) to being in a particular location (say the plains). For dummy variables (that is, variables recorded as 1 or 0) the marginal effect represents a predicted increase or decrease for a discrete change from 0 to 1.

Turning to the results, we find that most of our independent variables have a statistically significant effect on educational attainment for young people in both years. First and foremost, we find that minority status (or ethnicity) exerts a sizeable and statistically significant negative effect. For example, in 1988 minorities were 10 per cent less likely to complete four or more years of schooling, controlling for other factors. By 1995 this figure had dropped to only 5 per cent. Consistent with many other studies, we also find that household income is an important determinant of education in both years. Based on these results, a doubling of household income would increase the probability of completing at least four years of schooling by more than 7 per cent in 1988 and nearly 3 per cent in 1995.

Table 4.11 reveals that several other factors were also important determinants of educational attainment. For example, low levels of educational attainment by the household head exerted a statistically significant effect on the likelihood that children would complete at least four years of schooling. For 1988 our results show that if the household head had only one to three years of schooling, his/her children were roughly 18 per cent less likely to complete at least four years of schooling. In a similar fashion, if the household head was illiterate, this lowered the probability by approximately 12 per cent. By 1995 the magnitude of these

Table 4.11 Determinants of educational attainment in rural China (1988, 1995)

	(1) 1988 Logistic regression	(2) 1988 Marginal effects	(3) 1995 Logistic regression	(4) 1995 Marginal effects
A. *Minority status (ethnicity)*	-0.690** (0.34)	-0.102* (0.060)	-0.999*** (0.30)	-0.046** (0.020)
B. *Educational and other characteristics of household head*				
Head of household is illiterate	-0.763*** (0.24)	-0.117*** (0.044)	-1.011*** (0.27)	-0.048*** (0.019)
Head of household has completed four or more years of education	0.621*** (0.13)	0.073*** (0.014)	-0.024 (0.20)	-0.001 (0.006)
Head of household has completed 1–3 years of education	-1.060*** (0.22)	-0.175*** (0.047)	-1.116*** (0.27)	-0.056*** (0.020)
Head of household works in agriculture	-0.576*** (0.19)	-0.060*** (0.017)	0.092 (0.26)	0.003 (0.008)
Head of household is male	-0.199 (0.23)	-0.023 (0.024)	-1.023* (0.53)	-0.021*** (0.007)
Head of household is CP member	0.17 (0.16)	0.020 (0.018)	0.208 (0.23)	0.006 (0.006)
C. *Location and geography*				
Household is located in plains	0.378** (0.16)	0.045** (0.019)	0.062 (0.20)	0.002 (0.006)
Household is located in hilly region	0.698*** (0.16)	0.079*** (0.017)	0.285 (0.25)	0.008 (0.007)
Household is located in suburb	0.65 (0.45)	0.063* (0.033)	-0.878** (0.39)	-0.040 (0.025)
Household is located in designated poverty region	-0.638*** (0.13)	-0.087*** (0.020)	-0.095 (0.19)	-0.003 (0.006)
Household is located in designated minority region	0.197 (0.33)	0.022 (0.035)	-0.178 (0.32)	-0.006 (0.011)
D. *Per capita income*				
Logarithm of per capita income	0.614*** (0.10)	0.074*** (0.012)	0.904*** (0.14)	0.028*** (0.004)
Constant	-1.958*** (0.72)		-2.281* (1.23)	
Number of observations	2,570		3,627	
Pseudo R-squared	0.12		0.13	

Note: In both years these results are calculated from the CASS survey using data for the 19 provinces covered in the 1995 survey. Our dependent variable is a binary measure of completion of 4 or more years of schooling. We restrict our analysis to children between the ages of 13 and 18 years old, living with their parents. Robust standard errors are given in parentheses.
* significant at 10%; ** significant at 5%; *** significant at 1%. For dummy variables the marginal effects, (*) dy/dx, are calculated to measure the effect of a discrete change of dummy variable from 0 to 1.

influences had declined, but their negative influence remained. For both categories, low educational attainment by household heads reduced the likelihood of their children completing at least four years of schooling by approximately 5 per cent.

Geography also has a statistically significant effect on educational attainment, at least in 1988. For example, living in a suburb raised the probability of a young person completing at least four years of schooling by approximately 6 per cent compared to living further away from the urban centres. Moving from China's mountainous regions to the plains would increase the probability of a young person completing at least four years of schooling by nearly 5 per cent in 1988. Similarly, living in a hilly region increased the probability by nearly 8 per cent *vis-à-vis* a mountainous area. It is not clear why the probability for a hilly region is higher compared with the plains; it should in fact be lower. However, the difference is not great.

Another interesting difference between the two years is the way in which living in a designated poverty region affects the educational attainment of young people. We find that in 1988 living in such a region reduces the probability of completing at least four or more years of schooling by roughly 9 per cent. By contrast, in 1995 this designation has no statistically significant impact on educational attainment. Interestingly, in both years we find that living in a designated minority region has no discernible impact on educational attainment.

Taken together, these results indicate that locational factors have a relatively weak influence on educational attainment in rural China today. The diminishing importance of these factors is perhaps a sign of a strengthened educational infrastructure between the two years, particularly in underserved areas such as the mountainous regions in the far west.

Thus geography may now be an insufficient factor to identify or target those in need of better education. This is consistent with what Riskin (1994) describes as the 'impoverished regions' approach to poverty programmes, and how it is increasingly ineffective in reaching the poor (see Chapter 6).

Several other household characteristics have a statistically significant effect on educational attainment, at least in 1988. If the head of household worked in agriculture, this lowered the probability of young people completing four or more years of schooling by approximately 6 per cent. In 1995, if the household head was male, this lowered the probability of completing four or more years of schooling by roughly 2 per cent. Surprisingly, a household head's membership of the Communist Party (CP) had no statistically significant effect on educational attainment.

Educational policy for the minorities

The government policy towards the education of minorities is based on giving them special incentives to overcome their lack of access to education. These may include lower entrance requirements, 'bonus points' for taking examinations in the Chinese language instead of the minority languages, and exemption from payment of school fees. Preferential policies in education and employment include special funds to subsidize and promote minority education, e.g. Ethnic Minorities Education Aid Special Fund, Hope Project and the Border Areas Construction Aid Fund, special quotas for the minorities for admission to universities, giving preference to the minorities in hiring and promotions, and lower pass marks or scores in examinations. Although several preferences are restricted to the minorities residing in the autonomous areas, preferential admissions are extended to all the minorities irrespective of location, that is, one-quarter of the minority population living mainly in Han areas can also avail themselves of this policy (Sautman, 1999: 175). In 2000 the government started a Project for Schools in Eastern Regions to Aid Schools in Poverty-stricken Areas in the West and a Project for Large and Medium Cities in the West Aiding Schools in poor areas in their own provinces, which are generally autonomous regions or municipalities. The government has also formulated proposals to accelerate vocational education and training for the minority areas through the training of teachers and management personnel.[3]

The special admissions quota for the Chinese minorities is similar to the quota for the Indian scheduled castes and tribes, which form a significant proportion of the total Indian population (scheduled castes 16 per cent and scheduled tribes another 8 per cent). To promote equality of access to education, special seats are reserved for these castes and tribes at higher educational institutions such as medical colleges and universities (see Bhalla, 1995). The share of scheduled castes' enrolments into primary schools increased from 15.8 per cent in 1989–90 to 17 per cent in 1997–98; that of scheduled tribes from 8 per cent to 8.3 per cent during the same period (GOI, *Economic Survey 1999–2000*: 174).

Have the above preferential policies benefited the Chinese minorities by narrowing the gaps in access to education? A comparative analysis of minority autonomous areas, minority counties and minority households and non-minority regions, counties and households shows that these gaps have widened despite affirmative action. One scholar (Sangay, 1998) concludes that the bonus points system in favour of minority students is a failure, as it has not improved their access to education. However, the gaps would probably have been wider without the preferential policies. Are the widening gaps due to the poor implementation of the policies, lack of commitment to the betterment of minorities or inadequate resources for this purpose? Hansen (1999: xiii) notes: 'government regulations concerning special minority education are carried out only half-heartedly, either because they are rejected by local cadres or because the government fails to provide sufficient economic support'. This is a special and paradoxical case, however. The spread of education among the minorities, while improving their capabilities for income-earning employment opportunities, also has the danger of spreading ethnic demands.

There is another dilemma facing the educational policy makers, which pertains to the issue of minority languages versus the Chinese language. While the Chinese language helps minorities to integrate with the rest of Chinese society and prepares them better for the job market, the minority languages help them retain their identity and culture. But the diversity in minority languages also tends to hinder the popularization of education in the country. There is some resentment against the policy of bilingual education for economic rather than cultural reasons, as well as owing to the shortage of qualified teachers and suitable textbooks in a large number of minority languages (Johnson and Chhetri, 2000).

Concluding remarks

We have analysed the state of literacy and basic education in China with special reference to minorities in Tibet and other autonomous areas (Guangxi, Inner Mongolia, Ningxia and Xinjiang). Empirical evidence shows that all the five autonomous areas where the bulk of minorities live have made good progress in access to basic educational services. Actually in urban areas minorities enjoy a higher level of education than the Hans, suggesting that these areas are inhabited by successful minority people who put a high premium on education. The rather paradoxical situation may also be due to the government's preferential policies in favour of minorities. Although the minority urban literacy rate is higher, the share of the minority urban population is quite small except in Inner Mongolia and Liaoning. In rural areas the educational background of minorities is worse and literacy rates lower than those of the Han majority, as we show in Chapter 3.

We have compared the situation of Chinese minorities with that of minorities in India (Muslims and scheduled castes and tribes). This comparison suggests similarities between the two countries despite very different cultural and ethnic identities. The superiority of China in literacy and basic education does not hold when literacy rates are estimated separately for minorities and the Han majority population. Literacy rates for minorities in Tibet and other minority areas are very low, even lower than those for the scheduled castes and scheduled tribes in the poor state of Orissa in India. One can, of course, argue that the very low minority literacy rates in China affect a much smaller population (only 8–9 per cent compared to nearly 25 per cent for the Indian population of scheduled castes and tribes). While this is true, it is fair to note that the low minority literacy rates in China persist despite affirmative action, suggesting a general urban bias.

The low literacy rates in Tibet have a historical origin. The initial educational situation was much worse in Tibet than in the rest of China in 1951, when China took control of Tibet. Negative initial conditions, the poor natural environment (harsh climate and extremely cold temperatures) and low population density explain the government's failure to raise educational standards quickly. Despite adverse conditions, however, different educational indicators show considerable improvement between 1985 and 1999. Thus the facts do not confirm the Drèze–Sen assertion of a 'comprehensive neglect of Tibet in the promotion of elementary education'.

The results based on the CASS household surveys for 1988 and 1995 show that per capita income is an important determinant of educational attainment.

While locational factors played an important role in 1988, they were no longer important in 1995. The weakening of the locational factor suggests an improved educational infrastructure for the minorities between the two years. It would appear that the educational policy in favour of minorities discussed in this chapter has been quite effective.

5 Minorities and health status and services

A.S. Bhalla and Mark Brenner

In Chapters 3 and 4 we discussed access to such public goods as education as one non–income indicator of poverty. In this chapter our concern is to examine access to health services as another non–income indicator of poverty among minorities in China. Better health has a favourable effect on incomes through gains in worker productivity and a reduction in the cost of medical care. Furthermore, a decline in child mortality can also raise incomes by increasing the proportion of workers to dependants.[1]

Some would argue that health status and access are income determined.[2] As we show below, there is no conclusive evidence that this is actually so. This makes the case for non–income indicators of poverty stronger. Income is only one factor in determining access to health services in low–income developing countries. But it is a *necessary*, not a *sufficient* condition. Other factors, such as the nature of government policies and their effectiveness, adequate provision of public goods like health, institutional factors, food and nutrition, and cultural and social constraints, may be equally important.[3]

Different health indicators

Three aspects of health are relevant: health status, access and utilization. These are quite distinct even though interrelated. Indicators of each of these health aspects can also be distinct, as we note below:

(1) *Health status*: Common indicators of a population's health status may include:
   mortality rates – infant and overall;
   rates of death due to disease and life expectancy at birth;
   anthropometric status, which is the combined result of disease, nutrition and health care.
(2) *Access to health services*: Access can be defined in terms of:
   access of rural and urban areas and of social classes (e.g. ethnic minorities and majority population);
   actual utilization of available health services, which determines the level of satisfaction of health needs;

physical distance from available health facilities. For a large proportion of the population in poor countries like China and India, access is difficult, particularly when transport and communication are underdeveloped. Since many Chinese ethnic minorities live in remote and, therefore, inaccessible (mountain) areas, they are particularly likely to be denied whatever health services may be available.

Health access is generally measured in terms of delivery systems (e.g. doctors and beds per 1,000 population) and population characteristics (e.g. family income and insurance coverage). The most frequently used indicators of access to health services are doctors, hospitals and hospital beds per 1,000 population, which tell us about the availability of health facilities though not necessarily about their utilization, which would depend on physical access to and demand for those services. Neither do these aggregate indicators throw any light on the distribution of health services among different socioeconomic and population groups. Let us take the doctor–population ratio: unless it is linked to the income dimension which is necessary to determine access, it cannot indicate whether doctors' services are actually utilized and by which income groups of the population. Furthermore, the ratio implicitly assumes that health needs are uniformly distributed. In practice, interregional and inter-ethnic variations in disease prevalence, not to mention class differences, are quite common (Musgrave, 1986).

(3) *Utilization of health services*: It is important to consider the actual utilization of available health facilities, since access and equity are likely to have an impact on the health status of the population only if these facilities are actually utilized. The commonly used utilization indicators relate to:

the types of health services used (e.g. hospital, physician or home care);
the purpose of the health service (e.g. curative or preventive); and
the location of the health service rendered (home, clinic or in-patient hospital).

The above three types of health indicators are, of course, interrelated. For example, mortality rate as an indicator of health status may be related to that of access to health services. The higher the mortality rate, the more likely it is that access to health services is limited, with poor conditions of delivery, untrained medical attendants and a low rate of immunization.

One may argue that in developing countries low incomes are largely responsible for poor health. It is, therefore, not necessary to resort to independent non-income measures of poverty. It is true that among the poorest countries higher average incomes are associated with longer life expectancy. As countries develop and become richer, this relationship becomes rather weak. In a recent survey article Deaton (2003: 120) notes a 'widespread agreement that income has a direct causal effect [on health]'. Yet the bulk of the economics literature does not accept the existence of any causal effect running from income to health, arguing that other factors such as education and rates of time preference may be more important. In fact, causation may be in the reverse direction, from ill health to low earnings and low capacity to work.

Health indicators for the Chinese minorities

Having discussed above the various health indicators and their strengths and limitations, we now examine the Chinese data, which allow disaggregation of these indicators by racial composition of the population. The two sets of data come from the five autonomous areas dominated by ethnic minorities and the CASS household surveys for 1988 and 1995. Below we discuss the health indicators for minorities in the autonomous areas before analysing the rural household data.

Evidence from the autonomous regions/areas

Indicators of access to health services in the autonomous areas show even less improvement than the educational indicators (see Figure 5.1). Hospitals, hospital beds, doctors and medical personnel in the autonomous areas, as proportions of the total, were almost constant between 1980 and 1992. Between 1992 and 1998, while the autonomous-area share of hospitals started increasing, those of hospital beds, doctors and medical personnel gradually declined until 1996, before rising again.

The health indicators for the autonomous regions for 1994 and 1998 are presented in Table 5.1. The share of doctors in the autonomous areas and the west region declined during this period. The shares of senior minority doctors in the autonomous areas dealing with Western and traditional Chinese medicine, minority medical technical personnel and minority health care personnel are illustrated in Figure 5.2. Between 1980 and 1998, the trend for minority medical technical personnel and health care personnel was very similar except for a sudden jump of medical technical personnel in 1989. This unexpected rise may simply be due to a reclassification of health care personnel. The share of senior doctors rose sharply between 1981 and 1983, declined between 1983 and 1986, and rose sharply again from 1987 to 1988. It reached a peak in 1992; between 1992 and 1993, surprisingly enough, there was a steep decline in the share of senior minority doctors. Since the data are for 'senior' doctors with long experience, this situation may be explained by their older age. Many of them may have retired and died at more or less the same time. Their younger replacements would take many years before being classified as 'senior' doctors.

It is generally believed that the rural areas have fewer health centres and other facilities than the urban ones. What is the picture in the autonomous areas? To answer this question, we examine the shares of (1) rural doctors, (2) rural medical personnel, (3) a combination of (1) and (2), and (4) villages without health care stations for 1978–98 (see Figure 5.3). The share of villages without health care stations has been gradually declining since 1980. But between 1992 and 1998

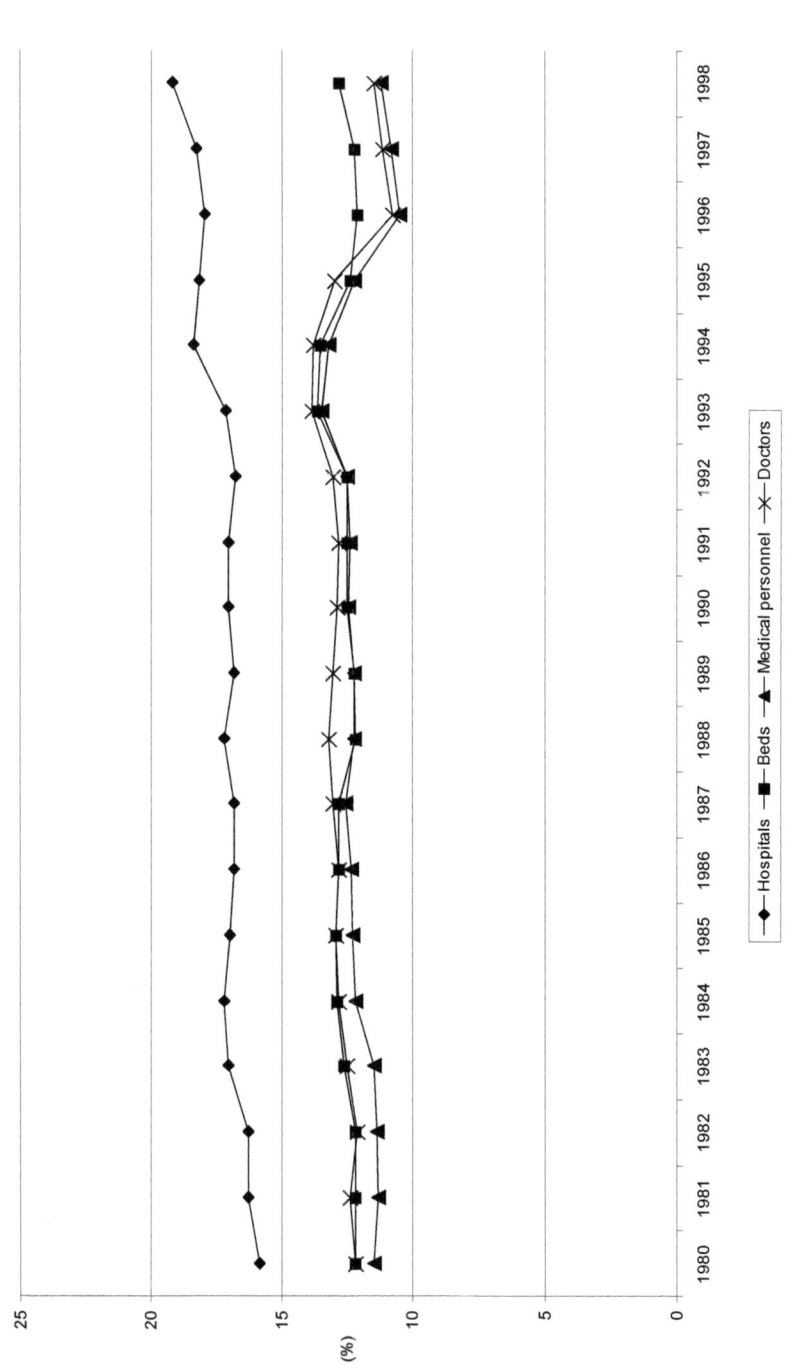

Figure 5.1 Hospitals, hospital beds and medical personnel in the autonomous areas (% of the total)

Sources: Based on data from *China's Ethnic Statistical Yearbook*; *Comprehensive Statistical Data and Materials on 50 Years of New China*, 1999.

Table 5.1 Health indicators for the autonomous areas (1994, 1998) (% of the total)

Province/indicator	1994					1998
	Total (1) (000)	Minority areas (2) (000)	(2) as % of (1)	Total (3) (000)	Minority areas (4) (000)	(4) as % of (3)
National total						
Hospitals	67.9	12.5	17.6	67.1	2.7	4
Hospital beds	2,831	380.6	13.4	2,914	272.2	9.3
Doctors	1,882	259.5	13.8	2,000	233.3	11.7
Autonomous areas						
Hospitals	6.2	6.2	100	6.4	1.7	26.6
Hospital Beds	223	223	100	228	178.8	78.4
Doctors	161	155.4	96.8	178	144.7	81.3
Tibet						
Hospitals	0.8	0.8	100	0.9	0.1	11.1
Hospital beds	5.3	5.3	100	6.3	4.6	73
Doctors	4.8	4.5	93.8	5.1	4.6	90.2
Guangxi						
Hospitals	1.7	1.7	100	1.8	0.5	27.8
Hospital beds	77.4	77.4	100	81	62.3	76.9
Doctors	53.1	53.1	100	60	47.1	78.5
Ningxia						
Hospitals	0.4	0.4	100	0.4	0.1	25
Hospital beds	12.3	12.3	100	11.5	11.5	100
Doctors	15.2	10.1	66.4	12.9	8.7	67.4
Xinjiang						
Hospitals	1.3	1.3	100	1.4	0.5	35.7
Hospital beds	66.7	66.7	100	52.9	52.9	100
Doctors	38.7	38.7	100	43.2	38.1	88.2
Inner Mongolia						
Hospitals	2.0	2.0	100	2	0.5	25
Hospital beds	61.4	61.4	100	62.5	47.5	76
Doctors	49	49	100	56.4	46.2	81.9
West Region						
Hospitals	19.4	7	36.1	18	1.42	7.9
Hospital beds	518	160.7	29.2	537	129.3	24.1
Doctors	385	110.9	28.8	401	111.2	27.7

Sources: Government of China, SSB, *China's Ethnic Statistical Yearbook*, 1995, 1999; *China Statistical Yearbook*; *Comprehensive Statistical Data and Materials on 50 Years of New China*. Autonomous areas include Guangxi, Tibet, Inner Mongolia, Ningxia and Xinjiang.

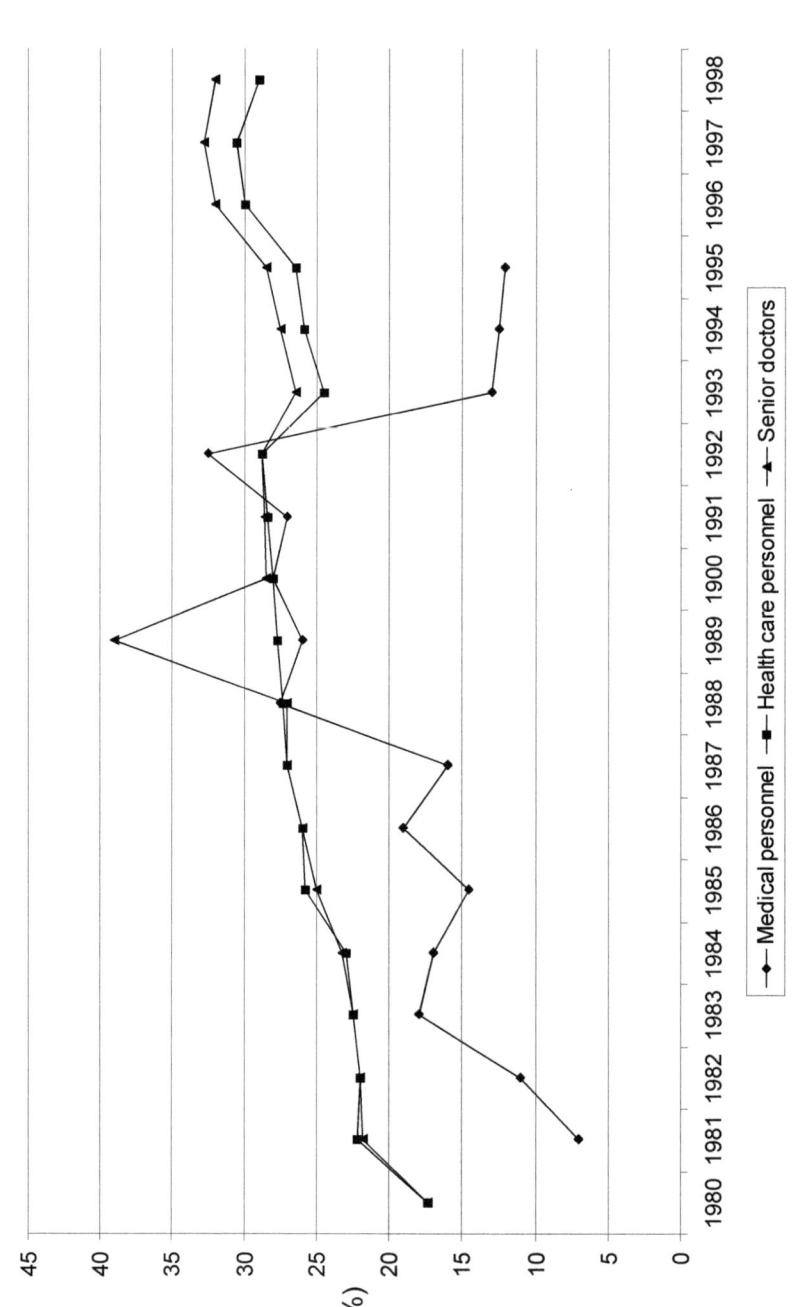

Figure 5.2 Minority medical and health care personnel in the autonomous areas

Sources: Based on data from *China's Ethnic Statistical Yearbook; Comprehensive Statistical Data and Materials on 50 Years of New China,* 1999.

villages without these facilities ranged between 16 and 20 per cent in the minority areas.

The share of rural doctors in the total rose steadily to reach a peak in 1998, but that of the rural medical personnel steadily declined and remained almost constant during the 1990s, thus bringing down the combined ratio for the medical personnel, which remained more or less unchanged during the 1980s and 1990s.

There are wide variations across different minority areas. In 1998 compared to the average of 0.9 rural doctors per 1,000 people, the ratio for Tibet was 1.4 and for Xinjiang 0.6 (see Table 5.2). The high ratio for Tibet is surprising. It is not clear whether this is due to a larger number of low-quality barefoot doctors than in other minority areas.

One cannot be too sure about the reliability of the health data presented above. For example, in Table 5.2 the health data for minority areas for 1994 are the same as those for the whole province/area, which cannot be true. There may be further problems due to under-reporting, over-reporting and even the manipulation of data.

Evidence from the CASS household surveys

Finally, we consider the evidence from the CASS surveys. As in the previous chapter, we restrict our analysis of sample means to households residing in the provinces of Hebei, Liaoning, Jilin, Hunan, Guizhou and Yunnan. However, unlike in the previous chapter, our analysis in this chapter takes the household as the unit of analysis (rather than the individual).

Table 5.3 compares the health situation and access to sanitary facilities for minorities and non-minority households in rural and urban areas separately. Table 5.4 compares different types of health insurance for minorities and non-minority households in urban and rural areas. Estimates are made using data from provinces with a sizeable ethnic minority population. In urban China these include Beijing, Liaoning, Anhui, Henan, Yunnan and Gansu. We had to modify the way insurance coverage was defined in the urban 1988 results to make it more consistent with the 1995 results. In rural China the provinces include Hebei, Liaoning, Jilin, Hunan, Guizhou and Yunnan. Child care expenses are calculated for the subset of families with children 5 years old or younger. The following tentative conclusions can be drawn from the estimates for urban and rural households.

Urban households

There were sizeable disparities in the access to running water in the 1988 survey, and there were still some disparities in 1995, but they were overwhelmed by an increase in the availability of running water in urban China in 1995.

Table 5.2 Medical doctors, health care personnel and hospital beds per 1,000
people in cities, counties and rural regions in the autonomous areas
(1994, 1998)

Province/ personnel	1994			1998		
	City	County	Rural	City	County	Rural
National total						
Doctors per 1,000	0.09	0.13	0.8	2.6	1.1	0.9
Health care personnel per 1,000	0.27	0.31	–	7.9	2.6	–
Hospital beds per 1,000	0.13	0.19	–	3.97	0.98	–
Autonomous areas						
Doctors per 1,000	0.84	0.86	0.78	0.78	0.73	0.83
Health care personnel per 1,000	2.41	2.25	–	2.40	1.85	–
Hospital beds per 1,000	1.07	1.32	–	3.33	0.70	–
Tibet						
Doctors per 1,000	0.47	1.43	1.0	4.9	1.5	1.4
Health care personnel per 1,000	1.47	2.83	–	14.9	2.98	–
Hospital beds per 1,000	0.58	1.68	–	6.3	1.4	–
Guangxi						
Doctors per 1,000	0.58	0.61	0.8	2.8	0.6	0.9
Health care personnel per 1,000	1.60	1.61	–	9	1.7	–
Hospital beds per 1,000	0.82	0.90	–	4.7	0.6	–
Inner Mongolia						
Doctors per 1,000	1.09	1.07	0.7	1.00	0.98	0.8
Health care personnel per 1,000	3.10	2.61	–	2.89	2.21	–
Hospital beds per 1,000	1.37	1.44	–	0.80	0.50	–
Ningxia						
Doctors per 1,000	1.05	0.96	0.8	3.7	1.0	0.8
Health care personnel per 1,000	3.09	2.19	–	12.4	3.4	–
Hospital beds per 1,000	0.06	1.00	–	6.4	0.9	–
Xinjiang						
Doctors per 1,000	1.20	1.17	0.8	2.7	1.7	0.6
Health care personnel per 1,000	3.64	3.41	–	8.0	4.99	–
Hospital beds per 1,000	1.74	2.35	–	1.7	1.1	–
West Region						
Doctors per 1,000	0.15	0.31	0.52	2.09	0.70	0.74
Health care personnel per 1,000	0.42	0.75	–	6.01	2.47	–
Hospital beds per 1,000	0.17	0.46	–	2.45	0.80	–

Sources: Government o China, SSB, *China's Ethnic Statistical Yearbook*; *Comprehensive Statistical
Data and Materials on 50 Years of New China*.
Autonomous Areas include Guangxi, Tibet, Inner Mongolia, Ningxia and Xinjiang. West
Region includes Guizhou, Sichuan, Gansu, Ningxia, Qinghai, Tibet, Yunnan and Xinjiang.

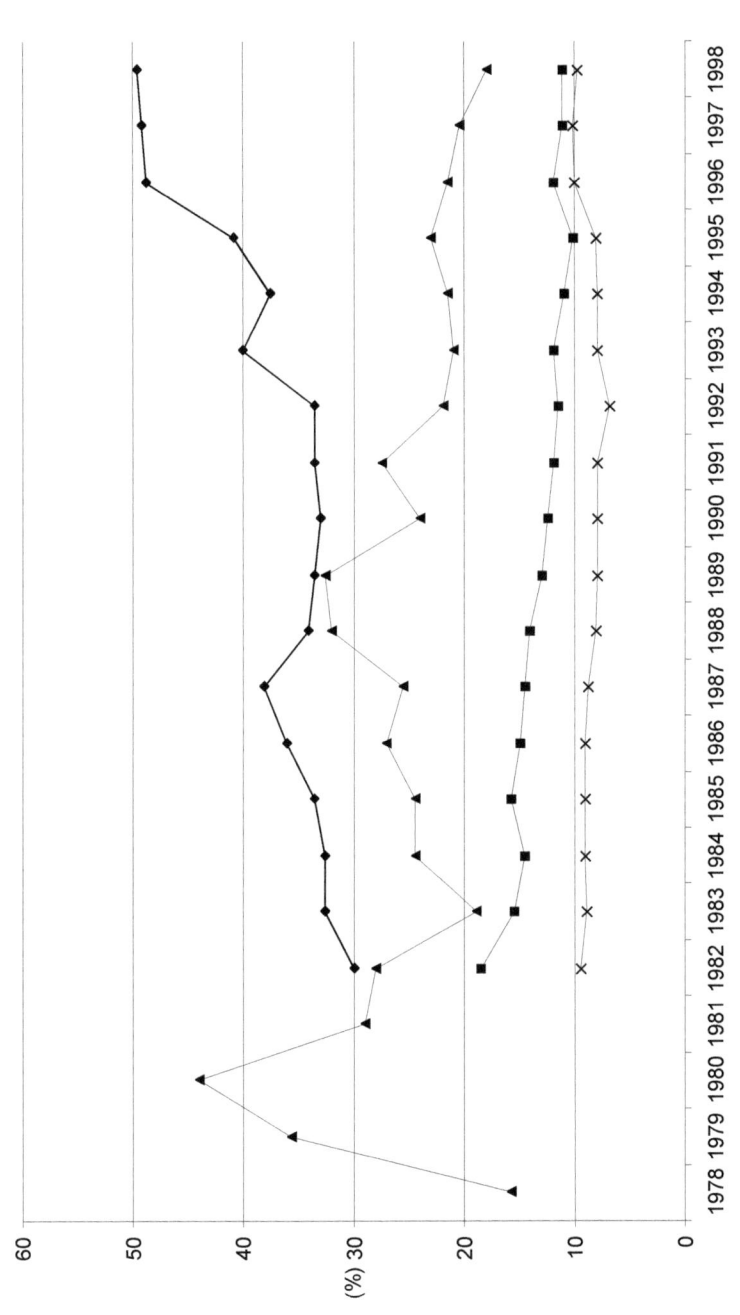

Figure 5.3 Rural health indicators for the autonomous areas

Sources: Based on data from *China's Ethnic Statistical Yearbook; Comprehensive Statistical Data and Materials on 50 Years of New China,* 1999.

There are meaningful differences in the access of urban minorities to sanitary facilities in both years, and the gap widened between the years. In 1988, 63 per cent of minorities lived in housing without sanitary facilities or with shared sanitary facilities, compared with 55 per cent of non-minorities. By 1995 that gap had widened to 55 per cent of minorities and 34 per cent of non-minorities.

Table 5.3 Health situation/status of Chinese minorities and non-minorities (1988, 1995) (%)

Health variable	Minorities		Non-minorities	
	1988	*1995*	*1988*	*1995*
Urban				
Access to running water	72.8	92.3	78.1	94.0
Sanitary facilities:				
lack of sanitary facilities	45.0	49.2	34.7	25.2
shared sanitary facilities	18.1	5.5	20.5	8.7
have toilet, lack bath	34.6	25.1	40.2	36.4
have bath and toilet	2.3	20.2	4.8	29.8
Medical expenses per capita (yuan)	57.3	64.7	46.9	70.4
Child care expenses per cpaita (yuan)	35.0	53.0	29.8	76.7
Rural				
Access to running water	–	16.6	–	28.1
Villages with health clinics	–	50.3	–	85.7
Medical expenses per capita (yuan)	2.1	11.4	4.4	16.2
Child care expenses per capita (yuan)	52.9	–	30.6	–

Table 5.4 Health insurance of rural/urban and minority/non-minority households (1988, 1995) (%)

	Minorities		Non-minorities	
	1988	*1995*	*1988*	*1995*
Urban				
Public health insurance	48.4	54.1	50.0	54.8
Semi-public health insurance	14.9	–	21.5	–
Private health insurance	–	5.3	–	8.6
Self-financed health insurance	22.4	38.2	17.0	29.4
Rural				
Public health insurance	1.5	0.2	0.8	0.7
Self-financed health insurance	86.0	87.5	92.8	87.6
Private health insurance	–	0.3	–	0.4

The proportion of minorities in households which self-finance their medical costs is higher than for non-minorities in both years, with the gap widening between 1988 and 1995. This could be in part due to the fact that in 1988 questions were asked in such a way that households could report some members being covered publicly and others being self-financed, whereas in 1995 the entire household was classified in only one way. Regardless, there is still an important differential between minority and non-minority households. There is not much difference in urban areas between minorities and non-minorities (especially in 1995) regarding public health insurance. However, the differences are more significant in the cases of semi-public health insurance and private health insurance.

Accordingly, minority households have a higher medical spending per capita in 1988. However, in 1995 the mean for minority households is lower, although one can see from the large standard error that it is not significantly different from the mean for non-minority households.

In the case of child care costs per capita for households with children under 5 years old, the pattern is similar to the health care per capita spending, although the standard errors are high. So it is not clear that the differences would be statistically significant.

Rural households

We have no data for rural China on access to running water for 1988. Data for 1995 are available and show that minorities had a much lower level of access to water from a tap (16.6 per cent) than non-minorities (28.1 per cent).

Data on medical costs per capita are available for both 1988 and 1995 for minorities and non-minorities. There does not appear to be much quantitative difference between the two in this case. Minorities spend less in both years, but the difference is less than 5 yuan, which may be statistically significant given the large number of observations, but is not substantively different.

Data are available only for 1995 on households with or without rural health clinics in their village. There were substantial disparities between minorities and non-minorities. While 50 per cent of the rural minority households had a health clinic in their village, nearly 86 per cent of rural non-minority households had a health clinic.

In the case of rural areas, public health insurance for minorities declined from 1.5 per cent of households in 1988 to only 0.2 per cent in 1995. Self-financed health insurance is the main mode of insurance in rural areas. It is generally acknowledged that rural health insurance in China has declined in the wake of economic and social reforms (Bhalla, 1995). A very small proportion of rural people is covered by health insurance (Kelaher and Dollery, 2003). In 1998, 87 per cent of villagers had no health insurance (Meng and Hu, 2000). Bloom and Fang (2003) note the rising cost of rural health services, smaller range of these services than before and poorer staffing.

Regression analysis

What factors influence this disparity in health care access between minority and non-minority households? To answer this question more formally, we explore household-level determinants of health care access using logistic regression analysis. As in the previous chapter, we closely follow the analysis of Gustafsson and Li (2003) when they were examining the influence of household factors such as income level and geography.

Unfortunately neither year's survey contains information on health status or utilization, but the 1995 survey asks several access-related questions, generating data which we use in this section. Specifically, the 1995 survey provides information on household access to drinking water, as well as on whether a clinic is present in the household's village. Although these data are not directly comparable with what we have presented above, they nevertheless offer an interesting glimpse into the disparities in health care access faced by ethnic minorities in rural China. For example, potable water is an essential element for sustained good health, while the presence of a clinic in the local village is likely to be necessary to allow regular access to health care.

Table 5.5 reports the results of our logistic regression model for 1995. In the first column in each case we report the coefficients from the logistic regression. The second column contains our estimates of the marginal effects. These marginal effects approximate an increased (or decreased) probability that a household will have access to potable water or have a clinic in its village, given a one unit increase in the independent variables. For dummy variables (i.e. variables recorded as 1 or 0) these marginal effects represent a predicted increase or decrease for a discrete change from 0 to 1.

Considering access to potable water first, our results indicate that several of our independent variables have an influence. First and foremost, we find that minority status exerts a sizeable and statistically significant negative effect. From these results it appears that minorities are roughly 6 per cent less likely to have access to potable water, controlling for other factors. Income is also important, with a doubling of household income increasing the likelihood of access by 7 per cent. Several characteristics of the household head also exert an influence. For example, if the household head is a Communist Party member, that increases the likelihood of having access to potable water by approximately 5 per cent. Surprisingly, we find that having a male head of household lowers the probability of having access to potable water by roughly 10 per cent, controlling for other factors. It is not clear if this reflects a conscious policy of extending basic infrastructure more readily to female-headed households, or if it is the result of some other factor.

Geography also plays an important part in access to clean drinking water. For example, households living in the suburbs were 21 per cent more likely to have clean drinking water. Households in the plains were 11 per cent more likely to have potable water. By contrast, living in hilly areas had no statistically significant effect on access to clean drinking water. For households in the plains

Table 5.5 Determinants of household access to potable water and local clinics in rural China (1995)

	(1)	(2)	(3)	(4)
	Household with potable water		Household with clinic	
	Logistic regression	Marginal effects	Logistic regression	Marginal effects
Minority status (ethnicity)	-0.309**	-0.058**	-0.859***	-0.106**
	(0.14)	(0.02)	(0.15)	(0.02)
Logarithm of per capita income	0.355***	0.071***	0.332***	0.031***
	(0.04)	(0.01)	(0.06)	(0.01)
Head of household is illiterate	0.051	0.010	-0.251*	-0.026*
	(0.11)	(0.02)	(0.13)	(0.01)
Head of household is male	-0.465***	-0.101***	0.231	0.023
	(0.12)	(0.03)	(0.17)	(0.02)
Head of household is a CP member	0.259***	0.054***	-0.097	-0.009
	(0.07)	(0.02)	(0.10)	(0.01)
Head of household works in agriculture	-0.097	-0.020	-0.314***	-0.027***
	(0.06)	(0.01)	(0.10)	(0.01)
Household is located in suburb	0.911***	0.209***	1.219***	0.074***
	(0.12)	(0.03)	(0.29)	(0.01)
Household is located in plains	0.530***	0.107***	1.513***	0.141***
	(0.07)	(0.01)	(0.10)	(0.01)
Household is located in hilly region	0.031	0.006	0.219***	0.020***
	(0.08)	(0.02)	(0.09)	(0.01)
Household is located in designated poverty region	-0.363***	-0.069***	-0.065	-0.006
	(0.07)	(0.01)	(0.08)	(0.01)
Household is located in designated minority region	-0.063	-0.012	-0.901***	-0.113***
	(0.15)	(0.03)	(0.15)	(0.02)
Constant	-3.330***		-0.958*	
	(0.36)		(0.51)	
Number of observations	7,967		7,967	
Pseudo R-squared		0.06		0.15

Note: These results are calculated from the CASS survey using data for the 19 provinces covered in the 1995 survey. In columns one and two our dependent variable is a binary measure of the household's access to potable water. In columns three and four it is a binary measure of the presence of a medical clinic in the household's village. Robust standard errors are given in parentheses.
* significant at 10%; ** significant at 5%; *** significant at 1%. For dummy variables the marginal effects, (*) dy/dx, are calculated to measure the effect of a discrete change of dummy variable from 0 to 1.

and hilly areas, the point of reference is households living in mountainous regions. Thus it is not surprising that the households in the plains have much higher probabilities of access to clean drinking water than those in the hills, which have access roughly on par with those in mountainous areas. Finally, our results indicate that households in poverty regions are 7 per cent less likely to enjoy access to clean drinking water than those outside.

How do these dynamics differ with respect to another key feature of the health care infrastructure in rural China, namely, access to a local village clinic? Columns 3 and 4 present logistic regression results and marginal effects. As before, minority status is a very important determinant of whether or not a household has access to a health clinic in the village. According to our estimates, minority households are roughly 11 per cent less likely to have access to a local village clinic than non-minority households. As with potable water, income is positively related to having a village clinic, although doubling a household's income only increases the probability of having a clinic by 3 per cent. Of all the individual characteristics of the household head, only two statistically lower the probability of having a local village clinic. In both cases, households are roughly 3 per cent less likely to have a village clinic if the household head reported being either illiterate or working in agriculture.

As before, geography is an important determinant of the presence of a village clinic. Households in the plains were 14 per cent more likely to have a village clinic, while those living in hilly regions were only 2 per cent more likely. For households in the plains and in hilly areas, the point of reference is households living in mountainous regions. Therefore, it is not surprising that both groups have a higher probability of having a local clinic.

Concluding remarks

In this chapter we have reviewed health access and utilization indicators for Chinese minorities and non-minorities on the basis of data for the autonomous regions from the *Ethnic Statistical Yearbooks* and data from the CASS household surveys. While the former uses the individual as the unit of analysis, in the case of the CASS survey data we use both individuals and households as our unit of analysis. Both sets of data indicate that minorities have less access to health services than the Han majority. The two data sets examine different health indicators. For example, health indicators pertaining to the autonomous regions include the doctor and health personnel to population ratio and the hospital beds to population ratio, whereas the CASS household survey data refer to access of minorities to potable water and village health clinics, medical expenses per capita including child care expenses, and public and private health insurance. Public health insurance for minorities declined significantly between 1988 and 1995. It is generally believed that rural public health insurance coverage declined in the wake of economic reforms. Today self-financed private health insurance is more common in rural China.

There is a much lower level of health care access for minorities in rural China compared with the Han majority. For example, in 1995 only 17 per cent of minority households report having access to clean drinking water, versus 28 per cent of households in the Han majority. These disparities are even sharper when we consider access to medical facilities, specifically local village clinics. Our survey indicates that approximately half of the minority population in rural China has a clinic in the local village compared with 86 per cent of the Han majority.

6 Anti-poverty policies and programmes

Chapters 1 to 5 have shown significant income and non-income poverty among the minorities despite past efforts to alleviate it. In this chapter and Chapter 7, we review the existing anti-poverty policies and programmes and examine the most suitable ones to create a dent in the problems of the minority poor.

In most developing countries, anti-poverty policies and programmes are designed to alleviate poverty by targeting assistance through credit or jobs to the poor who may not otherwise benefit from normal programmes. There are three main views on the basis of which anti-poverty policy and programmes are formulated. First is the view that rapid economic growth is the best means of poverty reduction. However, some public intervention may be necessary to make sure that the fruits of growth are widely shared. Second, measures may need to be designed to alleviate poverty directly. Third, even if direct measures are introduced, the damaging effects of poverty in terms of poor health, nutrition and education may not be addressed. Therefore, special action may be necessary to overcome the adverse *indirect* effects of poverty (Lipton, 1998).

In China during the reform period (1978 to date) economic growth rates have been very impressive and, at least until 1995, poverty was considerably reduced. However, despite a decline in the *proportion* of the population below the poverty line, a *substantial* number, especially in rural areas and minority regions, have remained absolutely poor. There is also the problem of *transient* or short-term poverty. Therefore, growth alone cannot be relied upon to tackle the poverty problem, especially in remote and mountainous areas where it is difficult to generate growth. Recognizing this, the Chinese government introduced two types of poverty reduction programmes: (1) those that specifically target poverty reduction, and (2) others, which provide social assistance and insurance against insecurity and hardship.

Poverty alleviation policies and programmes[1]

China's poverty alleviation policy can be analysed in terms of three distinct periods. The first period covers 1979 to 1985, when government efforts were concerned mainly with supporting (financially and in kind) – so-called 'money–food–cotton support' – the backward and remote areas. For example, during the 31 years since the establishment of the Tibet autonomous region, while output increased only fourfold (annual rate of growth of 5.4 per cent), the central budgetary grant increased by 65 times (at an annual rate of growth of 14.9 per cent) (Xu, 1997).

The second period, covering the Poor Area Development Programme and the 8-7 Poverty Reduction Plan, relates to 1986 to 1995. In 1986 the Leading Group for Economic Development of Poor Areas (LGEDPA) was established under the State Council in order to coordinate and make coherent various initiatives related to poverty alleviation. The Executing Agency of the Leading Group is the Poor Area Development Office, which coordinates $1 billion in annual central funding for poverty reduction programmes. Leading groups and poor area development offices have been set up at the provincial, prefecture and county levels on the model of the organization at the central level of government (Figure 6.1). An executive body of this group, namely, the Poor Area Development Office (PADO), reports directly to the State Council, which also funds three additional poverty reduction units within the framework of the Leading Group: China Development Foundation for Poor Areas, the Cadre Training Centre and the Economic Development Service Centre. In addition, the Ministry of Civil Affairs is responsible for income support and disaster relief and rural social welfare generally; the Ministry of Education for educational programmes for the poor; the Ministry of Health for rural health programmes and services; and the Regional Office of the State Planning Commission is responsible for the food-for-work programmes and other rural capital construction projects (Cook and White, 1998). All these programmes and institutions are geared for rural poverty reduction. There is no equivalent institutional arrangement for urban poverty reduction, although urban poverty and unemployment have been growing in recent years.

The third phase of the poverty alleviation policy started in 1996 with a State Council directive to shift the emphasis from area development to targeting of the poorest households. This change in policy may have occurred in the light of the experience that in many cases the anti-poverty programme did not reach the poor (see below). This phase is also distinct in another respect. For the first time during this period the government attempted to tackle the urban poverty problem by concentrating on three types of public intervention, namely, the guaranteeing of a minimum urban standard of living, the provision of the minimum basic needs of staff and workers laid off from state-owned enterprises, and the creation of an unemployment insurance fund.[2]

There are two types of regional poverty reduction programmes: those that are designed mainly for raising the rural productive capacity and capabilities, and others such as public works programmes intended for relief and social welfare.

Poverty reduction before the mid-1980s (when the LGEDPA was established) was considered as dependent almost entirely on economic growth and macroeconomic reform. However, since then the Chinese authorities have

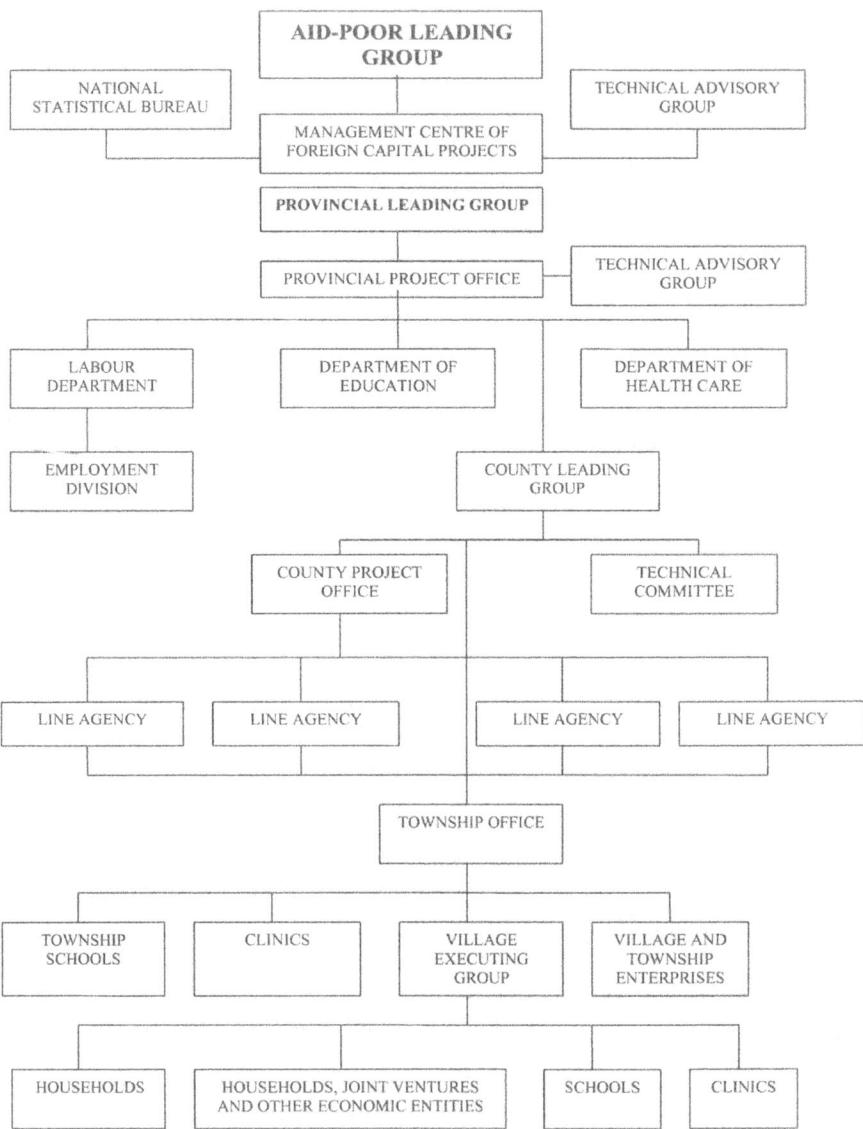

Figure 6.1 Organizational structure of the poverty reduction project in
      southwest China

Source: Poverty Reduction Office, Provincial Government of Yunnan, Kunming.

recognized the need to tackle seriously the growing poverty problem despite rapid economic growth by adopting a regional approach. In 1994 the government announced a national Poverty Alleviation Programme (popularly known as the 8-7 Poverty Reduction Plan) in order to reduce the number of remaining rural poor, then estimated at 80 million. This target was to be achieved by ensuring that most of the rural poor attain a per capita income standard of 500 yuan at 1990 prices. This is one of the most ambitious poverty alleviation programmes to be implemented by any developing country. An analysis and critical assessment of the programme and its potential for replication elsewhere are therefore highly desirable.

Poor and minority counties

Of the total number of 2,148 counties in China, 592 (or 27.6 per cent) were designated as 'poor' counties to which financial assistance for poverty reduction was to be confined. In addition to the centrally designated 'poor' counties, there are also 'poor' counties at the provincial levels. These latter counties receive financial assistance from the provincial governments. A quantitative estimate of a poverty line by the central and provincial governments determines which counties should be designated as poor. Apart from the income criterion, food consumption per capita in kilograms is also used. Additional criteria include accessibility to electricity, roads and water, health and education services, and remoteness. Apparently, the location of minority nationalities, which form the bulk of the poor in these counties, is not used as one of the selection criteria. Nevertheless, generally the autonomous counties, in which most of the minorities live, are designated as poor. But the minorities also live outside these counties in the non-autonomous and non-poor areas. Political pressures are not unknown in the choice of poor counties, which entitles them to central government or provincial government financial grants.

Besides receiving financial assistance from the central government, the centrally-designated 'poor' counties also benefit from lower agricultural tax and special agricultural produce tax, or its exemption altogether, and softer loans out of funds earmarked for poverty relief. Also the more developed coastal provinces and municipalities have entered into partnerships with poorer hinterland provinces and autonomous regions in order to provide technical advice and assistance (Government of China, 1999).

Plan targets

The Poverty Reduction Plan (1994–2000) aimed at achieving the following targets by the year 2000:

(1) net per capita income for the majority of the households in designated poverty counties to exceed 500 yuan at 1990 prices;

(2) assistance to poor households to create conditions to solve the food problem;
(3) provision of adequate drinking water for people and livestock;
(4) strengthening of infrastructure facilities linking most poor townships to highway systems, power grids and telecommunications networks in order to connect them to commodity and other rural product markets; and
(5) improvement of the cultural, educational and health situation in poverty counties.

The following were the main components of financial assistance:

(1) low-interest loans by the Agricultural Development Bank (56 per cent) for crop production, animal husbandry, agro-business and marketing;
(2) food-for-work programme financed by the State Planning Commission (26 per cent), which pays residents of poor areas (in cash and kind) for work on roads, water supply and other infrastructure projects;
(3) Training Fund financed by the Ministry of Finance (18 per cent) for the training of cadres and enterprise managers in poor areas.

Under the above programmes, emphasis is placed on the building up of the economic capacity of poor areas (through infrastructure, livestock development, agro-processing industries) rather than providing temporary relief.

Rural infrastructure investments (in water supply, rural access roads and electricity to poor remote areas) are a major feature of the programme. Besides rural infrastructure, other activities and programmes include the following:

(1) migration of the poor from 'pockets' of chronic poverty in remote and dryland areas to industrial zones and other high-growth areas where employment at higher wages can be provided. This programme (known as the 'labour mobility' programme) promotes labour redeployment as a means of poverty alleviation and productivity enhancement in rural areas. Such relocation of the poor is known to have been quite successful in Yunnan (see below).
(2) development of village and township agro-processing enterprises using raw materials supplied by small farmers;
(3) direct poverty reduction through the provision of micro credit;
(4) universal primary education, elimination of illiteracy among teenagers, and improved access of poor families to basic health services.

Between 1986 and 1996 the central government funding for poverty reduction consisted of (1) subsidized credit, (2) allocation for food-for-work programmes and (3) development fund for underdeveloped regions. The central funding increased from 4.2 billion yuan in 1986 to 10.8 billion yuan in 1996, representing an annual increase of nearly 10 per cent. The total cumulative central funding for the 1986–96 period amounted to nearly 72 billion yuan (Wang, 1997). In 1998 the budgeted funds for poverty reduction programmes were 18.3 billion yuan, including 10 billion yuan for special poverty reduction loans and 8.3 billion yuan for food-for-work programmes. The subsidiary funds of local governments amount to 30–50 per cent of the central government's inputs, which totalled 9.2 billion yuan in 1998. The above figures represent a significant increase over the total funding for poverty reduction in 1985, which amounted to a little over 3 billion yuan (UNDP, 1997a: 95). Total central government funding for the 1995–97 period for both poverty reduction and overall social development (education, health and pensions, for example) is given in Table 6.1.

Special anti-poverty policies for the minorities

The Chinese minority areas and populations receive especially favourable treatment. Under the fiscal contract system introduced in 1980 the minority autonomous areas were allowed to undertake their own fiscal management. However, under the state budget the central government continued to transfer resources to these areas. In 1992 these transfers to the five autonomous regions and Guizhou, Qinghai and Yunnan provinces amounted to 14 billion yuan, or 40 per cent of total revenues and about 32 per cent of expenditures of the poor regions (Zhu, 1995). Several special funds for minorities and poor regions include: flexible fund for minority nationalities, basic needs (*wu-bao*) fund for poverty-stricken counties of the minority areas, special fund for the education of minority nationalities, and development fund for the underdeveloped regions. The central government provides financial support to the minority autonomous administrations in the form of supporting funds, minority contingent funds and higher budgetary provisions. These special budgetary arrangements are called the 'three special treatment policies biased in favour of minority administrations in terms of central government budgetary fund allocation'.

The government has introduced preferential policies in favour of the minorities in view of their less advantaged position. These policies cover economic aspects (economic development and poverty reduction), social and

Table 6.1 China government expenditure on poverty reduction and social development (1995–97) (billion yuan)

	1995	*1996*	*1997*
Total central government expenditure	682	793	923
Central government expenditure on poverty reduction	10	11	15
Expenditure for social development, of which:	177	208	247
Expenditure on education, culture and hygiene	138	161	178
Expenditure on family pensions	11	13	14
Expenditure on other social development	28	34	55

Note: Figures have been rounded off.

Sources: Government of China (1999); UNDP (1997a).

cultural aspects (family planning, preservation of minority culture, languages and religion) and educational and labour market issues (lower entrance requirements and special funds to promote minority education, skill development and employment – see Chapter 4; for a discussion see Sautman, 1998, 1999).

The economic policies pay special attention to socioeconomic development in minority nationality areas with a view to narrowing the gaps in living standards. The 55 ethnic groups in China have a population of more than 100 million, or 8.5 per cent of the country's population, of which 75 per cent enjoy regional autonomy (the remaining live in non-autonomous areas). The central government makes a special allocation for the support of 'economically underdeveloped areas, among which minority nationality areas enjoy priority in the distribution of funds' (Government of China, 1999: 23). Special benefits to the minority areas also include reduction or exemption of business tax and income tax.

As we noted above, there are several special funds for minorities and poor regions, of which the basic needs (*wu-bao*) fund, established in 1990, is managed jointly by the State Minority Commission and other government organizations. Between 1990 and 1993, the total funds provided by the central government amounted to about 213 million yuan, for 221 poverty alleviation development projects, covering 117 counties (Wu, 1998). The coverage of the basic needs fund was subsequently extended to 257 counties. Since 1994, when the national 8-7 Poverty Reduction Plan started, the allocation for the basic needs fund has been more than doubled, from 45 million yuan to 100 million yuan.

The ethnic minority basic needs fund consists of two elements. The first is the fund provided by the Ministry of Finance, called the 'Basic needs fund budgetary loan'. It is limited to the 257 minority autonomous counties. The loan period is normally two years and, for special cases, three years. The second element is provided by the People's Bank of China, called the 'Basic needs fund poverty alleviation loan'. After 1994 the fund was transferred to the agricultural bank, although the method of fund allocation remained unchanged.[3]

In February 2001 the Standing Committee of the Ninth National People's Congress (NPC) made amendments to the Law Governing Regional Ethnic Autonomy. New elements of the law include an increase in investment in the ethnic minority areas for accelerating their development (*China Daily*, 10 April 2001).

In 1986, when the government determined the poor counties for additional support, the criteria for the autonomous minority counties to be included in the nationally designated poor counties were relaxed. The normal poverty line is rural net per capita income of 150 yuan, but this line was raised to 200 yuan (300 yuan for animal husbandry counties) for autonomous minority counties or counties within an old revolutionary base. As a result, 62 additional counties were included in the nationally designated poor counties, of which 51 were autonomous minority counties.

Preferential policies in the social and cultural domain, such as family planning, affect the poverty situation. The minorities are exempted from the one-child family rule. In the urban areas, they are allowed two or more children, especially if the first two are girls and one is handicapped. Rural couples are allowed three or even four children if they live in remote areas. This relaxation of the population control policy may partly explain the more rapid population growth among the minorities than among the Han. It may also have an adverse and countervailing effect on poverty-reducing measures by raising household size and dependency ratios. Amendments to the law governing minorities noted above stipulate that the People's Congresses of autonomous areas must include one or more people from the ethnic minorities. The head of an autonomous region, prefecture or autonomous county must be from ethnic groups. Among the deputies of the National People's Congress (NPC) the minority representation (over 14 per cent of the total) exceeds the minorities' share of the total population. However, minority representation among the cadres is much lower.[4]

Have the above preferential policies benefited the Chinese minorities by narrowing income gaps and promoting their access to education and health services? A comparative analysis of the minority autonomous areas, minority counties and minority households, and non-minority regions, counties and households, shows that the gaps have widened despite affirmative action. However, the gaps would probably have been even wider without the preferential policies. Are the widening gaps due to the poor implementation of policies, lack of commitment to the betterment of minorities or inadequate resources for this purpose? In the following pages we attempt to address some of these questions.

Poverty reduction programmes in southwest China

The bulk of the poverty counties in China (nearly 42 per cent) are located in the southwest region (see Figures 6.2 and 6.3, which give respectively areas and percentages of the poverty counties designated as national-level, provincial-level and non-poor counties in Guangxi, Guizhou, Sichuan and Yunnan). There are 257 minority nationality poverty counties, accounting for 43.4 per cent of the total number of poor counties. These counties receive special treatment in the allocation of funds and materials and fiscal exemptions, as noted above.

Under the poverty reduction programme, the central government provides to the centrally designated poor counties three types of funds: the subsidized loans, food-for-work funds, and budgetary grant. Subsidized loans are the most important component, accounting for more than three-quarters of the total poverty alleviation funds (PAF) for most years. The Poor Area Development Office (PADO) makes decisions about the total amount of subsidized loans and how to allocate them. Then the funds are channelled through the People's Bank of China under a special fund allocation plan.[5]

The special subsidized loans are approved and allocated project by project. Poverty alleviation offices at county level select projects, which are required to be approved by the PADO at the provincial level. The Agricultural Development Bank is authorized to set priorities among projects at the time of deciding loan

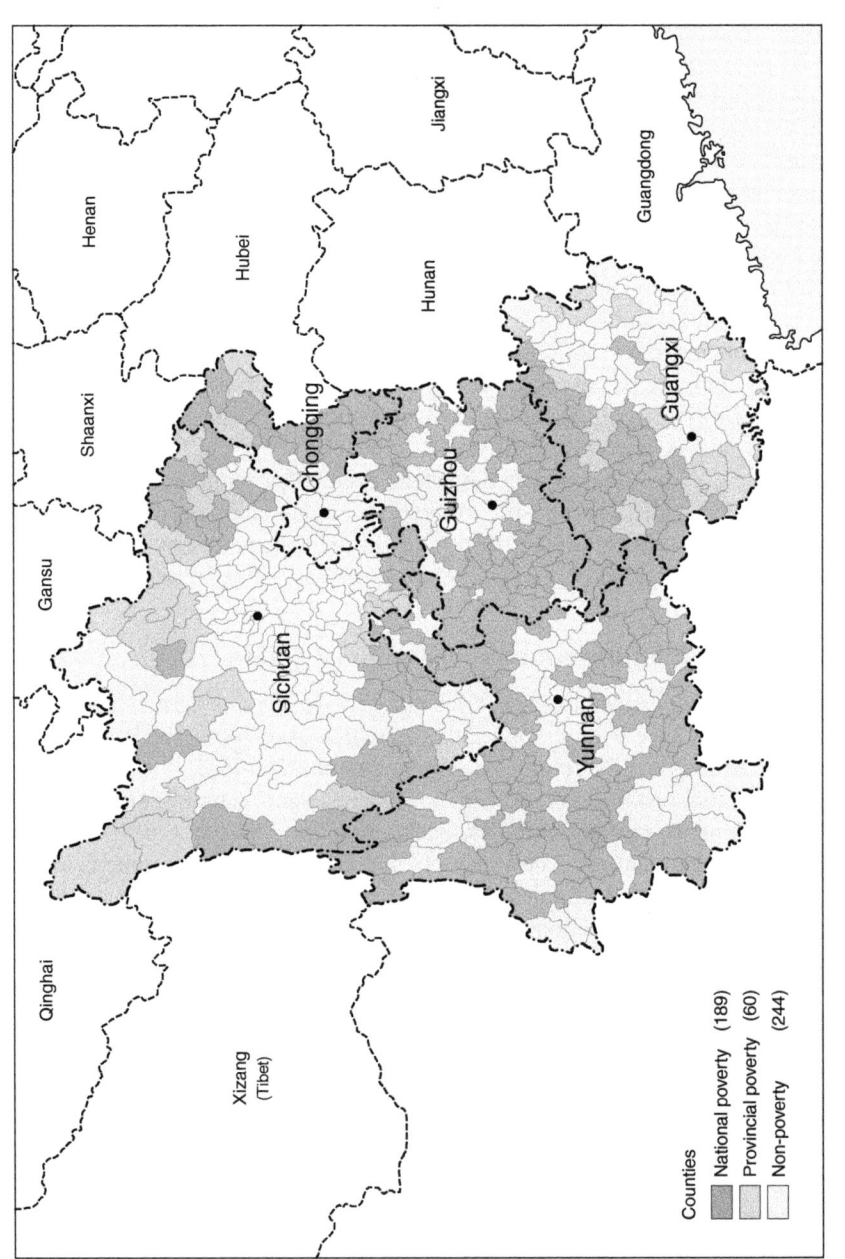

Figure 6.2 Number of national and provincial 'poverty counties' in southwest China

Source: Based on data supplied by the LGOPAD, Beijing.

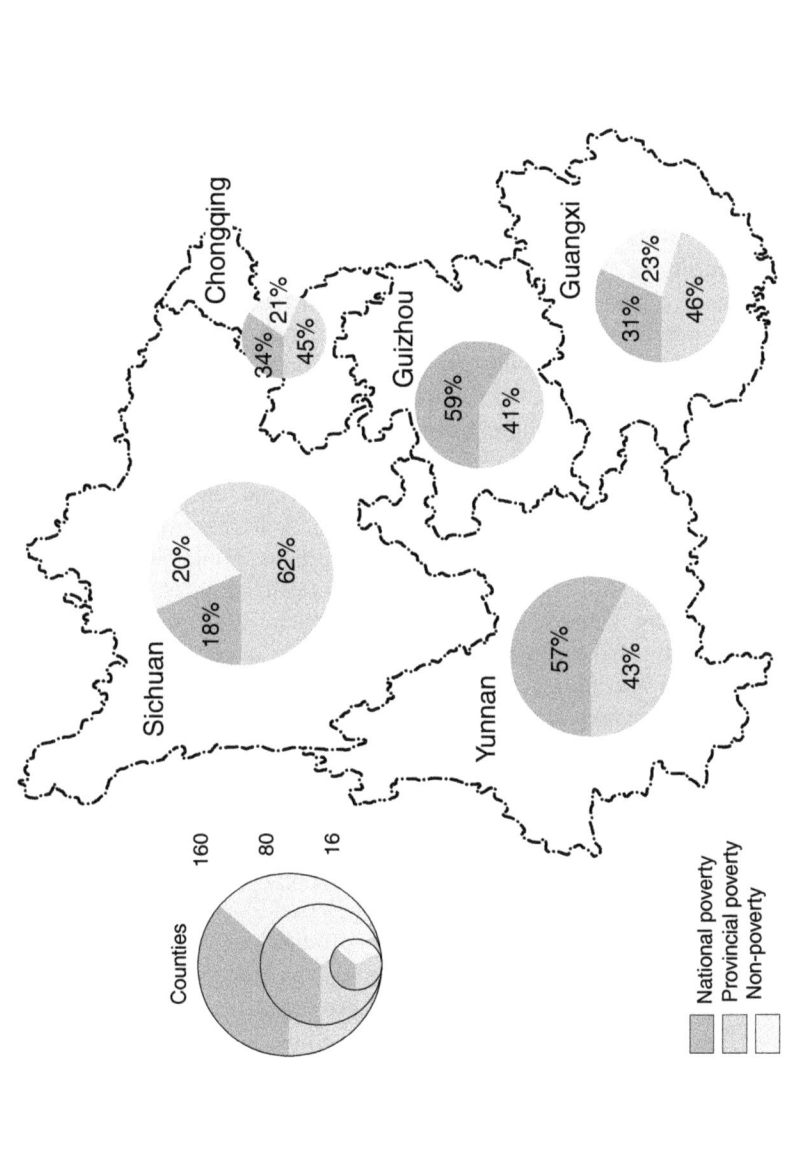

Figure 6.3 Percentage shares of national and provincial 'poverty counties' in southwest China

Source: Based on data supplied by the LGOPAD, Beijing.

allocation. The borrowers of below-market interest loans pay two different rates: an annual rate of 2.88 per cent for agricultural projects and 8.4 per cent for manufacturing projects. The difference between the market rate and the below-market rate is matched by government subsidies to the lending institution.

In Sichuan plan outlays for 1998-2000 show that central funding gave a higher priority to credit (which represents the highest allocation) than food-for-work programmes. However, the share of credit in the total central funding is forecast to decline and that for food-for-work to increase. Credit also accounts for the bulk of provincial government funds (see Table 6.2). The funding pattern for Sichuan is similar to that for China as a whole. From 1986 to 1998, the amount allocated to subsidized loans was higher than that for food-for-work programmes. In 1998 the amount allocated to food-for-work programmes was only half the amount allocated for credit (ADB, 1999).

Actual expenditures on budgetary grant, food-for-work programmes and subsidized loans are available for 1998 for Sichuan (see Table 6.3). We rank poverty-stricken counties in Sichuan by rural per capita net income. The five poorest counties are compared with the five least poor counties and the two minority autonomous counties. The central and provincial (local) government expenditures on anti-poverty programmes are presented in per capita terms in order to adjust for different sizes of counties. Several interesting comments can be made on the data in Table 6.3. First, as is to be expected, the poorest counties in general received higher central and local grants and loans per capita. But there were exceptions. Two counties, Xiangcheng in the poorest group and Yanbian in the second group, are outliers. As one of the poorest counties, Xiangcheng received exceptionally large grants per capita, which is difficult to explain without further study of the county. Similarly, Yanbian county has the highest rural net per capita income, yet it received substantially higher per capita budgetary grant than many poorer counties.

The situation of the two minority autonomous counties (the third, Ebian, is non-poor and therefore does not qualify for anti-poverty grants) also deserves comment. Although Muli county is the sixth poorest, it receives substantial per capita grant and loans. Mabian county is not so poor; therefore, it received very low per capita grant. This suggests that poverty is the relevant criterion for grants and loans rather than the size of the minority population in a county.

Poverty reduction activities are largely production-oriented: forestry, plantations, food processing and manufacturing. By the end of 1997 small loans for poverty reduction were granted to 11,627 poverty households in 14 pilot counties for the following activities: planting (1,365 households), livestock breeding (7,535 households), food processing (806 households), short-distance transportation by bus or truck (1,243 households) and long-distance transportation (199 households). Progress was also made in raising output and income per capita, and providing better access for the population and livestock to clean drinking water. The progress made in bringing new agricultural land under cultivation, employment generation and bringing the rural poor up to the poverty

Table 6.2 Funding sources and plan outlays for the poverty alleviation programmes in Sichuan (1998–2000) (million yuan)

		Central government funds					Provincial government funds				Prefectural government funds				
Year	Grand total for each year	Sub-sidized loans	Budgetary grant	Food for work	Develop-ment fund	Total	Sub-sidized loans	Budgetary grant	Addit-ional funds	Total	Budgetary grant	Funds through repay-ment of loans	Other funds **	Self financ-ing by enter-prises	Total
1998	2,139.01	722.90 (64.0)	119.31 (10.5)	251.77 (22.3)	36.49 (3.2)	1,130.47 (100.0)	78.80 (60.3)	31.57 (23.7)	21.07 (16.0)	131.44 (100.0)	55.65 (6.4)	56.12 (6.4)	328.93 (37.5)	255.45 (29.1)	877.10 (100.0)
1999	2,444.87	795.98 (62.0)	130.37 (10.1)	298.42 (23.2)	58.34 (4.5)	1,283.11 (100.0)	84.84 (57.0)	36.18 (24.1)	28.16 (18.8)	149.18 (100.0)	65.72 (6.5)	78.66 (7.7)	357.16 (35.3)	289.95 (28.6)	1,012.57 (100.0)
2000	2,672.73	869.06 (63.0)	143.01 (10.4)	317.47 (23.0)	50.81 (3.7)	1,380.34 (100.00)	93.05 (55.3)	44.59 (26.2)	30.68 (18.4)	168.32 (100.0)	71.31 (6.3)	114.77 (10.2)	374.89 (33.4)	303.62 (27.0)	1,124.06 (100.0)
Three-year total	7,256.60	2,387.95 (62.9)	392.69 (10.3)	867.65 (22.9)	145.64 (3.8)	3,793.92 (100.0)	256.69 (57.2)	112.34 (24.9)	79.91 (17.8)	448.94 (100.0)	192.68 (6.4)	249.55 (8.3)	1,060.98 (100.0)	849.02 (6.4)	3,013.74 (100.0)

* labour contribution by households.
** loans repaid by beneficiaries in earlier years.

Note: Brackets show percentages of the total.

Source: Based on the data provided by the Poor Area Development Office, Sichuan province, Chengdu.

Table 6.3 Per capita funding for the poorest counties in Sichuan (1988)

County	Per capita funding for food-for-work programme (yuan)	Per capita funding for subsidized loans (yuan)	Per capita budgetary grant (yuan)	Total county population (000)	Rural per capita net income of county (yuan)
Poorest counties					
Shiqu	105.31	201.3	130.0	62.1	570
Xiangcheng	187.21	528.1	111.7	25.8	588
Butuo	66.79	98.5	60.5	134	619
Xiaojin	113.43	127.5	51.4	73.7	661
Jinyang	73.80	101.2	28.2	137.4	665
Minority autonomous counties					
Muli	48.64	98.1	34.3	121.3	705
Mabian	43.31	10.3	6.8	169	1,170
Least poor among poor					
Junlian	4.20	35.6	7.7	371	1,803
Quxian	8.12	22.7	3.3	1,301.8	1,813
Yibing	3.94	20.3	1.8	973.6	1,836
Yanbian	39.80	41.0	41.0	177.9	1,854
Changning	6.28	30.50	8.02	420.3	2,118

Source: Based on data supplied by the Poor Area Development Office, Sichuan province, Chengdu.

line by selected counties is shown for Sichuan in Table 6.4. Only one county (Mabian) officially designated as a minority poor county is included in the table. Its progress in raising the number of poor up to the poverty line (only 1,030 persons) was the least good among all the counties listed. In Mabian county the area of new land brought under cultivation was also relatively small.[6]

Selected anti-poverty programmes

Below we discuss the three main anti-poverty programmes in China: the food-for-work programme (*Yigong-daizhen*), micro-credit programme, and rural labour mobility programme.

Food-for-work programme (Yigong-daizhen)

This is a public works programme, which replaced the earlier poverty relief measures under which work or job creation was not a condition for securing relief. The programme, started in 1984, differs from the regular capital

Table 6.4 Sichuan: progress in selected counties under the poverty reduction programme (1998)

County	New agricultural land under cultivation (ha) (1998)	Employment generated by projects (No.) (1998)	Total number of rural poor brought up to the poverty line (cumulative)	Total number of rural pool below the poverty line (cumulative)	Percentage of rural poor brought up to the poverty line (%) (cumulative)
Poorest counties					
Shiqu	32		6,124	3,335	64.74
Xiangcheng			3,718	3,195	53.78
Butuo	133	25	27,360	38,927	41.27
Xiaojin	67		10,559	6,370	62.37
Jinyang			23,851	39,220	37.82
Minority autonomous counties					
Muli	14		25,266	23,217	52.11
Mabian	286		34,591	21,461	61.71
Least poor among poor					
Junlian	365	21,500	20,300	2,767	88.00
Quxian	319	1,000	337,783	27,578	92.45
Yibing	110	1,450	86,938	22,962	79.11
Yanbian	362	467	29,851	12,104	71.15
Changning	12	11,000	37,183	1,970	94.97

Source: Data supplied by the Poor Area Development Office, Sichuan province, Chengdu.

construction projects in several respects. The central government provides partly in-kind investment and partly financial investment for the food-for-work programmes. The local governments are expected to allocate matching funds. The central government payments in kind (generally surplus food and goods) are paid to workers in the form of wages.

Initially the local public works projects consisted mainly of building and construction, besides work on the drinking water supply. More recently, projects have been diversified to include farming, water conservation, health care facilities, education and so on. Food-for-work programmes include grain and cotton cloth, medium and low-quality industrial products, flood relief through the harnessing of rivers and assistance to the poor sate farms. The central government investments in these programmes, and the nature of the works covered under each are given in Table 6.5.

Objectives

In most developing countries (notably, Bangladesh, India and Pakistan) the main purpose of public works and food-for-work programmes is to generate immediate short-term employment as a measure of poverty relief rather than the building of capital assets. The public works in Bangladesh and India are the largest measured in terms of the number of days of employment generated, for example in India the *Jawahar Rozgar Yojana* (JRY), whose main objective is to employ the rural poor below the poverty line. In China the provision of short-term employment is not the main objective of the food-for-work programme. Instead, the main emphasis of the programme is on capital construction and long-term economic development. However, employment generation remains one of the secondary objectives.[7]

Work requirement (workfare) as distinct from social welfare has become increasingly popular not only in developing countries but also in developed ones (see Besley and Coate, 1992). This requirement is designed partly to provide incentives to recipients of poverty relief, and partly to impart skills to improve their future employability.[8] Some authors (notably, Murray, 1984) suggest that

Table 6.5 Chinese central government investment in food-for-work schemes (1993)

Scheme	Planned period	Goods-in-kind invested	Equivalent monetary value of investment (billion yuan)	Project focus
1	1984–87	Cereals, cotton and cloth	2.7	Roads, drinking water supply
2	1989–91	Medium and low-quality consumer goods	0.6	Roads, drinking water supply
3	1990–92	Industrial goods	1.5	Roads, drinking water supply, farm improvement
4	1991–95	Foodgrains	5.0	Terracing, small-scale water conservation
5	1991–95	Foodgrains and industrial goods	10.0	Dredging of big rivers
6	1993–97	Cereals, cloth, edible oil, medium and low-quality consumer goods	10.0	Infrastructure, clinics and health care stations for women and children

Source: Zhu (1997). In 1993, 1$ was equal to 5.8 yuan.

welfare programmes, which do not insist on work requirements, have discouraged welfare recipients from acquiring the human capital necessary for poverty avoidance or reduction.

Nature of wage payments

The level of the wage paid under the food-for-work programmes is of critical importance for various reasons. First, if the wage is set too high (above the minimum wage for example), it will attract the non-poor and thus defeat the purpose of reaching the poor.[9] Second, high wage will also imply that only a limited amount of employment could be created for a given level of investment. In other words, the cost of the programme will be higher than if the wage was kept low. If the wage is set low (at least no higher than the prevailing market wage), a process of self-selection or targeting can be ensured. In general, low wage rates will improve self-targeting and attract only the poor (Ravallion, 1991a, 1991b). However, if the wage rate is kept too low, it may not attract rural workers, especially if they have alternative income-earning opportunities and if cost is involved in their participation in the food-for-work programme. In developing countries with limited administrative infrastructure and capacity, targeting of the poor on the basis of earnings or other criteria is considered costly and cumbersome. Experience of the programmes in many developing countries has shown that political and legal considerations prevent the programme wage being fixed below the minimum wage.[10]

In China there is no minimum wage. In the absence of landless labour (which is substantial in India and other developing countries) wage employment in rural areas is also rare. Therefore, neither a minimum wage nor a rural wage can be used as a yardstick to assess the level of the programme wage offered under food-for-work programmes. It may, therefore, be more appropriate to consider the level of rural per capita income to determine whether the programme wage is high or low. To some extent the level of the programme wage will be determined by whether the opportunity cost of labour is high or low and whether the cost of participation in public works is positive and significant. In the Chinese poor rural areas, the opportunity cost of labour is likely to be low or close to zero, especially during the slack agricultural season when rural public works are implemented. However, during the busy agricultural season it may not be all that low and rural labour may have to be attracted by paying a higher programme wage. This point, however, may not apply to minorities living in remote mountainous areas with little scope for agricultural activity. The opportunity cost of labour may also be positive at least in certain areas, since rural to urban migration is now much easier and is actually encouraged (see below). By moving to urban areas, the rural migrants can earn much more than they would by working on food-for-work programmes.

There appear to be wide variations in wage payments on the Chinese food-for-work programmes. The State Planning Commission notes 1 to 3 yuan per workday under the first food-for-work programme. Zhu and Jiang (1996) note that the programme wage varied between 3 to 6 yuan in 1991 in the counties surveyed, namely, Ningxia, Sichuan and Shandong. These variations seem to be a reflection of the local labour supply situation and the opportunity cost of rural labour. They also argue that the focus of the food-for-work programme on poverty alleviation was diluted by the lowering of the programme wages paid to farmers for work on sites. The provincial and county governments, expected to provide matching funds, have been using central government funds for other purposes, which leads to the lowering of wages and the raising of compulsory workdays. Thus the conditions of the poor may have actually become worse! Zhu and Jiang (1996: 130) note that, 'at most, projects' earnings compose one-sixth of disposable income for rural households'.[11]

UNDP (1997a) notes that the compulsory nature of labour mobilization without wage payment on the Chinese public works creates a disincentive to work. Under a law promulgated in the 1950s, each worker is expected to spend 20 man-days on building and repairing construction sites annually without payment. However, wage payments are made in excess of 20 man-days. If workers do not want to contribute physical labour, they have to pay a penalty to the Construction Committees, which can then finance the hiring of wage labour (Zhu and Jiang, 1996). Some Chinese scholars believe workers are unlikely to come forward to work on the food-for-work programmes in the absence of compulsion, presumably because of alternative income-earning opportunities, the cost involved in moving and sheer laziness.

Targeting

In China the food-for-work programme does not directly target the poorest segments of the population and may thus not reach the minority poor. However, if a low wage was a requirement for self-targeting, it is likely that at a low wage only the very poor (who cannot afford to stay idle for long) will come forward. Furthermore, China's anti-poverty strategy does seem to involve some targeting of the poor. As Lipton and Ravallion (1995: 2,617) note, it 'relies heavily on regional targeting'. This implies that the poor regions (that is, both poor and non-poor inhabitants) benefit from the programme. It may, therefore, be useful to make a distinction between targeting by location or region and targeting by poverty groups. Direct targeting of the minority poor is likely to achieve better results, if their poverty reduction is the main programme objective. However, one can argue that in a region/locality where everyone is absolutely poor, direct targeting may not be all that necessary.

The nature of the targeting will depend on the organizational pattern and the institutional arrangements of the public works projects. The projects target the village communities instead of rural individuals or households. The Chinese government chooses beneficiaries on the basis of the selection of project sites and the specific investment orientation of various projects. The village communities chosen as targets have generally been known to enjoy favourable socioeconomic conditions (Zhu and Jiang, 1996: 188).[12]

The case of Sichuan

The experience of Sichuan suggests per capita funding for food-for-work (FFW) programmes is generally lower than that for credit. However, in Mabian county (which is a minority county) this expenditure was higher in 1998 than the per capita expenditure for subsidized credit and budgetary grant (see Table 6.3). The outlays for FFW for Sichuan for 1998 to 2000 are also lower (only 22 to 23 per cent of the total) than the outlay for subsidized loans (62 to 64 per cent). Table 6.6 gives the total expenditure on FFW in Sichuan for the 1996–99 period.

As mentioned above, Zhu and Jiang (1996) argue that the focus of the food-for-work programme on poverty alleviation was diluted by the lowering of the programme wages paid to farmers. The situation is further complicated because the provincial funding for poverty reduction in Sichuan for expenditure outside the poor counties is extremely limited. The World Bank (2001: 45) notes: 'The problem is quite severe in Sichuan, and LGPR has allowed the province to use 30 percent of its share of the central government's poverty reduction program funding to assist three extremely poor minority areas not included in the list of nationally-designated poor counties.'

From subsidized loan programme to the micro-credit programme

Since the mid-1980s the most important funding source for poverty alleviation in China has been the subsidized loans provided to the designated poor areas. In China initially (until 1984) the central government provided funds for credit to the rural poor out of the state budget. However, since then additional funds for credit have been channelled through such financial institutions as rural credit cooperatives and the Agricultural Development Bank of China established in 1994.[13] Since 1995, much of the credit for rural projects has been channelled through the Agricultural Development Bank and various branches of the Agricultural Bank of China (the branches of the Agricultural Development Bank are limited to the provincial capital cities). Other sectoral banks also provide rural credit, which goes mainly to county enterprises and is, therefore, not particularly targeted at the poor. It is unlikely to have benefited the minority poor.

There are many different types of poverty alleviation loans depending on project activity, destination and sources. These loans include subsidized loans by

Table 6.6 Food-for-work funds for selected poor counties in Sichuan (1996–99) (1,000 yuan)

Prefecture/city	1996	1997	1998	1999
Dachuan prefecture:	20,900	17,200	23,400	21,000
Yihan	14,360	7,960	9,990	
Quxian	6,540	7,440	8,810	
Wanyuan		1,800	4,600	
Bazhong prefecture:	21,300	20,600	26,800	95,500
Tongjiang	12,150	8,000	9,460	
Nanjiang	9,150	8,000	9,090	
Bazhong City		2,740	3,590	
Pingchang	1,860	4,660		
Guang'an prefecture:	11,250	9,800	9,700	10,000
Guang'an county	11,250	9,800	9,700	
Yibing City:	9,950	1,360	22,600	25,900
Xingwen	9,950	7,800	8,000	
Yibing		850	3,200	
Changning		1,100	2,200	
Gaoxian		800	1,900	
Junlian		800	1,300	
Gongxian		900	2,950	
Pingshan		1,350	3,050	
Nanchong City:	35,800	41,200	53,600	46,600
Yilong	7,650	12,520	14,950	
Nanbu	8,840	9,030	11,350	
Liangzhong City	9,340	7,430	10,750	
Jialing District	9,970	9,220	9,430	
Xichong	1,300	1,200	3,000	
Yingshan	1,700	1,300	4,120	
Luzhou City:	15,250	16,200	20,800	18,000
Gulan	7,690	8,350	11,600	
Shuyong	7,560	7,850	9,200	
Guangyuan City:	28,150	28,600	34,700	34,700
Changxi	10,390	7,500	9,530	
Wanglun	7,890	6,500	6,670	
Chaotian District	9,870	8,100	6,550	
Shizhong District		1,950	3,300	
Qingchuan		2,350	2,900	
Jiange		1,050	2,800	
Leshan City	6,500	7,600	8,500	8,550
Panzhihua City	4,500	5,000	5,900	5,000
Ganzhi Prefecture	37,900	36,900	40,950	40,950
Aba Prefecture	31,550	29,600	39,800	39,800
Liangshan Prefecture	45,550	55,800	72,100	72,100
Yaan Prefecture	500	1,900	4,050	3,700
Mianyang City		2,000	6,100	7,100
Others	90,900	1,000		9,800
Grand total	360,000	287,000	369,000	370,000

Source: Data supplied by the Poor Area Development Office, Sichuan province, Chengdu.

the Agricultural Bank of China, special loans for industrial projects granted by the People's Bank of China, the Industrial and Commercial Bank of China and the Construction Bank of China, special loans for the old revolutionary bases, minority areas, remote areas and poor areas by the People's Bank of China; development loans for underdeveloped areas granted by the Agricultural Bank of China and special poverty alleviation loans granted by the local authorities (Wang and Zhu, 1997).

Loans for poverty alleviation are targeted at poor areas. They can be used for both agricultural and non-agricultural projects. The interest rate is different depending on the purpose of the project loan. For example, in 1998 the annual rate of the Agricultural Bank loans for projects on plantation and domestic husbandry was 2.88 per cent, while the rate for specialized loans for rural industrial projects was 8.4 per cent.

A poor county can obtain subsidized loans in one of two ways. One is to obtain allocation directly from the provincial government. The other is to submit project proposals to the Agricultural Bank and compete for loans granted by the bank. Generally speaking, the amount of loans a county can obtain depends on several factors: (1) *size of the population* below the poverty line in the county; (2) *location of the county* (whether it is located in an area of strategic industrial importance – a poor county in such an area will be preferred for loan allocation); (3) *ethnicity* – whether a county is autonomous with a significant minority population; and (4) *previous record of loan repayment*. A good repayment record entitles a county to more loans (Wang and Zhu, 1997).

Under the subsidized loan programme the Agricultural Development Bank sets credit ceilings for each county, which passes on this information to townships and villages within its jurisdiction, which in turn select poor households for loan applications.[14] The names of the selected households are reported to the Poor Area Development Office (PADO).

PADO centrally determines the planning and allocation of loans. There is a clear conflict of interest between PADO and the Agricultural Development Bank. While PADO favours the poor, the bank favours the non-poor with greater capacity to pay back loans.

Interest is charged for the use of loans for poverty alleviation, but the difference between the prevailing market rate and the rate for specialized loans is paid by the central government. The nominal interest rates for such loans (generally for one to three years) are at least 20 per cent lower than the normal official rates. Demand for rural credit in China remains very high because of the low or negative real interest rate.[15]

A centrally administered loan scheme follows a top-down approach under which loans are allocated in a hierarchical manner from the centre to the provinces and from there to the poor counties. The objectives of central, provincial and county governments are often different and in conflict. Collateral is not easily available to the poor farmers since until recently land leases were not transferable (see Hoff *et al.*, 1995). The rural credit cooperatives are still reluctant to accept land as collateral; they prefer financial deposits as a guarantee. Thus poor farmers are often denied access to formal credit. They have to rely on friends and relatives (who do not require either collateral or a guarantee) for informal credit for both consumption and investment purposes.

The Chinese poverty-alleviation loan programme has contributed positively to economic development and poverty reduction in poor areas. But the mechanism of loan grants and their allocation has caused many concerns among domestic and international scholars and government officials. One of the main criticisms is that subsidized loans are targeted at poor areas, not poor people. Often the local authorities and officials are the main beneficiaries. Zhu (1997) notes that the poor do not enjoy access to rural credit, although the programme was started to 'provide credit to assist the poor'. This is due to the way in which the loans are granted and used. The process of loan approval is quite subjective; it depends on the ability and preferences of the leaders of the PADOs. Furthermore, since the Agricultural Bank is responsible for the repayment of loans, a return from the subsidy on the interest rate is less important than the principal itself. Finally, the bank often uses delaying tactics in order to maximize profits. Very often it uses the subsidized loan funds for normal commercial lending. The really poor people do not have the ability or connections to set up a project, and the rural credit market is less developed in China than in other developing countries, particularly South Asia. The banks are reluctant to lend to the poor especially in remote areas for fear of non-payment (or inadequate collateral). A survey under the World Bank-assisted Poverty Reduction Project in southwest China showed that 32 per cent of the households did not receive any loan, and that lower priority was given to poor households in Guangxi and Guizhou project areas during 1998–99. A comparison of the loan grants and households by income levels shows that over 30 per cent of the loans went to households with incomes above 1,000 yuan and only 23 per cent to those with incomes below 500 yuan (see LGOPAD, 1999: 47).

To conclude, the subsidized loan programme suffered from two major weaknesses: it failed to reach the poor, and it encountered the low loan repayment rate. The poor (including the minority poor), especially in remote mountainous areas, may not seek loans due to the cost of the frequent meetings involved in taking a loan. Park and Ren (2001: 46) note costly and frequent meetings and remote location in mountainous areas as two reasons for the low demand for credit. Furthermore, the subsidized nature of credit attracts the more wealthy rather than the poor, especially as loans are generally granted for town and village enterprises (TVEs) with shorter gestation periods rather than for agricultural and livestock activities.[16]

Micro-credit

The above problems led the Chinese government to introduce a micro-credit programme along the lines of the Grameen Bank (GB) in Bangladesh. Micro-credit is regarded as one of the important components of public intervention for poverty alleviation by both donors and developing countries (Lipton, 1998; Zhao, 1999). Especially since the establishment of Grameen Bank in Bangladesh in 1974 as a group or cooperative lending institution for the poor, a large number of developing countries, including China, have been inspired by the Grameen approach.

The Grameen Bank is characterized by some unique features. First, unlike most banks the GB does not require any collateral in the form of land or other assets. Peer pressures, social sanctions and guarantees are used as substitutes for a collateral. Much against initial expectations, the loan repayment rate has been remarkably high thanks to group pressure, social sanctions and the grass-roots organization of the loan programme. The high loan repayment rate may also be due partly to the insistence of the bank on encouraging borrowers to save. The participation of the potential beneficiaries and the local cooperative nature of the lending are noted to be important reasons for the bank's success. Lipton (1998: 44) notes that 'mutual monitoring by small groups of borrowers, as in Grameen, was the central tenet of cooperative credit before it became politicized'. The Indian experience with credit programmes shows that local popular selection of borrowers by the village councils, for example, works much better than their selection/identification by the state bureaucracy (Lipton, 1998: 49).

Table 6.7 summarizes distinguishing features of the old Chinese subsidized loan programme and the new micro-credit programme. By 1998 this programme is reported to have reached 200 poor counties, accounting for investment of about 800 million yuan (World Bank, 2000).

Loans are targeted at the very poor who own less than 0.5 acre of land. This limit is not relevant in China, where there are no landless workers. The bank has

Table 6.7 A comparison between the subsidized loan programme and the micro-credit programme in China

The subsidized loan programme	*The micro-credit programme*
Targeting of project area	Targeting of group of poor households
Low rate of repayment	Higher rate of repayment*
Need for collateral	Absence of collateral
Mainly domestic sources of funding	Domestic and international financing
Centralized structure and administration	Decentralized structure and administration

* The Chinese micro-credit programme was introduced as an experiment only recently. Therefore, it is difficult to determine at this stage whether the loan repayment rate is actually higher. On the basis of a household survey data of six counties in different provinces in 1997, Park and Ren (2001) show that loan repayment is very high specially among the non-governmental programmes.

adopted a cooperative or group-based lending scheme, which requires a minimum group of five villagers, not relatives or from the same household (to avoid bias), to obtain a loan. Although each member of the group receives an individual loan, the group is collectively responsible for the total credit, which provides 'peer monitoring' and mutual insurance against default. Group lending is known to have been successful in reaching the poor target groups.

In December 1997 a survey was undertaken of six nationally designated poor counties in different provinces to determine the impact of micro-credit (based on the Grameen model) on poverty reduction (Park and Ren, 2001). Three types of programmes were covered: an NGO programme, a mixed (government and NGO) programme, and a government-funded programme. The survey results show that (1) loan repayments are particularly high under NGO programmes, but low under government programmes (repayment rates improve if the borrowers are female with more and better-quality land), (2) financial self-sufficiency is achieved even with low interest rates thanks to access to donor funds and low operating costs and (3) the government programme does not target the poor and is thus similar to the earlier loan subsidization programme.[17]

In China the Institute of Rural Development of the Chinese Academy of Social Sciences is responsible for a Grameen-type experiment at the grass-roots level with funding from both domestic and foreign sources, and joint efforts of local governments and village communities. Community participation raises the loan recovery rate to 85 per cent, which is much higher than that under the formal credit projects of the poverty alleviation programmes (Zhu *et al.*, 1997: 52). Other Grameen-type rural credit schemes in China are supported by the UNDP in association with IFAD, UNICEF and WFP. These projects, characterized by high commercial rates and compulsory group savings, are located in Yunnan, Guangxi, Guizhou, Sichuan and Inner Mongolia (Cook and White, 1998). The Mutual Assistance Credit Groups (MACGs) promoted by the Ministry of Civil Affairs since 1982 have some resemblance to the Grameen-type micro-credit programmes. MACGs grant credit for both consumption and production purposes unlike the official credit programmes for poverty reduction. Zhu *et al.* (1997: 48) note that 'this type of self-help group at the grass roots level … has linked villages' mobilization of savings to their utilization of credit, combined poverty reduction with disaster relief, performed effective credit supervision, and developed a model for integrating the poor in rural systems for credit service'.

The labour mobility programme

The government intervention in labour mobility can be classified into three categories: the population migration programme, induced labour mobility through public projects, and the employment promotion programme. We briefly discuss these below.

The population migration programme: In some areas natural conditions are so adverse that there is no hope of eliminating poverty through economic development. Therefore, the central and local authorities and some international institutions provide financial grants to organize the movement of people away from their homes to new and better areas.[18]

The induced labour mobility programme: In recent years the government has substantially increased its investment in infrastructure programmes, such as building roads, dams and bridges, as part of its fiscal policy to stimulate the sluggish economy and to reduce the income gap between coastal and inland provinces. These projects created a large labour demand and induced migration from the poor areas to fill job vacancies in urban areas.

The employment promotion programmes: The government provides a grant to set up employment agencies to bridge the gap between the demand for labour and its supply. This programme (funded partly by the World Bank) helps to transfer labour from the poor counties and areas with low labour demand to the high labour-demand areas either within the same province or other provinces, particularly the coastal areas. This public intervention is guided by the notion that economic and social development is essentially witnessed in an inter-sectoral shift of labour from agriculture to manufacturing and services. Within the Lewis–Fei–Ranis framework of labour surplus models, rural labour spontaneously moves out of agriculture and into higher income-earning opportunities in non-agricultural activities in the rural and urban areas. Labour demand has increased within rural areas through agricultural modernization (use of advanced biological and mechanical technologies, changes in cropping and cultivation patterns) and the development of village and township enterprises. Yet many of the poor counties have substantial labour surpluses, which cannot be absorbed in non-farm activities within those areas. Therefore, the labour mobility programme is intended to smooth the transfer of surplus labour from poor areas to more rapidly growing areas and regions.[19]

In Sichuan in 1998 over 57 per cent of rural migrants moved outside the province, whereas 42 per cent moved to other counties within the province. Very few migrants went abroad (see Table 6.8). Over 48 per cent of the migrants' income in 1998 was remitted back to their places of origin. In the case of some counties the proportion of remittances was extremely high. In Sichuan, during the last decade, between 8 and 9 million people migrated to other provinces in search of jobs, but they were not from the poorest areas (World Bank, 1997a). In Guangxi the labour mobility programme is noted to have had a significant impact on poverty reduction in the villages and counties from which the rural migrants moved. Information for selected counties for 1995 shows that per capita incomes and remittances per capita were significant. For example, the per capita annual income of rural migrants from Napo county was nearly 5,000 yuan.

Table 6.8 Sichuan: labour mobility of migrants from selected poverty counties and their remittances (1998)

| Region | Within counties/ cities (no.) | Labour mobility | | | | Income (1,000 yuan) | Remittance (1,000 yuan) | Remittance as % of of income |
| | | Total (no.) | External | | | | | |
			Outside counties but within province (no.)	Outside the province (no.)	Abroad (no.)			
Sichuan	1,358,865	1,422,035	596,004	813,562	1,446	7,599,520	3,658,650	48.1
Yanbian	7,105	2,386	2,252	134	-	11,260	-	-
Xuyong County	163,243	17,188	813,540	3,591	54	245,600	130,000	52.9
Gulin County	8,600	35,100	821,600	10,500	-	123,360	5,220	4.2
Beichuan	13,217	6,151	5,320	1,123	11	35,990	35,540	98.7
Pingwu	7,900	6,100	2,265	1,100	35	13,500	7,500	66.6
Wangcang	8,600	19,880	12,300	7,580	-	17,000	15,000	88.2
Qingchuan	2,000	7,661	4,600	3,061	-	5,000	1,000	20.0
Jiangxie	21,000	220,000	10,000	180,000	-	20,000	1,000	50.0
Cangxi	15,867	115,000	28,750	89,250	18	45,000	150,000	33.3
Muchuan	12,500	18,839	13,666	5,100	73	25,300	15,250	60.3
Mabian	6,350	5,253	1,350	3,903	-	-	-	-
Yibin County	150,000	21,000	4,000	17,000	25	121,500	23,500	19.3
Changning	36,824	37,630	26,620	11,010	-	1,405,200	96,500	6.9
Gao County	150,023	8,265	790	7,172	3	130,000	99,000	76.1
Junlian	19,300	27,066	11,106	17,317	-	13,000	11,010	84.7
Qi County	19,890	22,377	11,293	8,081	-	32,600	19,800	60.7

Source: Data supplied by the Poor Area Development Office, Sichuan province, Chengdu.

Organization of labour mobility

Government channels exist for organizing migrants from poor upland counties to urban areas within the provinces or to neighbouring provinces. Employers from the southern coastal provinces and cities with growing labour shortages approach the Labour Departments to recruit surplus rural labour. They describe their specific requirements, in the light of which the relevant Labour Department identifies the supply pool of workers from which employers select a certain number and train them for their new jobs. The provincial Labour Departments do not bear the cost of transporting workers, who are themselves responsible for it.[20]

Causes of migration

Several factors account for rural-to-urban migration from the southwest provinces: worsening income gaps and terms of trade between rural and urban areas, the unprecedented boom in coastal cities in the south, relaxation by the government of resident permits and residency regulations, and the slow growth of the urban population due to the one-child policy. Discussions with the Yunnan Labour Department in 1999 suggest that rural labour redundancy rather than better income prospects in urban areas was the main factor explaining migration, at least from that province. Thus the Todaro model, according to which the driving force is the wage differential between rural and urban areas, does not seem to apply at least to conditions in Yunnan. It would, however, be surprising if this economic factor did not play any role. Single-factor explanations for such complex and multi-faceted issues as migration are rarely satisfactory.

Socioeconomic characteristics of rural migrants

The poorer the people, the lower their mobility to go elsewhere. This is due partly to the cost of moving and partly to the fear of the unknown. In southwest China most of the very poor people (especially minorities) live in remote mountainous areas. They are attached to their homes and their religious, cultural and linguistic environment. This is particularly true of older people. On the other hand, young people migrate more easily. There seems to be no clear evidence on migration patterns by gender; both men and women migrate. However, male members of households are more likely to move in search of jobs than female members, who generally stay back to do farming and rear children.

In 1996 the Chinese State Statistical Bureau (SSB) conducted a detailed survey of rural migrants (within the framework of the World Bank-assisted poverty reduction project) in a selected number of villages of Guangxi, Guizhou and Yunnan. The survey shows that employers and local government agencies play a very limited role in placing migrants, who find jobs by themselves or through informal networks of friends and relatives. The bulk of migrants are engaged in manufacturing and construction activities. With the exception of

Guizhou, farming is not an important occupation for migrants. Most of the migrants spend 10–12 months away from home.

Very short-term migrants form only a small proportion in all three provinces. Rapidly growing coastal provinces suffering from labour shortages are the most attractive destination for the majority of rural migrants. The net per capita annual income of migrants is much higher than the average rural net per capita income. Many migrants earn more than 5,000 yuan per annum. In 1999 remittances per capita were highest for Guizhou. followed by Guangxi (see Table 7.11, Chapter 7).

The CASS household surveys provide some information on remittances separately for minorities and non-minorities which is presented in Table 6.9. The results are estimated on the basis of survey data for 1988 and 1995, using the 19 Chinese provinces common to the two surveys. An individual is the unit of analysis. The first row of the table shows the percentage of households that report receiving remittances. One can see a growing gap between minority and non-minority households with regard to remittances, but the absolute differences are not large. The average per capita values are very small because very few households report any remittances. While the absolute gap in terms of yuan is growing, the relative gap between the minority and non-minority is shrinking.

One of the important benefits of migration is the flow of remittances back to the rural areas, which can help raise rural incomes and productivity, especially if they are used for capital investment. Thus remittances can be an important equalizing factor for reducing rural–urban income disparities. In 1994, according to estimates by the Chinese Ministry of Labour, 37 million rural migrants in 23 large cities remitted 75 billion yuan to their families in rural areas.[21]

Social costs of migration

Rural migrants from Guangxi, Guizhou and Yunnan encountered several difficulties in moving to other areas: language problems, finding jobs and

Table 6.9 Remittances: minority vs non-minority (1988, 1995)

	1988		1995	
	Minority	*Non-minority*	*Minority*	*Non-minority*
Household receiving remittances (%)	5.3	6.1	4.5	7.1
Annual average remittance per capita (1988 yuan)	2.7	7.5	5.2	12.1

Note: Remittances are inflation-adjusted to 1988 yuan.

Source: Based on the CASS household survey data for 1988 and 1995.

housing, social prejudices and cultural differences. The two most important factors militating against labour mobility in all three provinces were finding jobs and housing.

Large influxes of migrants to urban areas strain the existing limited economic resources and social and physical infrastructure, leading to environmental hazards. Further costs involved include the growth of urban slums and social and cultural problems arising from difficulties faced by rural migrants in assimilating into unknown environments.

One cannot argue against the movement of people from low-productivity areas to high-productivity areas. After all, this is the whole purpose of economic development. But rural-to-urban migration is by no means an unmixed blessing. The social costs of the dislocation of rural people need to be taken into account in designing and implementing the labour mobility programme for poverty alleviation. Illiterate and semi-literate migrants, many of whom are from ethnic minorities, women and older people, are particularly vulnerable to poor working conditions and low incomes and employment security in urban areas. Migrants moving on their own accord often work in very bad and unhygienic conditions in coal mines and on construction sites at wages below the legal minimum. Many of the jobs are of a contract or casual nature, involving risk and insecurity.

Urban unemployment has been increasing in China with the retrenchment of workers from state-owned enterprises. This means that rural migrants (particularly the minorities) will have to compete with these redundant state workers, who are better trained to the extent that they look for the same sorts of jobs. To some extent, the segmented labour market will prevent or mitigate such competition. Furthermore, the educational and training profiles of rural migrants will keep them in non-competitive markets. However, increasing unemployment pressures can break down the walls between the two types of labour market.

Thus, appropriate policies and action programmes (in addition to simply ensuring labour mobility) are needed in order to minimize the social costs of migration. Measures required may include: better labour market information about jobs by strengthening Labour Bureaus' employment service systems, training schemes for rural migrants, and a monitoring system to ensure safety and good living conditions (including housing). The provincial and local governments have an important role to play in introducing new and innovative institutional arrangements for the placement of migrants, improving job information networks, providing housing, and channelling migrants' remittances into productive investments in rural areas.

The Chinese poverty reduction programme: a review

There is no systematic assessment and evaluation of the 8-7 Programme either at the centre or in the provinces. However, sporadic commentary on and critique of the programme have been made to assess whether it has created a dent in the poverty problem. Riskin (1993a) notes that only 37 per cent of the poor households in the 1988 rural survey reported that they were located in the poor-designated areas to which the anti-poverty programme is confined. This suggests that at least at that time, nearly three-fifths of the poor outside the area did not benefit from the programme. Similarly, Jalan and Ravallion (1998b: 69, fn 12) note that during 1985–90 nearly half the poor did not live in centrally or provincially designated poor counties. Using household data for Guangdong, Guangxi and Guizhou for 1985–90, Jalan and Ravallion (1998b: 68) conclude: 'an unconditional comparison of areas in Southern China covered by the poor-area program and those not covered suggests that the program has done nothing to help poor areas catch up with other areas—the program benefits seem to have vanished'. The effectiveness of the anti-poverty programme is measured by the consumption growth of households, which was higher in the programme areas. They conclude that the anti-poverty programme led to gains which prevented an absolute decline in living standards. However, these gains were not strong enough. Although Jalan and Ravallion (1998b) present a rigorous and neat attempt to estimate the impact of the anti-poverty programme on the household standard of living, it is not certain that all growth of consumption can be attributed to the programme. The incidence of poverty may well be influenced by other exogenous factors. It is, therefore, impossible to isolate the effects of the programme on household living standards especially in the absence of any regular and systematic poverty-monitoring exercises by the provincial PADOs.

No poverty alleviation programmes exist for the rural poor outside the designated poverty counties, who in 1998 constituted about 21 million (World Bank, 2001: 44). This is a substantial number of the poor, who are expected to benefit from economic growth and such economic policies as agricultural pricing, rural–urban terms of trade, and investment allocation.

Targeting

The programme is largely locational and is thus not targeted at the poor. The poor households in rural areas are usually not the direct project beneficiaries. The Chinese anti-poverty programme targets poor areas instead of poor households. Jalan and Ravallion (1998b: 70) note that 44 programme counties out of the 131 covered in their sample provinces targeted poor areas. Since 1996 (State Council decision of October of that year), the Chinese government has shifted emphasis from area development to targeting the poorest households. This shift in policy seems to have been induced by Western criticism that the anti-poverty programme was not reaching the poor and the fact that nearly 70 per cent of the funds allocated for the programme were being used by counties for other purposes.

Targeting the poor reinforces the importance of micro-credit, discussed above. However, in the past this credit programme was targeted more for social development than for poverty alleviation. Poor farm households do not enjoy direct access to the micro-credit programmes (UNDP, 1997a: 99). Beneficiaries have included local governments, project organizers and the non-poor. As we noted above, the credit programme has not been very effective, especially if it is judged by the loan repayment rate, which has been quite low. It is estimated that about one-third of the loans are not recovered. This can be seen by the lack of any correlation between subsidized loans and rural per capita income. The subsidized loan programme has several inherent problems, as discussed above.

In comparison, the smaller food-for-work funds and some other development funds tend to be more beneficial for the poor. These funds are used for improving the agricultural infrastructure and land productivity, with possible significant long-term effects on the incomes of the poor households in rural areas.

Targeting the rural poor minorities directly is more likely to prevent leakages of benefits to the non-poor. World Bank (2001: 44–5) recommends targeting the poor townships instead of counties and claims that this will benefit the minorities living outside the poor counties. It is, however, not clear whether this method will necessarily reach the minority households, which need to be specifically targeted rather than the townships as such. Furthermore, the administrative cost of reaching the townships may be prohibitive. At present, the administration at the township level suffers from having too few (and poorly qualified) staff.

Coordination and financing of activities

There have been organizational and administrative problems in the coordination of the projects and activities funded under the anti-poverty programme. These problems are caused by the number of different bodies and agencies involved and the different sources of funding. We illustrated in Figure 6.1 the organizational structure of the Leading Group for Poverty Reduction (LGPR) at the central, provincial and county levels and the large number of bodies which have their own mandates and funding sources. Furthermore, the requirement for the formulation and implementation of long-term production-oriented projects differ from those for the more immediate relief-type of projects. The Leading Group does not seem to have direct control over funding which comes from such diverse sources as the State Planning Commission, the Ministry of Finance and such international funding agencies as the World Bank.[22]

Fiscal decentralization has reduced central government revenues for direct poverty alleviation programmes. During the 1990s the central revenue to GDP ratio was consistently declining, which has weakened the central government's redistributive role through fiscal transfers to poor localities. The centre granted fixed subsidies to the poorest regions in nominal terms, which implies their decline in real terms (Gai, 1996; Gao, 1995). It has thus reduced the ability of poor local governments to finance anti-poverty programmes. The poor localities with more limited human resources, almost no industrial base and adverse initial conditions are less able to generate their own resources than other localities with better local conditions and resources.[23]

The programme is mainly production-oriented; it does not integrate such social objectives as provision of access to health and educational facilities, which is important for reducing minority poverty. Thus a multi-pronged approach to poverty, which is highly desirable, has not yet been implemented (Khan and Riskin, 2001). Neither is there any complementarity between the overall development policies and the micro-interventions. Khan and Riskin (2001: 123) note that 'fostering economic growth through policies that steer resources away from poor areas and people, and then trying to compensate with a poverty alleviation program, turns out to have been an ineffective overall strategy for coping with poverty'.

The World Bank-assisted project in southwest China

A report on poverty monitoring for the World Bank project in southwest China (Yunnan, Guizhou and Guangxi) surveys and assesses the progress achieved in the first three years (1995 to 1997). In 1995 the State Statistical Bureau (SSB) conducted a baseline survey of 35 project counties, including 3,500 households, and collected data at the community, household and individuals levels. Of these in 1996 and 1997, 20 counties covering 2,000 households were surveyed. The survey shows that at least in these counties in the three southwest provinces the living standards of the households improved considerably, which is reflected in a rise in annual per capita income of nearly 9 per cent, a decline in the head-count poverty ratio from 31.5 per cent in 1995 to 21.3 per cent in 1997, and a decline in the proportion of the population with less than 150 kg grain production per capita from 17.7 per cent to 7.5 per cent during the same period (LGOPAD, 1997: 48). Since the minorities are concentrated in these provinces, it may be reasonable to assume that they have also benefited.

The above survey did a controlled experiment under which the poverty situation of project villages was compared with that of non-project villages. The results show that the decline in the incidence of poverty in project villages was faster than in non-project villages. The project villages showed better results in respect of more production-oriented activities (for example, agricultural development) than in terms of social development activities, including the promotion of accessibility to electricity and road infrastructure. Another noteworthy finding of the above survey is that the rate of participation of the poorest households in project activities is much lower than that of the not so poor. The majority of the participating households are near or at the poverty line rather than below (or far below) it. One explanation for this situation is that the very poor are not being targeted because the rate of implementation of the programme would be lower if they were; the extremely poor are unable to repay loans, for example, and are reluctant to be resettled under the 'labour mobility' programme (LGOPAD, 1997: 88). In terms of the performance of individual provinces, it is not surprising that Guizhou, the poorest province with the worst initial conditions, lags behind the other southwest provinces in poverty reduction (see

Chapter 7). According to the *Poverty Monitoring Report* (LGOPAD (1997: 49), for example, the village coverage rate in the province for the health, rural infrastructure and labour mobility components of activities is relatively low.

The Poverty Reduction Programme has helped reduce the number of poor. By 1997 over 12 million poor people were brought up to the poverty line, and 40,000 were resettled in 11 areas. By the end of 1998 the poor population had dropped by 38 million, down to 42 million from 80 million in 1994. The problem of feeding and clothing 10 million rural poor still remains, however. Besides, there are extremely poor people living in remote and inaccessible areas. Poverty persists here because of harsh natural conditions and low-productivity mountainous terrain (Government of China, 1999: 12).[24]

Concluding remarks

This chapter has discussed three distinct phases of the poverty alleviation policies and programmes in China. The first period covered 1979 to 1985, when government efforts were concerned mainly with supporting (financially and in kind) – so-called 'money-food-cotton support' – the backward and remote areas. The second period, covering the Poor Area Development Programme and the 8-7 Poverty Reduction Plan, related to 1986 to 1995. The third phase started in 1996 with a State Council directive to shift the emphasis from area development to targeting of the poorest households. This change in policy was a response to the actual experience that in practice the anti-poverty programme did not reach the poor. This phase was also distinct in another respect. For the first time during this period the government attempted to tackle the urban poverty problem by concentrating on three types of public intervention, namely, the guaranteeing of a minimum urban standard of living, the provision of the minimum basic needs of staff and workers laid off from the state-owned enterprises, and the creation of an unemployment insurance fund. However, initial findings suggest that this switch in policy has not had any significant effect on poverty reduction (World Bank, 2001).

Three main anti-poverty programmes, namely, the food-for-work programme, loan subsidization and micro-credit, and labour mobility, have been discussed with special reference to Guizhou, Yunnan and Sichuan in southwest China. Three types of labour mobility interventions were examined: population migration, induced labour mobility (through public projects) and employment promotion through the establishment of employment agencies. Using county-level data for each province, per capita funding for food-for-work (FFW) and subsidized loans were compared between the poorest and least poor among the poor and minority counties. The sample number of counties was too small to make any generalizations. However, it is clear that the food-for-work programme tended to be more beneficial for the (minority) poor than the subsidized loan scheme and micro-credit.

A comparison was made between the Chinese FFW programme and similar programmes in other developing countries such as Bangladesh, India and Pakistan. In these latter countries, the programmes were aimed mainly at generating short-term employment, whereas in China the main objective of the programme was long-term capital construction and accumulation. The Indian subcontinent suffers from the problem of landless labour (absent in China), which partly generates pressures to create rural wage employment.

There is no systematic assessment and evaluation of the 8-7 Programme either at the centre or in the provinces. However, it is generally believed that the programme has not reached the poor. No poverty alleviation programmes exist for the rural poor outside the designated poverty counties. We do not know of any assessment of whether the minority poor have benefited from the anti-poverty programmes discussed in this chapter. But it would seem that the lack of minority community participation in the anti-poverty projects has resulted in a failure to adapt these projects to cultural differences between minorities and the Han majority. Anti-poverty programmes for Guizhou province are discussed, and their impact on minorities, assessed in Chapter 7.

7 Anti-poverty programmes in Guizhou

In this chapter we present a case study of Guizhou province in southwest China. The choice of Guizhou is guided by several considerations: existence of acute absolute poverty, a substantial minority population and limited Western literature on the province. Guizhou is one of the poorest provinces of China. It accounted for 5.3 per cent of China's rural poor in 1988 and 7.6 per cent in 1996. Between 1988 and 1995 the incidence of poverty, based on the head-count ratio, rose from 58 per cent to nearly 62 per cent. The poverty-gap ratio declined only slightly from 21 per cent to 19 per cent (Khan and Riskin, 2001). According to Table 1.3 in Chapter 1, the incidence of poverty in Guizhou in 1999 (measured by head-count ratio, poverty-gap ratio and weighted poverty-gap ratio) was higher than that in Guangxi and Sichuan but lower than in Yunnan.

Among the southwest provinces/regions considered, Guizhou has the largest proportion of the total population represented by minority nationalities (nearly 40 per cent). In Chapter 1 we showed their poorer economic situation compared to the Han majority. For example, while the minorities form nearly 40 per cent of Guizhou's total population, they account for only 4.7 per cent of total employment. Over 80 per cent of the land area of Guizhou is mountainous and thus non-cultivable. The province is known as a place where 'one has to climb eight mountains before one can find a river and a piece of cultivable land' (Zuo, 1992). However, despite difficult terrain, GDP has grown surprisingly rapidly, from 6 billion yuan in 1980 to 92 billion yuan in 1997 (that is, an annual real growth rate of 8.7 per cent). The province has the highest birth rate of all the southwest provinces, and its death rate is also quite high. The average family size and dependency ratio are also quite large. The province is largely rural with the bulk of its population at subsistence level. The majority of the population depends on the cultivation of rice, potatoes and tubers. In 1997 the share of primary sector GDP was 34 per cent and that of secondary and tertiary sectors 37 per cent and 29 per cent respectively. The sectoral composition of employment shows a similar picture: over 72 per cent of the labour force is employed in the primary sector, 10 per cent in the secondary sector and 18 per cent in the tertiary sector, suggesting a rather low rural/agricultural productivity. The above factors contribute to the high incidence of poverty in Guizhou.

The CASS household survey data enable a disaggregation of income levels between minorities and non-minorities for 1988 and 1995 for Guizhou and other provinces. Table 3.4 in Chapter 3 gives information on the average household size, per capita income and growth rate of per capita income for Guizhou and Yunnan. It shows some interesting results: (1) average household size is slightly larger among minorities in both provinces, (2) minority per capita income was lower than the majority per capita income in 1988 but higher in 1995 in both provinces, and (3) per capita income growth between 1988 and 1995 in both provinces was much higher for the minority than for the majority, which may explain (2). We noted in Chapter 4 on basic education that several locational factors were important in determining schooling in 1988 but not in 1995. Expansion of the basic education of minorities and the narrowing of educational gaps between minorities and non-minorities is one of the factors explaining why minorities in Guizhou and Yunnan have done better in 1995 in terms of per capita income. As we discussed in Chapter 3, other factors explaining a more rapid income growth among rural minorities in Guizhou and Yunnan include a more rapid increase in 'the proportion of working members fully engaged in nonfarm work', growth of tourism and the opening up of border trade.

To obtain an impression of the micro-poverty situation at the county and township levels we consider below in Table 7.1 the income and non-income poverty situation of Puding county and its various townships, with the shares of minority populations in each. The county is located in the karst mountains in Guizhou, and the southern townships are separated from the northern by the Sanfen river. Minorities are concentrated more in the northern townships, in which their share of the agricultural population is as high as 38 per cent compared to a maximum of 24 per cent in the southern townships. Townships with a high concentration of minorities are generally poorer in terms of per capita incomes and such non-income poverty indicators as per capita irrigated area, physical per capita grain output and road access.

Programmes for poverty reduction

We discuss below three main micro-interventions for poverty reduction, namely, the food-for-work programme (FFW), the micro-credit programme and the labour mobility programme.[1] As the poverty situation in Guizhou remains acute, it is important to analyse the impact of various government measures adopted to reduce poverty.

Figure. 7.1 shows poverty alleviation fund (PAF) allocations for subsidized loans, food-for-work (FFW) and budgetary grant to cover deficits of the local county governments.[2] We notice that since 1993 the allocation for subsidized credit has been growing far more rapidly than allocations for the other two items. This situation is similar to that in Sichuan discussed in Chapter 6. Between 1990 and 1997, although the percentage shares of subsidized loans, FFW funds and budgetary grants did not change much, in absolute terms the annual total PAF

Table 7.1 Poverty indicators for Puding county and townships (Guizhou) (1992)

	Agricultural population		Per capita income (yuan)	Per capita grain output (kg)	Irrigated land per capita (mu)	Share of administrative villages with road access (%)
	Total (no.)	Minorities (%)				
Southern townships	224,646	13.2	379	237	0.40	77.1
Machang	33,148	10.9	369	258	0.33	73.7
Longchang	27,619	10.0	331	191	0.25	68.8
Chengguan	47,967	23.6	419	267	0.39	87.8
Baiyan	27,620	17.0	391	260	0.46	76.0
Huachu	44,228	3.8	371	223	0.33	69.8
Maguan	44,064	12.7	373	219	0.52	83.9
Northern townships	115,200	33.3	233	213	0.24	47.2
Jichangpo	28,300	36.7	248	216	0.25	70.8
Pingshang	22,800	32.0	235	248	0.20	40.0
Bulang	19,500	34.9	222	222	0.23	50.0
Houchang	19,000	37.9	224	238	0.20	41.2
Maodong	25,600	26.2	230	153	0.30	34.6
All Puding	339,846	20.0	329	229	0.34	67.2

Source: Data supplied by the Poor Area Development Office, Guizhou Province, Guiyang.

increased dramatically for the 48 poor counties of Guizhou from 181.7 million yuan to 1,314 million yuan, an increase of over 632 per cent (see Table 7.2).

More detailed official statistics not presented here show that since 1993 the FFW funding has flattened out, which suggests that the grant element in the total PAF has become less important. A shift in priority is based on the assumption that grants create disincentives.

The destination of PAF by economic activity (see Figure 7.2) shows a relative neglect of manufacturing in the early 1990s, when the overall PAF amount was low. With a gradual increase in PAF since 1993, the allocation to manufacturing picked up significantly during 1994–95, exceeding that for agriculture. This may be due to an increase in emphasis on town and village enterprises (TVEs). However, since then funding for agricultural activities under PAF has increased.

One of the major difficulties faced by anti-poverty micro-interventions in achieving their objective and targets in Guizhou is the relatively large size of the poor population. In southwest China, Guizhou has the largest proportion of extremely poor people (the bulk of whom are ethnic minorities), who mostly live in limestone areas with serious soil erosion and a poor ecological system generally. Despite efforts at poverty reduction through various economic and social activities, several poverty counties have no access to a main road,

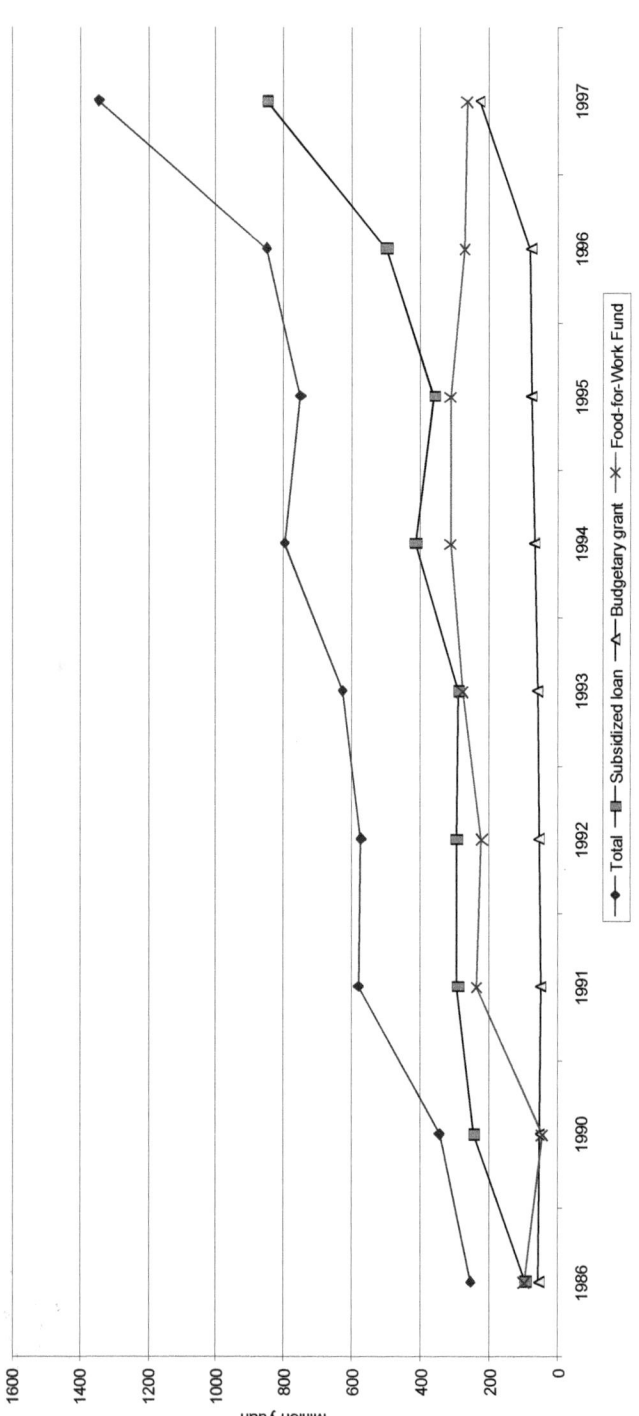

Figure 7.1 Poverty alleviation funds by category for 48 poor counties in Guizhou (1986, 1990–97)

Source: Data provided by the Poverty Alleviation Office, Guizhou, Guiyang.

Table 7.2 Guizhou: rural per capita accumulated poverty alleviation fund
(1990, 1997) (yuan)

	1990		1997
Xifeng	270.35	Jianhe	429.04
Panxian	225.91	Taijiang	459.92
Liuzhi special zone	214.40	Liping	188.03
Shuicheng	352.84	Rongjiang	358.12
Zheng'an	203.32	Congjiang	404.65
Wuchuan	405.67	Leishan	524.86
Fenggang	272.81	Majiang	284.93
Xishui	132.24	Danzai	569.08
Shiqian	268.24	Libo	424.31
Yinjiang	299.76	Dushan	256.20
Dejiang	388.49	Pingtang	262.71
Yanhe	268.34	Luodian	903.05
Suntao	149.09	Changshun	522.86
Xingren	246.33	*Sandu*	395.47
Pu'an	416.57	Xiuwen	39.06
Qinglong	340.62	Zhongshan District	215.25
Zhenfeng	402.04	*Daozheng*	96.44
Wangmo	461.99	Chishui	15.69
Ceting	515.44	Tongchuan City	141.07
Anlun	210.82	Jiangkuo	61.23
Dafang	165.67	*Yuping*	89.29
Zhijin	146.86	Sinan	24.30
Nayong	200.78	Wanshan special zone	144.82
Weining	137.61	Bijie city	49.54
Hezhang	235.54	Qianxi	60.79
Puding	204.75	Anshun city	20.00
Guanling	339.62	Pingba	26.88
Zhengning	472.77	Kaili	201.04
Ziyun	378.47	Zhenyuan	137.86
Huangping	454.52	Jingping	57.23
Shibing	270.96	Fuquan	
Shanshui	220.67	Guiding	
Chenggu	285.57	Lunli	
Tianzhu	191.95	Huishui	47.33

Note: Minority counties are in bold italics.

Source: Based on data supplied by the Poor Area Development Office, Guizhou province, Guiyang.

electricity, a health clinic or a school (see Table 7.3); and 2.7 million people in 1997 had no access to clean drinking water (LGOPAD, 1997).

The tenth Five-Year Plan (2001–2005) aims at the provision of two-thirds of Guizhou's population with minimum living standards and the elimination of poverty among the remaining three million poor. The new anti-poverty component of the plan also aims at the stabilization of production conditions to ensure sustainable development and to prevent poor people (brought above the

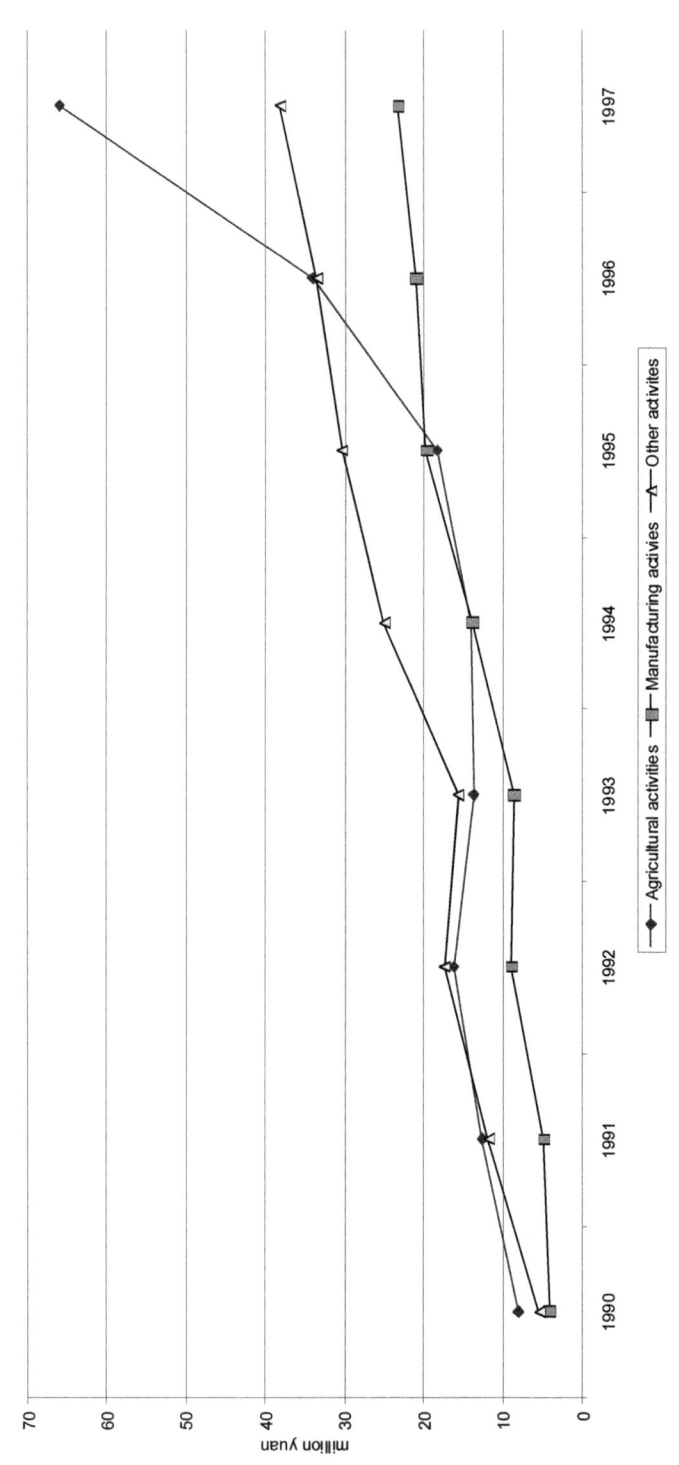

Figure 7.2 Poverty alleviation fund allocation by activities in 48 poor counties in Guizhou (1986, 1990–97)

Source: Data supplied by the Poverty Alleviation Office, Guizhou.

Table 7.3 Guizhou: income and non-income poverty in selected villages
under the World Bank-assisted project on poverty alleviation (1995–97)

	1995	1996	1997
Income aspects			
Gross annual income per capita	1,064	1,147	1,293
Net annual income per capita	704	845	985
Average wage per worker	69	64	79
Average gross expenditure per capita	977	1,110	1,101
food	466	559	601
clothing	46	47	41
medicine and medical service	16	9	11
Non-income aspects			
(a) Access indicators			
% of villages with electricity	71	87	87
% of villages linked to main road	89	89	89
% of villages with a primary school	79	82	87
% of villages with a health clinic	13	13	42
% of villages with a qualified health attendant	26	39	58
% of villages with distance to school 1–2 kms	–	–	73
(b) Education	83	85	83
Enrolment rate of children aged 7–15	91	89	85
Enrolment of boys aged 7–15	76	77	81
Enrolment of girls aged 7–15	–	87	57
% of female teachers	–	32	28
% of female to total teachers	–	40	45
% of female to total students			
(c) Health			
Number of children under 5 years immunized (%)	–	–	60

Source: LGOPAD, 1997.

poverty line) from falling back into poverty. The government has advanced the target date of nine years of compulsory schooling from 2010 to 2005.[3]

Table 7.4 ranks poor counties in the ascending order of rural per capita net income. Table 7.5 compares per capita funding of the poor and least poor counties in Guizhou under PAF with their net rural per capita income and shares of minority population in total population in 1997. We chose the five poorest of the poor counties, which are all minority counties, designated poor by the central government, and the five least poor, of which one was centrally designated poor and the others provincially designated poor. In 1997 the poorest of the poor counties received much higher funding than the less poor counties. Per capita funding for the poorest five for FFW and subsidized credit is generally higher than that for the five least poor among the poor counties. The only exception is Fenggang county, which is centrally designated poor and thus receives a much higher allocation than the other provincially funded poor counties in that group.

Table 7.4 Guizhou: ranking of poor counties by rural net per capita income (1990, 1997) (yuan in current prices)

	1990				1997		
County	Rural net per capita income	County	Rural net per capita income	County	Rural net per capita income	County	Rural net per capita income
Danzai	146	Dushan	285	Leishan	866	Jingping	1,156
Qinglong	167	Shiqian	286	Qinglong	877	Xingren	1,157
Dejiang	173	Bijie city	294	Wangmo	893	Wanshan	1,161
Yanhe	175	Majiang	306	Rongjiang	935	Zhengning	1,162
Pu'an	175	Anshun	316	Yanhe	945	Liuzhi	1,164
Ceting	179	Liping	317	Jianhe	947	Puding	1,165
Yinjiang	183	Wuchuan	328	Congjiang	955	Majiang	1,167
Zhenfeng	186	Sinan	329	Daozheng	961	Panxian	1,171
Leishan	192	Rongjiang	331	Ceting	978	Jiangkuo	1,173
Shuicheng	206	Zhongshan	332	Nayong	983	Wuchuan	1,181
Xifeng	208	Cishui	333	Huangping	994	Chenggu	1,184
Wangmo	210	Tianzhu	336	Danzai	1,023	Xishui	1,187
Panxian	214	Anlun	338	Zhenyuan	1,041	Shibing	1,204
Weining	214	Shanshui	339	Liping	1,042	Libo	1,206
Jianhe	214	Libo	340	Suntao	1,045	Shanshui	1,224
Taijiang	215	Jingping	354	Hezhang	1,046	Zhongshan	1,265
Puding	218	Xishui	361	Yinjiang	1,071	Dejiang	1,268
Dafang	219	Chenggu	375	Shuicheng	1,072	Lunli	1,286
Ziyun	226	Guiding	391	Zhenfeng	1,082	Guiding	1,301
Zhijin	231	Yuping	397	Sinan	1,083	Anlun	1,311
Huangping	234	Daozheng	398	Sandu	1,087	Kaili	1,315
Luodian	235	Wanshan	404	Weining	1,091	Fuquan	1,328
Suntao	240	Lunli	404	Changshun	1,095	Xifeng	1,353
Hezhang	240	Zheng'an	414	Zheng'an	1,098	Bijie city	1,364
Guanling	251	Fenggang	429	Pu'an	1,101	Dushan	1,370
Zhengning	252	Shibing	440	Taijiang	1,101	Pingba	1,408
Congjiang	253	Jiangkuo	442	Dafang	1,102	Qianxi	1,416
Changshun	260	Zhenyuan	443	Luodian	1,110	Tongchuan	1,427
Sandu	267	Pingba	449	Ziyun	1,113	Yuping	1,455
Liuzhi	268	Xiuwen	451	Shiqian	1,118	Huishui	1,460
Xingren	268	Huishui	478	Guanling	1,126	Anshun	1,498
Nayong	274	Fuquan	482	Tianzhu	1,128	Cishui	1,510
Qianxi	282	Tongchuan	507	Pingtang	1,131	Fenggang	1,599
Pingtang	283	Kaili	554	Zhijin	1,143	Xiuwen	1,610

Source: Based on data supplied by the Poor Area Development Office, Guizhou province, Guiyang.

Table 7.5 Per capita funding of poor counties in Guizhou (1997)

County	Per capita funding for food-for-work (yuan)	Per capita funding for subsidized loans (yuan)	Per capita budgetary grant (yuan)	Minority population in county (%) of total population	Rural per capita net income (yuan)
Poorest counties					
Leishan *	20.13	61.00	10.64	87.25	866
Qinglong *	21.10	60.13	25.16	51.05	877
Wangmo *	2.81	116.19	18.43	79.08	893
Rongjiang *	5.78	51.88	23.71	72.91	935
Yanhe*	14.73	38.52	5.62	53.52	945
Least poor among poor					
Huishui	3.82	5.18	4.08	58.21	1,460
Anshun city	–	10.69	2.01	17.33	1,498
Chishui	3.52	0.00	0.37	1.40	1,510
Fenggang*	13.51	32.50	17.57	3.68	1,599
Xiuwen	1.65	3.12	1.08	7.08	1,610

* Centrally designated poor; others are provincially designated poor.

Source: Based on data supplied by the Poor Area Development Office, Guizhou province, Guiyang.

Table 7.6 links the performance of selected poor counties to the PAF grants/loans for the period 1990–97. Several features of the table are worth noting. First, the top performers (measured by growth in rural net per capita income during 1990–97) receive larger per capita (cumulative) PAF (almost twice as much if one compares the top performers with the bottom performers) than the weakest performers. Their population growth during the period was generally lower than that of the weakest performers. Second, minority counties are found in both the top performers and weak performers. This suggests that these counties are not necessarily the poorest; neither do they necessarily lag behind the non-minority counties. The top performers may be better off because of a more diversified production structure, reflected in the existence of TVEs.

The real per capita income of all the weakest performers declined between 1990 and 1997, which means that their poverty situation actually worsened despite the PAF. On the basis of the above information, one cannot conclude that the best performers necessarily owe their better performance to higher PAF allocations. There may be two other factors at work, namely, the superior initial conditions of these counties when PAF was introduced, and differences in rural population growth during the period. However, rather surprisingly, rural population growth rates are generally higher among the top performers than

Table 7.6 Linking the performance of selected poor counties to poverty alleviation funding (1990–97)

County	Growth of real rural per capita income (%)	Rural population growth (%)	Change in rural population share in total population	Minority population share (%)	Per capita cumulative poverty alleviation fund (yuan)
	(1990–97)	*(1990–97)*		*(1990)*	*(1990–97)*
Top performers					
Deijing*	430.4	14.2	1.5	61.3	362.2
Danzai*	398.1	13.3	0.8	83.7	526.9
Xifeng*	347.9	15.2	2.8	49.3	239.5
Pu'an*	326.5	21.0	2.2	24.8	385.4
Yinjiang *	282.7	13.3	1.7	69.1	280.1
Weakest performers					
Jiangkuo**	-37.2	14.7	1.8	49.3	53.0
Zheng'an*	-37.4	15.5	1.4	4.5	190.8
Daozheng**	-61.1	9.8	0.24	57.3	173
Kaili**	-65.2	9.6	-5.1	62.2	133.9
Zhenyuan	-67.6	11.5	2.0	37.5	123.4

*   Centrally designated poor counties.
** Provincially designated poor counties.

Source: Based on data supplied by the Poor Area Development Office, Guizhou province, Guiyang.

among the weak performers, which suggests that the population factor is not important (even though there are wide variations in rural population growth among the 48 poor counties, as shown in Table 7.7).

Having given a brief general picture of poverty reduction in Guizhou, we now turn to the particular anti-poverty interventions: the food-for-work programme (*Yigong-daizhen*), micro-credit programme, and rural labour mobility programme.

Food-for-work programme (Yigong-daizhen)

In Guizhou the total central government expenditure for the food-for-work programme amounted to 3.6 billion yuan between 1984 and 2000. The provincial government provided additional funding of 1.6 billion yuan, which included contributions from prefectures and counties. A comparison of PAF funding in Guizhou, Sichuan and Yunnan shows that the importance of FFW declined and that of subsidized credit increased in all three provinces. However, in 1995, the FFW share in Guizhou was much larger (see Table 7.8).

Table 7.7 Population changes in poor counties of Guizhou (1986–97)

	Percentage change in total population	Percentage change in rural population	Percentage change in the share of rural population in total population
Xifeng	11.66	15.18	2.82
Panxian	18.45	17.90	-0.42
Liuzhi special zone	14.45	15.56	0.80
Shuicheng	-22.91	-3.42	20.47
Zheng'an	13.85	15.49	1.39
Wuchuan	*15.59*	*16.64*	*0.87*
Fenggang	15.62	16.75	0.94
Xishui	19.10	20.92	1.44
Shiqian	12.67	14.77	1.78
Yinjiang	*11.27*	*13.31*	*1.75*
Dejiang	12.40	14.24	1.54
Yanhe	*16.04*	*18.33*	*1.89*
Suntao	*14.51*	*16.44*	*1.63*
Xingren	20.94	23.57	2.05
Pu'an	18.26	21.02	2.21
Qinglong	17.09	20.29	2.51
Zhenfeng	16.47	19.21	2.23
Wangmo	14.64	16.57	1.63
Ceting	18.87	19.84	0.78
Anlun	18.55	20.77	1.75
Dafang	18.17	21.21	2.47
Zhijin	13.40	15.97	2.18
Nayong	15.82	18.45	2.20
Weining	*19.43*	*21.80*	*1.92*
Hezhang	17.93	21.13	2.58
Puding	20.16	21.96	1.44
Guanling	*18.54*	*20.71*	*1.72*
Zhengning	*19.38*	*23.71*	*3.33*
Ziyun	*22.93*	*24.85*	*1.51*
Huangping	9.83	11.37	1.34
Shibing	11.92	12.63	0.60
Shanshui	13.94	15.71	1.47
Chenggu	15.41	16.94	1.26
Tianzhu	12.43	13.99	1.32
Jianhe	16.09	16.79	0.57
Taijiang	13.11	12.04	-0.90
Liping	16.40	17.92	1.25
Rongjiang	17.57	19.52	1.56
Congjiang	15.00	16.49	1.25
Leishan	11.90	13.02	0.95
Majiang	12.08	13.71	1.39
Danzai	12.33	13.34	0.85

Table 7.7 continues

Table 7.7 continues

	Percentage change in total population	Percentage change in rural population	Percentage change in the share of rural population in total population
Libo	12.67	13.67	0.84
Dushan	18.03	18.45	0.32
Pingtang	10.81	13.63	2.45
Luodian	13.83	15.26	1.22
Changshun	12.58	14.42	1.54
Sandu	*18.50*	*20.92*	*1.97*
Xiuwen	10.08	17.71	5.88
Zhongshan District			
Daozheng	*9.54*	*9.81*	*0.24*
Chishui	10.31	9.72	-0.43
Tongchuan City	15.09	13.86	-0.83
Jiangkuo	12.42	14.66	1.85
Yuping	*15.59*	*12.77*	*-2.13*
Sinan	13.12	15.90	2.33
Wanshan special zone	-4.38	8.92	9.50
Bijie city	15.05	17.11	1.65
Qianxi	14.81	14.35	-0.37
Anshun city	20.86	21.06	0.47
Pingba	15.77	17.68	1.35
Kaili	17.97	9.63	-5.06
Zhenyuan	9.06	11.54	2.03
Jingping	13.93	15.82	1.54
Fuquan	18.45	15.92	-1.94
Guiding	9.83	15.50	4.28
Lunli	11.26	13.18	1.60
Huishui	13.95	16.92	2.39

Source: Based on data supplied by the Poor Area Development Office, Guizhou province, Guiyang.
Note: Minority counties are in bold italics.

These PAFs were spent on the following types of economic activities: road building, land improvement, irrigation, drinking water supply for rural people and animals, forestation, generation of hydropower, installation of new telephone lines, and resettlement of poor people to new areas. Building of roads and other infrastructure is one of the major components of the FFW programmes under which the government supplies the equipment and materials while the local people supply free labour, especially if they benefit directly. As we noted in Chapter 6, the free labour contribution amounts to 15 days per year; this regulation also applies to Guizhou. Any additional labour input is rewarded by wage payment in cash, which varies from county to county and project to project, depending on the local labour supply situation, opportunity cost of labour or the

Table 7.8 Poverty Alleviation Fund allocations for Guizhou, Sichuan and
Yunnan (1995–97) (million yuan and percentages)

	Guizhou		Sichuan		Yunnan	
	1995	*1997*	*1996*	*1997*	*1995*	*1997*
Food for work	313.4	265.0	262.4	286.1	292.7	312.3
	(41.7)	(19.7)	(29.9)	(18.3)	(28.2)	(14.2)
Subsidized loans	360.0	850.0	462.3	972.3	465.6	1032
	(47.9)	(63.3)	(52.8)	(62.3)	(44.9)	(47)
Fiscal grant	78.0	228.0	139.7	280.5	181	516.7
	(10.4)	(17.0)	(15.9)	(18)	(17.5)	(23.5)

Note: Figures in brackets are percentage shares of the total.

Source: World Bank (2000) for Sichuan and Yunnan.
Data for Guizhou were supplied by the Poor Area Development Office, Guiyang.

level of rural farm incomes. No wage payments are made when workers benefit from the infrastructure. Instead, 1 yuan a day are paid as compensation for foregone production. Infrastructure which does not benefit the farmers directly is built by contractors and contracts are won through a bidding procedure. In Zhenning county, in the western part of Guizhou, contractors hired labour by paying an average wage of 12–15 yuan a day, which is well above the average rural farm income of 5–6 yuan a day (information collected during a field visit in April 2001).

It is reported that 110 million workdays were created in Guizhou in 82 to 94 per cent of the counties covered by the food-for-work programme (State Planning Commission, 1992).

From subsidized loan programme to micro-credit programme

In Chapter 6 we discussed at length the impact of the subsidized loan programme and the micro-credit programme in China. Below we examine the experiences of Guizhou in bank lending and lending by credit cooperatives compared to those of Guangxi and Yunnan. Bank lending is much less important than lending by friends and relatives in all the three provinces, which is generally for both consumption and investment purposes (see Table 7.9). The loan repayment rate is extremely low in Guizhou, the lowest for 1996 and 1997. On the other hand, in Guangxi and Yunnan it varies between 49 per cent and 69 per cent (see Table 7.9), which compares favourably with the average recovery rate of 57 per cent or less for the special subsidized loans by the Agricultural Bank of China since 1991 (see Zhu, 1997: 14). Several reasons explain the delay in loan repayments: political interference by the local governments which prevents banks from selecting bankable projects, poor accounting systems, short periods of loan repayment and the long period for returns to accrue on capital investment. Generally, the loan repayment rate is higher in the informal credit market than in the formal credit market. Under the former, symmetric information between borrowers and lenders, peer pressure and ethical norms (including fear of social unrest) keep the monitoring of loans and their repayment more orderly and at lower cost.

Loans made to poor households are used for various purposes: agricultural development (for example, crop planting, animal husbandry, crop tree management and terracing), rural infrastructure, and education and health. The bulk of the loans are used for agricultural improvements (see Table 7.10).

Micro-credit

In Guizhou under the Grameen-type micro-credit scheme, loans of up to 2,000 yuan, repayable in one to two years, are granted when a minimum of five households together offer a guarantee of repayment. Between 1998 and 2000 the Agricultural Bank provided 1.8 billion yuan. In 1998 the interest rate charged was

Table 7.9 Bank loans vs borrowing from friends and relatives in southwest China (per household) (1995–97)

	1995	1996	1997
Guizhou			
Loans from banks and credit cooperatives (yuan)	28.0	10.6	30.3
Borrowing from friends and relatives (yuan)	41.6	104.0	62.4
Repayment of bank loan (yuan)	–	2.7	2.9
Rate of repayment (%)	–	25.5	9.5
Guangxi			
Loans from banks and credit cooperatives (yuan)	31.8	20.9	33.4
Borrowing from friends and relatives (yuan)	91.8	151.0	81.4
Repayment of bank loan (yuan)	–	14.5	16.3
Rate of repayment (%)	–	69.3	48.8
Yunnan			
Loans from banks and credit cooperatives (yuan)	36.3	30.1	32.7
Borrowing from friends and relatives (yuan)	54.7	63.3	56.4
Repayment of bank loan (yuan)	–	19.0	20.8
Rate of repayment (%)	–	63.1	63.6
Average			
Loans from banks and cooperatives (yuan)	31.9	20.1	32.2
Borrowing from friends and relatives (yuan)	64.0	109.7	67.6
Repayment of bank loan (yuan)	–	13.4	13.2
Rate of repayment (%)	–	66.6	41.0

Source: LGOPAD, 1997.

Table 7.10 Loans/subsidies to survey households by economic activity in
southwest China (1997) (000 yuan)

	Guangxi	Guizhou	Yunnan	Total
Agricultural development	162.8	139.3	49.1	351.2
Crop planting	63.2	34.8	13.2	111.2
Animal husbandry	74.8	86.8	21.8	183.4
Crop tree management	24.8	9.3	14.0	48.1
Terracing	0	8.4	0	84.0
Infrastructure	10.7	1.2	1.8	13.7
Education	2.3	0.8	1.6	4.8
Health	1.9	0.02	0.2	2.1
Total	177.8	141.3	52.7	371.8

Source: LGOPAD, 1997: 158.

2.8 per cent, but since 1999 a unified interest rate of 3 per cent has been charged for all types of loans, against a commercial rate of 5.2 per cent. Like the Grameen loans, there is no collateral required although a clause in the loan agreement states that non-repayment when the household has capacity to repay can lead to seizure of property. The loan repayment rate is lower than that in neighbouring Guangxi province, where repayment is at more frequent intervals. As Guizhou is quite poor, loan repayment is required at the end of one year. The lower repayment rate is explained by two main factors: transport difficulties, especially in remote mountainous areas, and the relative inefficiency of the Agricultural Bank in collecting repayments.

In Zhejin county (Guizhou), between 1998 and 2000, 3.20 million yuan were spent on micro-credit, which covered 32 townships and towns and 32 villages, 3,338 poor households, and 14,000 poor people. Loans were granted for agriculture and animal husbandry. The criteria for loan grants include annual household net income of 600 yuan and less than 325 kg of grain output. In this county 70 per cent of the poor are from ethnic minorities and only 50 per cent of those receive micro-credit, which suggests that the ethnic minorities are not granted any preference. As loans are targeted at the poor, the bulk of whom are from minorities, it is assumed that ethnic minorities would benefit (interviews with county staff in April 2001). Micro-credit cannot be granted in the following situations:

(1) if financial support is received from the welfare and civil affairs office;
(2) if an earlier loan is not repaid;
(3) if a household fails to comply with family planning rules.

Loans cannot be used to repay an old loan, or to pay agricultural tax or to pay any penalty. Neither can loans be used for any purpose other than that proposed under the agreement. Local county agents and representatives of the Agricultural Bank undertake periodic monitoring to ensure that the loan is properly utilized. Households are also trained in self-monitoring.

The labour mobility programme

In Chapter 6 we discussed the labour mobility programme and its main components. In this chapter we carry that discussion further with a case study of Guizhou, which is one of the poorest provinces in southwest China. Extreme poverty pushes people out either to other areas within the province or outside the province. Of the total number of migrants from Guizhou, about 0.5 to 0.8 million represent rural-to-urban migration within the province. On a field visit to Guiyang (Guizhou) in April 2001, we discussed the labour mobility programme with the Development Research Centre (DRC) of the provincial government. We were told that two million migrants went from Guizhou to such other provinces as Guangdong, Fujian, Jiangsu and Zhejiang. These four provinces account for over 70 per cent of the migrants. Although the bulk of them at present go to Guangdong, more and more migrants are going to Zhejiang. Owing to rapid development, the Guangdong economy requires more and more highly skilled labour for industry, which is not available in Guizhou. On the other hand, in Zhejiang there continues to be demand for low-skilled workers in industry and services.

Migration is induced by both push and pull factors. The push factor is the large rural surplus of labour, estimated at nearly 8 million, or 55 per cent of the total rural labour force. The TVEs can absorb no more than about 1.6 to 2 million, which means that nearly 6 million people need to migrate to other provinces every year.

The supply of labour in poorer regions of Guizhou, especially those with a significant minority population, has been growing more rapidly than in other regions thanks to the more liberal population policies for the ethnic minorities (see Chapter 6). For example, while the national rural labour force grew at the rate of 1.3 per cent per annum between 1990 and 1997, that in Guizhou grew at 2.3 per cent, in Guangxi at 2 per cent and in Ningxia at 3.3 per cent (World Bank, 2001:28).

The bulk of migrants are engaged in manufacturing and construction activities. A survey (undertaken by the DRC) of 168 migrants returning home showed that the migrants engaged in construction constituted 20 per cent, whereas 9 per cent were absorbed in loading and unloading, and 5 per cent in casual work. With the exception of Guizhou, farming is not an important occupation for migrants. In Guizhou income from migrants is equivalent to the entire tax revenue of the government from the tobacco industry. Between 1987 and 2000 there were 13 million migrants from Guizhou, who remitted 21 billion yuan. During our field visits in April 2001, we were told that the experience of Ludian county of Guizhou in labour mobility was particularly successful. In 1996 this county had 290,000 inhabitants, of which 10,000 were migrants. The remittances of these migrants amounted to 120 million yuan, which was three times the county's budgetary revenue. However, the remittance per capita as a proportion of income per capita in 1995 was much lower for this county (about 6 per cent) than the figures for many other counties (e.g. Ziyun and Changshun, where the figures were respectively 43 per cent and 41 per cent; Table 7.12).

We have not come across any evidence to suggest that the remittances per capita and total remittances are necessarily higher for counties and villages with substantial minority populations. Table 7.12 shows that Puding county of Guizhou (which has a 20 per cent minority population according to Table 7.1) had in 1995 a per capita remittance equivalent to nearly 23 per cent of income per capita, which is fairly significant and is close to the figure of about 27 per cent for Guizhou as a whole. The national rural household surveys do not give separate figures for remittances (which are included under 'transfer' income), not to speak of separate information on remittances by minorities and the Han majority. World Bank (2001: 21) notes: 'the national statistics suggest that wage and remittance incomes' shares of net rural household income have remained relatively stable, but they give few clues about the situation for poor households'. Neither is it clear whether rural migrants necessarily come from the poorest households.

In principle, remittances can be an important factor, that can help equalize rural–urban income disparities in the long run. But the equalization goal can only be achieved if and when remittances go disproportionately to the poorer households left behind. Income disparities will remain as long as remittances go to rich as well as poor households.

It is not very easy for migrants to find jobs in large-scale factory manufacturing because of their low skills and education. Many of the migrants are from minority nationalities, whose level of education is even lower. About 11 per cent of the rural migrants have primary education, 27 per cent secondary education and only 2 per cent high school education. Because of their poor education, the average earnings of rural migrants are low: between 3,000 yuan and 10,000 yuan per annum, or 400–500 yuan per month.

Large-scale migration from Guizhou has not adversely affected agriculture or food production. The survey cited above shows that the available land continues to be cultivated by remaining family members and relatives. In Guizhou a new phenomenon of leasing land to friends and relatives on payment of wages is

Table 7.11 Characteristics of rural migrants in selected villages in Guizhou, Guangxi and Yunnan (1997, 1999)

	Guangxi		Guizhou		Yunnan	
	1997	1999	1997	1999	1997	1999
Means of finding a job (%)						
Relatives/friends	42	37	34	40.3	33	38.3
Oneself	52	60	61	56.5	62	59.6
Employer	1.1	1.2	4.9	–	4.2	–
Local government agency	3.4	0.8	–	3.2	–	2.1
Economic activity (%)						
Farming	3.9	2.8	17.4	3.2	2.1	–
Industry	49.4	56	36.6	24.2	33.3	23.4
Construction	21.9	23.4	17.1	33.9	39.6	53.2
Services	13.5	10.5	19.5	17.7	22.9	21.3
Duration away from home						
1–3 months	9.3	–	6.4	–	6.3	–
4–6 months	15.2	–	11.2	–	35.4	–
7–9 months	14	–	4.9	–	31.3	–
10–12 months	68	–	41.5	–	16.7	–
Migrants' destination (%)						
Other counties within province	12.4	19	4.9	9.7	66.7	46.8
Other inland provinces	24.2	7.7	7.3	8.1	8.3	19.1
Other coastal provinces	36	54.4	75.6	54.8	–	6.4
Income (yuan/year/head)	4,016	–	3,429	–	2,861	–
% of migrants earning:						
500–1,000 yuan	16.3	–	24.4	–	10.4	–
more than 5,000 yuan	28.1	–	26.8	–	8.3	–
Per capita annual living expenditure (yuan)	2,217	1,893.1	1,794	1,849.8	1,923	2134
Remittances per capita (yuan)	1,119	1,482.6	897	1,734.1	557	896.3

Source: LGOPAD, Report 1997, 1999.

emerging as a result of rural-to-urban migration. A portion of output is made as payment for the leasing of the land.

Apart from the substantial amount of remittances, one of the other benefits noted by the DRC staff was the saving of food grains to the tune of 2.6 million tons due to the departure of migrants. Formerly, Guizhou used to be a food-deficit

Table 7.12 Guizhou: per capita income, expenditure and remittances of migrant labour (1995) (yuan)

County	Income per capita per annum	Living expenditure per capita	Remittances per capita	Remittances per capita as % of income per capita
Guizhou province	2,270.8	1,389.8	606.2	26.7
Liuzhi	2,079.2	1,006.9	806.5	38.8
Wangmo	725.0	465.0	260.0	35.9
Dafang	3,605.8	2,533.3	485.3	13.4
Guanling	3,373.8	2,328.3	722.1	21.4
Luodian	2,562.5	912.5	150.0	5.8
Zhijin	2,179.8	1,272.6	805.5	36.9
Ziyun	1,368.9	638.2	587.6	42.9
Panxian	3,034.7	2,162.7	871.9	28.7
Qinglong	1,855.3	1,185.3	316.4	17.0
Zhenfeng	2,409.4	1,550.3	484.4	20.1
Ceheng	2,466.7	1,600.0	733.3	29.7
Puding	2,464.3	1,738.6	555.7	22.6
Changshun	1,232.9	517.6	502.1	40.7

Source: Based on data from LGOPAD, 1995,

province, which had to import food grains from other provinces. Now it is food self-sufficient, even though it does import some food grains which it does not grow itself. Guizhou has insufficient land for crop production, only about 0.8 *mu* per capita.[4]

There is one negative aspect of the return of migrants to their villages, that is, transport bottlenecks, especially during New Year. This factor is, however, exaggerated. While it creates temporary problems, it also creates additional demand for goods, tourism and other services.

Do minorities benefit?

In this chapter we have discussed the three main anti-poverty programmes, namely, the food-for-work programme, micro-credit and labour mobility, with special reference to Guizhou. Further, we have described three types of labour mobility interventions: population migration, induced labour mobility (through public projects) and employment promotion through the establishment of employment agencies. Using county-level data for Guizhou, per capita funding for food-for-work (FFW) and subsidized loans were compared between the poorest and least poor among the poor counties. A comparison between the minority counties (with ethnic minorities forming more than 50 per cent of the population) and non-minority counties suggests that the former are not necessarily the poorest. Linking the performance of the selected poor counties to the poverty alleviation funding (PAF) during 1990–97 showed that those with rapid growth in rural per capita net income received larger per capita cumulative PAF than those with slow growth in rural per capita income.

A comparison of the subsidized loan programme with the more recent micro-credit programme suggests that the loan repayment rate is generally higher under the latter. In 1996 and 1997 the loan repayment rate in Guizhou was much lower than in Guangxi and Yunnan, due partly to transport shortages in remote mountainous areas. The Chinese government places a good deal of emphasis on labour mobility programmes for reducing poverty. One of the significant benefits of this programme is the substantial amount of remittances, which for Guizhou equalled the entire government tax revenue from the tobacco industry.

Since 1996 the poverty reduction programme in Guizhou (following the national policy shift) has targeted the poorest households instead of concentrating on the poor regions. Targeting the poor has reinforced the importance of subsidized credit and micro-credit, which has not been very effective judging by the low loan repayment rate. It is estimated that about one-third of the loans are not recovered. There is a lack of any correlation between subsidized loans and rural per capita income. In comparison, the food-for-work funds, which are much smaller, and some other development funds tend to be more beneficial for the poor than the subsidized loan scheme. These funds are used for improving agricultural infrastructure and land productivity, with possible significant long-term effects on the incomes of the poor households in rural areas.

Can we conclude from the above that the anti-poverty programmes are benefiting the minorities and that they have created a dent in their poverty situation? It is difficult to give a conclusive or categorical answer since information on the impact of the programmes separately for minorities and the Han majority is generally not available. Whatever information is available suggests that both the minority poor and other poor have benefited from the government programmes but not as much as they could have if measures had been targeted more directly at the poorest ethnic minorities.

We do not know of any information on the benefits of specific anti-poverty programmes such as micro-credit and labour mobility on the poverty situation of ethnic minorities. In general, it may be assumed that the situation of the ethnic minority poor would not be very different from that of the Han poor in respect of access to micro-credit. However, the former living in remote areas and the mountains may be particularly disadvantaged, as their access to micro-credit would be more difficult than that of the Han population. The latter is known to live in more prosperous, agriculturally fertile low lands. For example, in Guangxi 'the Han tend to be concentrated in the coastal region and more productive southern part of the province, sinicized Zhuang occupy the less fertile northeast, less sinicized Zhuang dominate in the karst regions of the northeast, and Yao occupy the most remote areas of the karst region. Guizhou shows a similar pattern, with the Miao, or Buyi and Miao, occupying the most remote, mountainous areas' (World Bank, 2001: 9).

It is generally believed that minorities would benefit from anti-poverty programmes that target poor areas because they are concentrated there. However, nearly half the poor people live outside poor areas (designated poor counties) and many of these poor are from the ethnic minorities. Not all the minority populations reside in the autonomous areas, which receive preferential treatment. Therefore, one can conclude that minorities have not so far particularly benefited from anti-poverty programmes. This is especially true to the extent that ethnic minorities live in remote and mountainous areas, which have been beyond the reach of these programmes. World Bank (2001: xxi) notes that minorities are heavily represented in these areas. To quote: 'Minorities constitute such a large proportion of the remaining absolute poor because past programs have often not reached out to the most remote areas where the obstacles to poverty relief are greatest'. The report implies that targeting these remote areas will automatically benefit the minorities, an assertion which may or may not be true. Those minorities which are currently living outside the boundaries of the poor counties and the minority regions have not benefited from either the anti-poverty programmes discussed in this and the last chapter or the special types of relief measures administered in the autonomous regions. The minorities are likely to benefit much more if they are directly targeted, but they are not.

Distance reduces the access of minorities to such programmes as micro-credit and food-for-work. Minority migrants from remote rural areas are likely to be particularly handicapped, as they are generally less educated, lack the Han Chinese language and are thus more risk averse and fearful of the unknown in distant urban areas. In theory these migrants should be prepared to migrate in view of their extreme poverty, but in practice they may be less prone to move for the reasons given above. Thus, the situation of minority migrants is likely to be somewhat different from that of the Han migrants.

Do our results on the effect of locational factors in Chapter 4 confirm the above argument? Not necessarily. As we showed in Chapter 4, the effect of locational factors on the schooling of minorities was negligible in 1995, when educational gaps between minorities and the Han majority narrowed considerably. Our conclusion regarding the targeting of minorities for educational programmes suggests that targeting by poverty regions may not be an adequate approach to reaching the poor minority population.

Anti-poverty programmes specifically for the minorities have suffered from lack of funding from the central government. Under the policy of fiscal decentralization, local authorities kept a greater proportion of tax revenues, thus reducing the revenue going to the central government. As a result minorities may have suffered in two ways: (1) the wealthier Han areas retained larger absolute funds, (2) the central government was unable to subsidize the poorest areas. Palmer (1997: 281) notes that the central government transferred limited resources to minorities as it has 'lost much of its redistributive power owing to the fiscal decentralization reforms'.

Deng's policy of economic efficiency at the expense of equality, and his support of the coastal areas at the expense of the hinterland, may also have adversely affected minorities. To quote Palmer (1997: 281), 'although the policy did not directly target minority regions for reduced investments, given the geographic distribution of nationalities, the policy effectively redirected funds away from minorities to the Han'. However, this policy of helping the coastal areas has now been reversed and it remains to be seen what effect this reversal will have on minorities in the future.

The Western Development Strategy of the Chinese government is intended to narrow the gaps between the coastal areas and the hinterland. The White Paper on Poverty Reduction in rural China issued on 15 October 2001 emphasizes the positive role that the Western Development Strategy will play in poverty reduction in the central and west regions where ethnic minorities are concentrated. The White Paper puts great faith in the cooperation between the more developed eastern region and the west region. It notes: 'such cooperation between the eastern and western regions focuses on improving the production conditions and ecological environments in the poor areas as well as solving the food and clothing problem in these areas'. However, the past experience of this induced cooperation has been rather mixed. The White Paper further states that 'from 2001 to 2010, the Chinese Government will concentrate its poverty alleviation efforts on the ethnic minority areas, old revolutionary base areas, border areas and destitute areas in the central and western regions'. This statement suggests that the government has not entirely abandoned the approach of targeting areas in favour of more direct targeting of the poor households.

In this book we have shown that several factors account for poverty among minorities: low incomes, geographical location or remoteness, mountainous terrain, underdeveloped infrastructure (roads and communications), low educational levels, poor access to health services and concentration on farming as a major economic activity. A very small proportion of minorities are engaged in trade, light industry and manufacturing, which are the major growth sectors. And the hinterland in southwest China has attracted very limited foreign direct investment (FDI). We have shown that these economic forces have been far more important in explaining poverty among the Chinese minorities than their cultural backwardness, religion or social values.

Notes

1 Poverty and ethnicity

1   It is not possible to fix a minimum below which a person will simply die. Experience shows that human beings can survive even at a very low level of consumption though their faculties and efficiency are impaired. But mere human survival is not the issue. The real issue is survival with good health.
2   Estimates by Barton and Prais-Hauthakker (see Deaton and Muellbauer, 1980: 202–5).
3   Two works by Muellbauer (1974, 1977) contain references to several other studies of equivalence scales for welfare purposes.
4   For example, the adoption of subjective poverty thresholds in the United States would substantially increase the measured incidence of poverty from the current official estimate, which for poor people in the US is 14 per cent, but an estimate based on a subjective poverty line would be 42.2 per cent (De Vos and Garner, 1991).
5   For example, in 1941 Lord Beveridge in the United Kingdom explicitly adopted the Rowntree poverty standard as a basis for deciding the rates of benefit to be paid out under the new social security plan. The subsistence concept played an important role in deciding the Social Security Administration Poverty Index in the United States. The US government's 'poverty index' is based on estimates prepared by the Department of Agriculture of the costs of food needed by families of different composition.

Appendix to Chapter 1: The measurement of poverty

1   Actually if the ratio of expenditure on food to family income can be obtained, the ratio itself will serve as a cut-off line which can be directly used to identify the poor from the population. Thus the poverty line in terms of income becomes redundant.
2   Townsend sets δ at 0.50 for a very low poverty line and 0.80 for a low poverty line. The value chosen by OECD (1976) is 0.66.
3   The advocates of a median income include Fuchs (1967) and Lansley (1980).
4   It should be noted that in the poverty literature the term income-gap ratio is often used interchangeably with the term poverty-gap ratio (see Sen, 1976; Kanbur, 1987).
5   At the extreme, if all the population in a community is poor, n would be equal to m. Therefore, the income gap would make no difference to the poverty gap, the I_r would be an indicator of how poor the poor really are.
6   Sometimes the ratio of the aggregate poverty gap to GDP is used to show the percentage of GDP needed at the national level to eradicate poverty (see Beckerman, 1979). Anand (1977) obtains an alternative measure by expressing the aggregate

poverty gap as a ratio of the aggregate income of the non-poor. He treats it as an indicator of the ease of poverty alleviation rather than as a measure of poverty.

7 There is another axiom which was only implicitly presented in Sen's original paper but used explicitly in his later work, that is, the so-called focus axiom. This axiom requires that the poverty measure should depend on the incomes of the poor, not on the incomes of the non-poor (Sen, 1981; Foster, 1984).

8 For example, Anand (1977) presents two distribution sensitive measures whereas Kakwani (1980b) and Thon (1979) are concerned with the way the Sen measure treats certain income transfers to the poor. They propose alternative measures that satisfy Sen's transfer axiom.

9 Authors who take this route include Blackorby and Donaldson (1980) and Takayama (1979).

10 Economists often present the Rawlsian difference principle as maximizing the welfare of the least advantaged in a society. Actually, Rawls presents two principles: one is to give priority to basic liberties and the other is concerned with a least fortunate group; people belonging to this group have an income level less than half of the median income and wealth. People cannot enjoy basic liberties without reaching a necessary level of wealth (see Atkinson, 1987).

11 The best life expectancy at age one is 77.6 years achieved by Japan (UNDP, 1992).

12 This section draws heavily on UNDP (1990, 1992, 1993).

13 The adjustment of real GDP per capita is based on the theory of diminishing marginal utility of income and the formulation for utility of income by Atkinson is used: $W(y_i) = \frac{1}{1-\varepsilon} y_i^{1-\varepsilon}$ where $W(y_i)$ is the utility or well-being derived from the income y, and ε represents the elasticity of the marginal utility with respect to y and it is set a value between 0 and 1, and is an inverse function of the level of real GDP per capita of the country concerned, dependent on the relationship between its real GDP per capita and the world poverty line z^*. HDI sets z^* at real GDP per head of \$4,829. If the country's real GDP per capita y_i is equal to or less than z^*, ε takes a value of 0, meaning that there are no diminishing returns to income: therefore, the adjusted real income per capita is $W_a = y_i$ for all developing countries. But for countries with real GDP per capita larger than z^*, the adjusted figure should be worked out by the following formula:

$$W_a = z^* + \sum_{a=2}^{n-1} a(z^*)^{\frac{1}{a}} + n\left[y_i - (n-1)z^*\right]^{\frac{1}{n}}$$

where n is the ratio of the country's y_i to z^*, a takes values from 2 to n-1.

2 Socioeconomic characteristics of minorities

1 Sautman (1999) notes that between the 1982 and 1990 censuses about 14 million minority people (who had earlier opted to be classified as Han Chinese) got themselves reclassified as minority groups, presumably to take advantage of positive discrimination in favour of the minorities. Such reclassifications vitiate intercensal comparisons of population.

3 Poverty and inequality among minorities

1 For more details see Bhalla and Nachane (2001).

2 The only statistical sources on minorities (namely, population censuses, ethnic statistical yearbooks and household surveys) appear quite infrequently. For example, population censuses are generally undertaken every ten years whereas the ethnic statistical yearbooks appear every four years.

4 Literacy and basic education

1 Using population census data (1 per cent sample of China's population in 1996), Rong and Shi (2001) show that the illiteracy rate was reduced to 16 per cent of the total population in 1996, from 18 per cent in 1990.
2 Drèze and Saran (1995: 190) note: 'the available information on the age-specific literacy rates in India indicates that 7+ literacy rates are typically a little *higher* than 15+ literacy rates. Thus the gap between the Indian and Chinese literacy rates would be slightly larger if an identical age cut-off of 15 had been applied in both countries.' They further state that 'in 1981 the All-India 7+ literacy rate was higher than the 15+ literacy rate by 2.8 percentage points'. They made this estimate on the basis of the Census of Population of India for 1991, Table C9.
3 In 2000 there were 925,000 full-time minority teachers and 18.5 million minority students in different schools throughout the country. Minority students in primary schools, secondary schools and colleges account for 9 per cent, 6.8 per cent and 5.7 per cent respectively of the total number of students in each category.

5 Minorities and health status and services

1 For a detailed discussion on interrelationships between health, productivity and economic growth, see World Bank (1993).
2 An analysis of 42 countries showed a positive correlation between low per capita income and poor health standards. In the sample which covered countries with infant mortality rates of over 100 per 1,000 births, 26 countries had per capita incomes below US$400, 9 had per capita incomes between US$400 and 670 and a very small number had incomes per capita above US$800 (see World Bank, 1985).
3 In a comparative study of access to health services in China and India, Bhalla (1995) shows the importance of such non-economic factors as government policies, effectiveness in policy and programme implementation and organizational/institutional endowments.

6 Anti-poverty policies and programmes

1 The Poverty Alleviation Programme is entitled the '8–7' programme because it aims to reduce the numbers of poor by 80 million in 7 years.
2 It is reported that 'up to the end of 1998, 1,702 cities (counties) of the country had established the system of minimum standard of living, and 1.84 million urban residents living below the guaranteed minimum standard of living had received poverty relief and assistance' (Government of China, 1999: 11).
3 The fund available was 20 million yuan annually from 1990 to 1993, which increased to 80 million yuan in 1997. The loan period is normally one to three years and in some special cases loans can be extended to four to five years.
4 In 1992–93, 2.28 million were minorities out of the 32–34 million cadres, or about 6–7 per cent (Sautman, 1998).
5 Until 1995 the Agricultural Bank of China was charged with the management and day-to-day operation of the fund. With the creation of the Agricultural Development Bank in 1995 at the central and provincial levels for policy lending for rural development, this new bank was entrusted with the main responsibility for managing the subsidized loans for poor areas.
6 The provincial authorities claim that as a result of the agricultural reforms in 1978 and the subsequent poverty alleviation programme, the magnitude of poverty was significantly reduced from nearly 26 million people in 1978 to 4.5 million in 1997, that is, from about 40 per cent of the population to about 7 per cent (based on personal interviews with government officials in July 1999). As of October 1998, 34 counties

(including 13 centrally-designated ones) were classified as having moved out of poverty. By the end of 1998 there were 3 million poor people. This figure, based on data collected by the Provincial Statistics Bureau and the Poor Area Development Office, excludes those who returned to poverty. Of the 3 million poor, 300–400,000 came from the non-poor counties. According to the provincial plan, about half a million poor people were expected to be brought above the poverty line in 1999.

7   It is reported that the implementation of the first food-for-work programme led to the creation of 600 million workdays annually.

8   In the developed countries poverty alleviation programmes were known in the nineteenth century. Under the English system the Poor Law of 1834 is a good example, whereby poverty relief was provided on the basis of residence in a workhouse. Workfare was also common in France where poverty relief was granted in 'charity workshops' (see Besley and Coate, 1992).

9   On the basis of the National Sample Survey (NSS) data for 1987-88 Gaiha (2000) concludes that the Indian rural public works programme could have benefited the poor more if the wage rate relative to the agricultural wage was lower.

10 Cross-country comparisons of the level of programme wage show wide variations: in Chile, the programme wage was set at 70 per cent of the minimum wage whereas in India under the *Jawahar Rozgar Yojana* (employment generation scheme) the wage was set at the level of the minimum wage which was well above the market wage in many regions of the country (Subbarao, 1997).

11 Here again the Chinese situation seems similar to that on the Indian JRY programme where many workers interviewed during an evaluation noted that the programme wage was too low (Neelakantan, 1994).

12 The poorest villages and the poorest people may not necessarily benefit since the village communities are responsible for the mobilization of labour for the projects. The benefits may also leak to the non-poor counties and to people who are not so poor (see Zhu and Jiang, 1996). This is also true of the Indian JRY programme which is administered by the local village *panchayats* (councils). But unlike the Chinese programme, the JRY is directly targeted towards women and the poor low-caste groups (scheduled castes and tribes) (Gaiha, 2000).

13 It is reported that between 1984 and 1993, the combined resources for poverty alleviation out of the state budget and the banking system amounted to over 38 billion yuan, out of which the bank credits accounted for 74 per cent (Wu, 1994).

14 Before 1995 the Agricultural Bank of China was responsible for the management and operation of loans for poverty alleviation. Since the establishment of the Agricultural Development Bank, the latter has taken over the management of specialized agricultural loans.

15 During the second half of 1993, the official annual rate for capital construction projects was 12.4 per cent, whereas it was about 3 per cent for rural credit for poverty alleviation (Zhu *et al.*, 1997: 29). Since the inflation rate during the same period was about 15 per cent, interest on rural credit implied a significant element of subsidy.

16 Recognizing this problem, the National Poverty Reduction Conference held in 1996 decided that 70 per cent of subsidized loans should be allocated to agriculture (World Bank, 2001: 47).

17 Park and Ren (2001: 59) conclude: 'there is considerable evidence that only some of the poor will benefit from greater credit access, so that there is a real danger that the recent surge in donor funding of micro-finance programs may overlook more pressing needs facing many of the poor'.

18 For example, from 1993 onwards 180,000 people migrated from the mountain areas in the north of Guangdong province. The local authority provided a special grant of 5,000 yuan to each migrating household. Living conditions of 80 per cent of the households

that moved were considered adequate in the first year of migration. These migrants began to move out of poverty in the second and third years (see Zhou, 1997).

19 Although there is sizeable unemployment in cities, many job vacancies exist because of a mismatch between available jobs and people's expectations. The urban unemployed people are not willing to accept some of the jobs opportunities due to low rates of pay, adverse working conditions and low social prestige. Many of these vacancies are filled by workers from rural areas.

20 During a trip to China (Yunnan, Guizhou and Sichuan) in April and July 1999, we were told that loans were sometimes granted to workers within the framework of the World Bank-funded Poverty Reduction Project to enable them to finance transport costs.

21 According to the Sichuan Labour Bureau 6 million migrants accounted for remittances worth more than 16 billion yuan annually. Per capita remittances are estimated at 2,000 yuan, a figure much higher than the per capita income of poor households (530 yuan at 1995 prices) (information collected during field visits to Beijing and Chengdu in April and July 1999).

22 The World Bank and the Asian Development Bank (ADB) do not wish to relinquish control of these funds. Loans by such financial agencies as the ADB are also handled separately from food-for-work funds and projects. Thus the programme structure militates against a comprehensive approach to poverty alleviation.

23 In contrast, even under the condition of budget constraint, the central government managed to substantially raise government financial resources for the programme – by 1.5 billion yuan annually in central government budgetary allocations and by 3 billion yuan annually for government loans for poverty reduction (UNDP, 1997).

24 According to one estimate, by the beginning of the twenty-first century, 21 million people in China will still be extremely poor (see Zhao, 1999). These facts clearly suggest that the target of the 8-7 poverty reduction programme, of eliminating the 80 million has been far from achieved, although significant progress in that direction has been made.

7 Anti-poverty programmes in Guizhou

1 During a field trip to China in July 1999, the officials of the Guizhou Poverty Alleviation Office told us that by the end of 1998 nearly 2 million people and 18 counties were expected to be brought up to the poverty line. This target is unlikely to have been met.

2 Guizhou has made institutional arrangements for poverty reduction similar to those elsewhere and at the national level (see Chapter 6). The Leading Groups for Poverty Reduction and Poor Area Development Offices have been established to promote and implement anti-poverty policies and programmes. The PADO in Guizhou consists of a staff of 2,489 of which 1,365 are engaged in full-time work on poverty reduction. There are five divisions with a full-time staff of 29 at the provincial level; 106 full-time staff at the prefecture level, 420 full-time staff at the county level covering 48 nationally designated poor counties; and 810 full-time staff at the township level covering 555 townships.

3 By the end of 2000, only 35 per cent of the school-age population received nine years of schooling compared to 85 per cent for China as a whole (information provided by the Provincial Planning Commission during a meeting in April 2001).

4 A *mu* is a Chinese measure of land. One hectare is equal to 15 *mu*.

Bibliography

Abdul, R., Mohamed, J. and Lloyd, D. (eds) *The Nature and Context of Minority Discourse*, Oxford: Oxford University Press.

Acharya, A. and Wall, H.J. (1994) 'An Evaluation of the United Nations' Human Development Index', *Journal of Economic and Social Measurement*, 20, 1.

Adelman, I. and Morris, C.T. (1973) *Economic Growth and Social Equity in Developing Countries*, Stanford, CA: Stanford University Press.

Adelman, I. and Robinson, S. (1988) 'Income Distribution and Development', in Chenery, H.B. and Srinivasan, T.N. (eds), *Handbook of Development Economics*, I, Rotterdam: North-Holland.

Ahluwalia, M.S. (1976) 'Inequality, Poverty and Development', *Journal of Development Economics*, 3.

Ahluwalia, M.S., Carter, N.G. and Chenery, H.B. (1979) 'Growth and Poverty in Developing Countries', *Journal of Development Economics*, 6, 3.

Ahmad, E. and Wang, Y. (1991) *Inequality and Poverty in China: Institutional Change and Public Policy 1978–88*, London School of Economics (LES) Development Economics Research Programme.

Ahuja, V. and Filmer, D. (1995) 'Educational Attainment in Developing Countries: New Estimates and Projections Disaggregated by Gender', *World Bank Policy Research Working Paper* 1489, Washington, DC: World Bank.

Alderman, H., Behrman, J.R., Khan, S., Ross, D.R. and Sabot, R. (1993) 'Public School Expenditures in Rural Pakistan: Efficiently Targeting Girls and a Lagging Region' (mimeo), Washington, DC: World Bank.

Alesina, A. and Spolaore, E. (1997) 'On the Number and Size of Nations', *Quarterly Journal of Economics*, CXII.

Alesina, A., Baqir, R. and Easterly, W. (1999) 'Public Goods and Ethnic Divisions', *Quarterly Journal of Economics*, CXIV, 4.

Anand, S. (1977) 'Aspects of Poverty in Malaysia', *Review of Income and Wealth*, 23,1.

—— (1983) *Inequality and Poverty in Malaysia: Measurement and Decomposition*, Oxford: Oxford University Press.

—— (1991) 'Poverty and Human Development in Asia and the Pacific', in UNDP, *Poverty Alleviation in Asia and the Pacific*, New York: UNDP.

Anand, S. and Harris, C. (1985) *Living Standards in Sri Lanka, 1973–1981/82: A Partial Analysis of Consumer Finance Survey Data*, Development Research Department, Development Strategy Division, Washington, DC: World Bank (mimeo.).

—— (1994) 'Choosing a Welfare Indicator', *American Economic Review – Papers and Proceedings*, 84, 2.

Anand, S. and Sen, A.K. (1993) 'Human Development Index: Methodology and Measurement', *UNDP Occasional Paper no. 8*, New York: UNDP.

Asian Development Bank (ADB) (1992) 'Rural Poverty in Asia', Part III of *Asian Development Outlook*, Manila: Oxford University Press.
—— (1999) *A Study on Ways to Support Poverty Reduction: Projects/Workshop Papers* (ADB/TA 3150-PRC), Manila: Asian Development Bank, August.
Atkinson, A.B. (1983) *The Economics of Inequality*, Oxford: Clarendon Press.
—— (1987) 'On the Measurement of Poverty', *Econometrica*, 55, 4.
—— (1989) *Poverty and Social Security*, New York: Harvester Wheatsheaf.
—— (1991) 'Comparing Poverty Rates Internationally: Lessons from Recent Studies in Developed Countries', *World Bank Economic Review*, January.
—— (1995) *Incomes and the Welfare State*, Cambridge: Cambridge University Press.
Banister, J. (1987) *China's Changing Population*, Stanford, CA: Stanford University Press.
—— (1992) 'Ethnic Diversification and Distribution', in Poston, D.L. Jr., and Yaukey, D. (eds), *The Population of Modern China*, New York: Plenum Press.
Bao, Jirui (1987) 'An Investigation of the Qian Xi nan (Southwest Guizhou) Autonomous Prefecture of Buyi and Miao', *Social Sciences in Guizhou*, 5, May.
Bardhan, P.K. (1970) 'On the Minimum Level of Living and the Rural Poor', *Indian Economic Review*, 5.
—— (1984) *Land, Labour and Rural Poverty*, Berkeley, CA: University of California Press.
—— (1996) 'Efficiency, Equity and Poverty Alleviation', *Economic Journal*, September.
Basu, K. and Foster, J.E. (1998) 'On Measuring Literacy', *Economic Journal*, 108, 451.
Batchelder, A.B. (1971) *The Economics of Poverty*, New York: Wiley.
Bates, R. and Yackovlev, I. (2002) 'Ethnicity, Capital Formation and Conflict: Evidence from Africa', in Grootaert, C. and van Bastelaer, T. (eds), *The Role of Social Capital in Development: An Empirical Assessment*, Cambridge: Cambridge University Press.
Baulch, B. and Hoddinott, J. (2000) 'Economic Mobility and Poverty Dynamics in Developing Countries', *Journal of Development Studies*, 36, 6.
Beckerman, W. (1979) 'The Impact of Income Maintenance Payments on Poverty in Britain', *Economic Journal*, 89, 354.
—— (1981) 'The Measurement of Poverty', in Riss, Thomas (ed.) *Aspects of Poverty in Early Modern Europe*, Odense: Odense University Press.
Behrman, J. (1991) 'The Action of Human Resources and Poverty on One Another: What We Have Yet to Learn', *Working Paper 74, Living Standards Measurement Study*, Washington, DC: World Bank.
Beijing Review, various issues.
Berry, A. and Cline, W.R. (1979) *Agrarian Structure and Productivity in Developing Countries*, Baltimore, MD: Johns Hopkins University Press.
Besley, T. (1990) 'Means Testing Versus Universal Provision in Poverty Alleviation Programmes', *Economica*, 57, 225.
Besley, T. and Coate, S. (1992) 'Workfare vs. Welfare: Incentives Arguments for Work Requirements in Poverty Alleviation Programs', *American Economic Review*, 82, 1.
Besley, T. and Kanbur R. (1988) 'Food Subsidies and Poverty Reduction', *Economic Journal*, 98.
Bhagwati, J. (1993) *India in Transition: Freeing the Economy*, Oxford: Clarendon Press.
Bhalla, A.S. (1995) *Uneven Development in the Third World: A Study of China and India*, second revised and enlarged edition, London: Macmillan.
—— (2002) 'Sino-Indian Growth and Liberalization: A Survey', *Asian Survey*, XLII, 3.
Bhalla, A.S. and Lapeyre, Frédéric (2004) *Poverty and Exclusion in a Global World*, second revised edition, London: Palgrave Macmillan.
Bhalla, A.S. and Nachane, D.M. (2001) 'The Impact of the Asian Crisis on China and India', in Bhalla, A.S. *Market or Government Failures? An Asian Perspective*, London: Palgrave Macmillan.

Bhalla, A.S., Yao, S. and Zhang, Z. (2003a) 'Regional Economic Performance in China', *Economics of Transition*, 11, 1.

—— (2003b) 'Causes of Inequalities in China, 1952 to 1999', *Journal of International Development*, 16, 8.

Birdsall, N. (1980) 'Population and Poverty in the Developing World', *Staff Working Paper no. 404*, Washington, DC: World Bank.

Biswas, Margaret and Per Pinstrup-Andersen (1985) *Nutrition and Development*, Oxford: Oxford University Press.

Blackorby, C. and Donaldson, D. (1980) 'Ethical Indices for the Measurement of Poverty', *Econometrica*, 48.

Blackwood, D.I. and Lynch, R.G. (1994) 'The Measurement of Inequality and Poverty: A Policymaker's Guide to the Literature', *World Development*, April.

Bloom, Gerald and Fang, Jing (2003) 'China's Rural Health System in a Changing Institutional Context', *Institute of Development Studies (IDS) Working Paper* 194 (July) (Brighton).

Bourguignon, F. (1989) *Optimal Poverty Reduction, Adjustment and Growth: An Applied Framework*, World Bank Human Resources Division, Technical Department, Latin America and the Caribbean, December.

Bourguignon, F. and Fields, G. (1990) 'Poverty Measures and Anti-Poverty Policy', *Recherches Economiques de Louvain*, 56.

Bramall, Chris (2000) *Sources of Chinese Economic Growth, 1978–1996*, Oxford: Oxford University Press.

—— (2001) 'The Quality of China's Household Income Surveys', *China Quarterly*, 167.

Bramall, Chris and Jones, M.E. (1993) 'Rural Income Inequality in China since 1978', *Journal of Peasant Studies*, 21, 1.

Brinker, P.A. and Klos, J.J. (1976) *Poverty, Manpower, and Social Security*, Austin, TX: Austin Press.

Brown, P. and Park, A. (2001) *Education and Poverty in Rural China*, Ann Arbor, MI: University of Michigan.

Cai, Fang (1998) 'Economic Reasons for Migration, the Organization of the Labour Force, and the Selection of Jobs', *Social Sciences in China*, 1.

Cannon, T. (1989) 'National Minorities and the Internal Frontier', in Goodman, D.S.G. (ed.), *China's Regional Development*, London: Routledge.

Carsten, A.H. (2003) 'Fast, Clear and Accurate: How Reliable Are Chinese Output and Economic Growth Statistics?', Research Report, *China Quarterly*, 173.

Carvalho, S. and White, H. (1997) *Combining the Quantitative and Qualitative Approaches to Poverty Measurement and Analysis: The Practice and Potential*, Washington, DC: World Bank.

Chai, Joseph C.H. (1996) 'Divergent Development and Regional Income Gap in China', *Journal of Contemporary Asia*, 26, 1.

Chambers, R., Longhurst, R. and Pacey, A. (eds) (1981) *Seasonal Dimensions of Rural Poverty*, London: Pinter.

Chan, H.L. and Chan, K.T. (2000) 'The Analysis of Rural Regional Disparity in China', *Asian Economic Journal*, March.

Chan, R.C.K., Hsueh, T. and Luk, C. (1996) *China's Regional Economic Development*, Hong Kong: Chinese University.

Chander, R., Grootaert, C. and Pyatt, G. (eds) (1980) 'Living Standards in Developing Countries', *Living Standards Measurement Study Working Paper no. 1*, Washington, DC: World Bank.

Chang, Gene H. (2002) 'The Cause and Cure of China's Widening Income Disparity', *China Economic Review*, 13, 4.

Chathukulum, J. and Kerien, V.K. (1995) '*Jawahar Rozgar Yojana*: An Assessment', *Economic and Political Weekly*, 11 February.

Chaubey, P.K. and Chaubey, G. (1997) 'Gender Equity Sensitive Literacy Rate: An Alternative Approach', *Margin*, April–June and July–September.

Chaudhuri, S. and Ravallion, M. (1994) 'How Well Do Static Welfare Indicators Identify the Chronically Poor?', *Journal of Public Economics*, 53, 3.

Chen, Qingde (1994) 'The Growth of the Minority Nationalities' Market Economy in Yunnan Province and the Reformation of Production Organizations', *Minzu Yanjui*, 1.

Chen, S. and Ravallion, M., (1996) 'Data in Transition: Assessing Rural Living Standards in Southern China', *China Economic Review*, 7, 1.

Cherry, R. (1995) 'The Culture-of-Poverty Thesis and African Americans: The Work of Gunnar Myrdal and Other Institutionalists', *Journal of Economic Issues*, 29, 4.

Chiao, C. and Tapp, N. (eds) (1989) *Ethnicity and Ethnic Groups in China*, Hong Kong: University of Hong Kong, Special Issue of *New Asia Academic Bulletin*, VIII.

China's Underdeveloped Regions, Beijing: Foundation for Underdeveloped Regions in China.

Chowdhury, O.H. (1991) 'Human Development Index: A Critique', *Bangladesh Development Studies*, September.

Clark, C. (1951) *Conditions of Economic Progress*, third edition, London: Macmillan.

Clark, S., Hemming, R. and Ulph, D. (1981) 'On Indices for the Measurement of Poverty', *Economic Journal*, 91, 362.

Clavijo, S. (1992) 'Variations on the Basic Needs Yardstick: An Application to Colombia', *World Development*, August.

Clay, E.J. (1986) 'Rural Public Works and Food-for-Work: A Survey', *World Development*, 14, 10/11.

Colasanto, D., Kapteyn, A. and Gaag, van der J. (1984) 'Two Subjective Definitions of Poverty: Results from the Wisconsin Basic Needs Study', *Journal of Human Resources*, 19, 1.

Collier, P. (1999) 'The Political Economy of Ethnicity', in Pleskovic, B. and Stiglitz, J.E. (eds), *Annual Bank Conference on Development Economics, 1998*, Washington, DC: World Bank.

—— (2000) 'Ethnicity, Politics and Economic Performance', *Economics and Politics*, 12, 3.

—— (2001) 'Implications of Ethnic Diversity', *Economic Policy*, 32.

—— (2002) 'Social Capital and Poverty: A Microeconomic Perspective', in Grootaert, C. and van Bastelaer, T., *The Role of Social Capital*, op. cit.

Cook, S. (1998) 'Who Gets What Jobs in China's Countryside? A Mulitnational Logit Analysis', *Oxford Development Studies*, June.

Cook, S. and White, G. (1998) 'The Changing Pattern of Poverty in China: Issues for Research and Policy', *Institute of Development Studies (IDS) Working Paper no. 67*, Brighton: IDS.

Crafts, N.F.R. (1997) 'The Human Development Index and Changes in Standards of Living: Some Historical Comparisons', *European Review of Economic History*, December.

Danziger S. and Gottschalk, P. (1986) 'Do Rising Tides Lift All Boats? The Impact of Secular and Cyclical Changes on Poverty', *American Economic Review*, 76, 2.

Dasgupta, P. (1990) 'Well-Being and the Extent of Its Realisation in Poor Countries', *Economic Journal*, 100, 4, supplement.

—— (1992) 'The Economics of Destitution', in de Zeeuw, A. (ed.), *Advanced Lectures in Quantitative Economics*, 2, New York: Academic Press.

—— (1993) *An Inquiry into Well-being and Destitution*, Oxford: Oxford University Press.

Dasgupta, P. and Weale, M. (1992) 'On Measuring the Quality of Life', *World Development*, 20, 1.

Datt, G. and Ravallion, M. (1993) 'Regional Disparities, Targeting, and Poverty in India', in Lipton, M. and van der Gaarg, J. (eds) *'Including the Poor'*, Washington, DC: World Bank.

—— (1994) 'Transfer Benefits to the Poor from Public Works Employment', *Economic Journal*, November.

—— (1998) 'Why Have Some Indian States Done Better Than Others at Reducing Rural Poverty?', *Economica*, February.

Davis, S.P. (1979–80) 'The Concept of Poverty in the *Encyclopaedia Britannica* from 1810 to 1975', *Labour History*, 21, 1.

Dayal-Gulati, A. and Husain, A.M. (2002) 'Centripetal Forces in China's Economic Take-off', *IMF Staff Papers*, 49, 3.

Deaton, A. (1980) 'The Measurement of Welfare: Theory and Practical Guidelines', *Living Standards Measurement Study Working Paper no. 7*, Washington, DC: World Bank.

—— (2003) 'Health, Inequality, and Economic Development', *Journal of Economic Literature*, XLI, 1.

Deaton, A. and Muellbauer, J. (1980) *Economics and Consumer Behaviour*, Cambridge: Cambridge University Press.

De Haan, Arjan and Laier, Julie Koch (1997) 'Employment and Poverty Monitoring', *Issues in Development Discussion Paper no. 19*, Geneva: ILO.

Desai, Megnad (1991) 'Human Development: Concepts and Measurement', *European Economic Review*, April.

—— (1995) 'Poverty and Capability: Towards an Empirically Implementable Measure', in Desai, Megnad, *Poverty, Famine and Economic Development, The Selected Essays, II*, Aldershot: Edward Elgar.

Desai, M. and Shah, A. (1988) 'An Economic Approach to the Measurement of Poverty', *Oxford Economic Papers*, October.

Desai, M., Sen, A. and Boltvinik, J. (1992) *Social Progress Index – A Proposal*, Bogota: UNDP.

Dessaint, A.Y. (1980) *Minorities of Southwest China*, New Haven: Hraf Press.

Dev, S. Mahendra (1995) 'Economic Reforms and the Rural Poor', *Economic and Political Weekly*, 19 August.

De Vos, Klass and Garner, Thesia (1991) 'An Evaluation of Subjective Poverty Definitions: Comparing Results from the US and the Netherlands', *Review of Income and Wealth*, 3, 3.

Diamond, Norma (1995) 'Defining the Miao', in Harrell, S. (ed.) *Cultural Encounters on China's Ethnic Frontiers*, Seattle, WA: University of Washington Press.

Dikotter, F. (1996) 'Culture, "Race" and Nation: The Formation of National Identity in Twentieth Century China', *Journal of International Affairs*, 49.

Dilger, B. (1984) 'The Education of Minorities' *Comparative Education*, 20, 1.

Dojiecaidan (1991) *Education in Tibet*, Beijing: China's Tibetan Studies Publishing House.

Drèze, Jean (1990) 'Poverty in India and the IRDP Delusion', *Economic and Political Weekly*, 29 September.

Drèze, J. and Loh, J. (1995) 'Literacy in India and China', *Centre for Development Economics Working Paper Series no. 29*, May, Delhi: Delhi School of Economics.

Drèze, J. and Saran, M. (1995) 'Primary Education and Economic Development in China and India: Overview and Two Case Studies', in Basu, K., Pattanaik, P.K., and Suzumura, K. (eds), *Choice, Welfare and Development*, Oxford: Clarendon Press.

Drèze, J. and Sen, A.K. (1989a) *Hunger and Public Action*, Oxford: Clarendon Press.

—— (1989b) 'Public Action for Social Security: Foundations and Strategy', *STICERD Development Economics Research Programme Paper no. 20*, London: STICERD.

—— (1990) *Hunger: Economics and Policy*, Oxford: Oxford University Press.

—— (1995) *INDIA: Economic Development and Social Opportunity*, Delhi: Oxford University Press.

Dryer, June (1976) *China's Forty Millions: Minority Nationalities and National Integration in the People's Republic of China*, Cambridge, MA: Harvard University Press.

Easterly, W. and Levine, R. (1997) 'Africa's Growth Tragedy', *Quarterly Journal of Economics*, 112.

Eberhard, W. (1982) *China's Minorities Yesterday and Today*, Belmont, CA: Wadsworth Publishing Co.

Editorial Board of Modern China (1991) *Tibet in Modern China*, Beijing: Modern China Publishing House.

Edmundson, W. and Sukhatme, P. (1990) 'Food and Work: Poverty and Hunger?', *Economic Development and Cultural Change*, 38, 2.

Ezaki, M. and Sun, L. (1999) 'Growth Accounting in China for National, Regional and Provincial Economies, 1981–1995', *Asian Economic Journal*, 13, 1.

Feder, G., Lau, L.J., Lin, J.Y. and Luo, X. (1995) 'The Nascent Rural Credit Market in China', in Hoff, K., Braverman, A. and Stiglitz, J.E. (eds), *The Economics of Rural Organization*, New York: Oxford University Press.

Fields, G. (1980) *Poverty, Inequality, and Development*, Cambridge: Cambridge University Press.

—— (1989) 'Changes in Poverty and Inequality in Developing Countries', *World Bank Research Observer*, 4, 2.

—— (1994) 'Data for Measuring Poverty and Inequality Changes in Developing Countries', *Journal of Development Economics*, 44, 1.

Forbes, K.J. (2000) 'A Reassessment of the Relationship between Inequality and Growth', *American Economic Review*, 90, 4.

Foster, J.E. (1984) 'On Economic Poverty: A Survey of Aggregate Measures', *Advances in Econometrics*. 3, 2.

Foster, J. and Sharrocks, A.F. (1991) 'Subgroup Consistent Poverty Indices', *Econometrica*, May.

Foster, J., Greer, J. and Thorbecke, E. (1984) 'A Class of Decomposable Poverty Measures', *Econometrica*, 52, 3.

Frank, C.R., Jr. and Webb, R.C. (eds) (1977) *Income Distribution and Growth in the Less Developed Countries*, Washington, DC: Brookings Institution.

Friedman, Milton (1957) *A Theory of the Consumption Function*, Princeton, NJ: Princeton University Press.

Friedman, R. (1965) *Poverty: Definition and Perspective*, Washington, DC: American Enterprise Institute for Public Policy Research.

Fuchs, V. (1967) 'Redefining Poverty and Redistributing Income', *Public Interest*, summer.

Gai, Jianling (1996) *China's Fiscal System after the 1994 Reform* (Paris: OECD Development Centre) (draft preliminary version) January.

Gaiha, R. (2000) 'Do Anti-Poverty Programmes Reach the Rural Poor in India?', *Oxford Development Studies*, 28, 1.

Galbraith, J.K. (1979), *The Nature of Mass Poverty*, Cambridge, MA: Harvard University Press.

Gao, Qiang (1995) 'Problems in Chinese Intergovernmental Fiscal Relations, Tax-sharing System, and Future Reform', in Ahmad, E., Gao, Q. and Tanzi V. (eds), *Reforming China's Public Finances*, Washington, DC: IMF.

Geng, Dechang (1991) *Survey of Economic Activities and Working Hours in Chinese Farm Household*, Beijing: China Statistical Publishing House.

—— (1996) *Study on Disparity in Wealth among Farmers: Analysis of Economic Activities of Chinese Farm Households*, Beijing: China Financial Economy Press.

Genne, M. (1992) 'Reflexions sur les indicateurs de développement humain', *Canadian Journal of Development Studies*, 13, 1.

Gibson, J., Huang J. and Rozelle, S. (2001) 'Why Is Income Inequality So Low in China Compared to Other Countries?', *Economics Letters*, 71, 3.

Girardin, E. and Ping, Xie (1997) 'Urban Credit Cooperation in China', *OECD Development Centre Technical Papers no. 125*, August, Paris: OECD.

Gladney, D. (1995) 'Economy and Ethnicity: The Revitalization of a Muslim Minority in Southeastern China', in Walder, A.G. (ed.), *The Waning of the Communist State, Economic Origins of Political Decline in China and Hungary*, Berkeley, CA: California University Press.

Glewwe, P. and Gaag, van der J. (1988) 'Confronting Poverty in Developing Countries', *LSMS Working Paper no. 48.*

—— (1990) 'Identifying the Poor in Developing Countries: Do Different Definitions Matter?', *World Development*, June.

Goedhart, T., Halberstadt, V., Kapteyn, A. and van Praag, B. (1977) 'The Poverty Line: Concept and Measurement', *Journal of Human Resources*, 12, 4.

Goodman, D.S.G. (ed.), (1989) *China's Regional Development*, London: Routledge.

Gormely, P.J. (1995) 'The Human Development Index in 1994: Impact of Income on Country Rank', *Journal of Economic and Social Measurement*, 21, 4.

Government of China (1999) *National Report on the Implementation of the Outcome of the World Summit for Social Development*, Beijing.

—— National Minority Affairs Commission (1981) *China's National Minorities* (Chinese), Beijing: People's Press.

—— National Minority Affairs Commission (1990) *Statistical Abstract of Minority Work (1949–1989)*, Beijing: Nationalities Press.

—— Office of National Population Sampling Survey (1997) *Data of the National One Per Cent Sample Survey in 1995*, Beijing: China Statistical Press.

—— State Council (2001) *White Paper on Rural China's Poverty Reduction*, Beijing.

—— State Council Population Census Office and State Statistical Bureau (SSB) Department of Population Statistics (1991) *Ten Per Cent Sampling Tabulation on the 1990 Population Census of the People's Republic of China* (Chinese), Beijing: China Statistical Publishing House.

—— State Planning Commission (1992) *China's Work-for-Food Programme*, Beijing, October.

—— State Statistical Bureau (1949–94, 1995, 1999) *China's Ethnic Statistical Yearbook*, Beijing: Ethnic Publishing House.

—— State Statistical Bureau (1990) *Tabulation on the 1990 Population Census*, Beijing: SSB, I to IV.

—— State Statistical Bureau (1992) *Chinese Rural Statistical Yearbook*, Beijing: SSB.

—— State Statistical Bureau (1992–95) *Gross Domestic Product of China, 1992–95*, Beijing: SSB.

—— State Statistical Bureau (1999) *Comprehensive Statistical Data and Materials on 50 Years of New China*: Beijing: SSB.

—— State Statistical Bureau (2000) *Tibet Statistical Yearbook*, Beijing: SSB.

—— State Statistical Bureau (2003) *2000 Population Census*, Beijing: SSB.

—— State Statistical Bureau (several years) *China Labour Statistical Yearbook*, Beijing: SSB.

—— State Statistical Bureau (various years) *China Statistical Yearbook*, Beijing: SSB.

Government of India, Department of Economic Affairs (1999) *Economic Survey 1999–2000*, New Delhi: Government Printer.

Gregory, C.A. (1999) 'South Asian Economic Models for the Pacific? The Case of Micro Finance', *Pacific Economic Bulletin*, 14, 2.

Grootaert, C. and van Bastelaer, T. (eds) (2002) *The Role of Social Capital in Development: An Empirical Assessment*, Cambridge: Cambridge University Press.

Guhan, S. (1995) 'Social Expenditures in the Union Budget 1991–96', *Economic and Political Weekly*, 18–19 May.

Guizhou Social Sciences Bulletin, various issues.

Gustafsson, B. and Li, Shi (1998a) 'The Structure of Chinese Poverty 1988', *Developing Economies*, December.

—— (1998b) 'Inequality in China at the End of the 1980s: Locational Aspects and Household Characteristics', *Asian Economic Journal*, March.

—— (2002) 'Income Inequality within Counties in Rural China, 1998 and 1995', *Journal of Development Economics*, 69, 1.

—— (2003) 'The Ethnic Minority–Majority Income Gap in Rural China during Transition', *Economic Development and Cultural Change*, 51, 4.

—— (2004) 'Expenditures on Education and Health Care and Poverty in Rural China', *China Economic Review*, 15, 3.

Gustafsson, B. and Zhong Wei (2000) 'How and Why Has Poverty in China Changed? A Study Based on Poverty Data for 1988 and 1995', *China Quarterly*, 164.

Hagenaars, A. (1986) *The Perception of Poverty*, Amsterdam: North Holland Publishing Co.

Hagenaars, A. and Devos, K. (1988) 'The Definition and Measurement of Poverty', *Journal of Human Resources*, 23.

Hagenaars, A. and van Praag, B.M.S. (1985) 'A Synthesis of Poverty Line Definitions', *Review of Income and Wealth*, 31, 2.

Hannum, E. and Zie, Y. (1998) 'Ethnic Stratification in Northwest China: Occupational Differences Between Han Chinese and National Minorities in Xinjiang 1982–1990', *Demography*, 35, 3.

Hansen, M.H. (1999) *Lessons in Being Chinese: Minority Education and Ethnic Identity in Southwest China*, Seattle, WA: University of Washington Press.

Haq, Mahbub ul (1995) *Reflections on Human Development*, New York: Oxford University Press.

Harrell, S. (ed.), (1995) *Cultural Encounters on China's Ethnic Frontiers*, Seattle, WA: University of Washington Press.

Hassan, M.K. and Renteria-Guerrero, L. (1997) 'The Experience of the *Grameen* Bank of Bangladesh in Community Development', *International Journal of Social Economics*, 24, 12.

Haveman, Robert H. (1987) *Poverty Policy and Poverty Research*, Madison, WI: University of Wisconsin Press.

Hayhoe, Ruth (ed.), (1992) *Education and Modernization: The Chinese Experience*, Oxford: Pergamon Press.

He, Yaoquan (1994) 'On the Poverty-stricken Regions' Ways to Improve Their Poor Economy', *Journal of Yunnan Institute for Nationalities*, 3.

Heckman, J.J. (2003) 'China's Investment in Human Capital', *Economic Development and Cultural Change*, 51, 4.

Hershkovitz, L. (1996) *China's 80 Million: Dimensions of Poverty*, University of Toronto-York University Joint Centre for Asia Pacific Studies.

Hicks, D.A. (1997) 'The Inequality-Adjusted Human Development Index: A Constructive Proposal', *World Development*, August.

Hill, R.D. (1993) 'People, Land and an Equilibrium Trap: Guizhou Province, China', *Pacific Viewpoint*, 34, 1.

Hoff, K., Braverman, A. and Stiglitz, J.E. (eds), (1995) *The Economics of Rural Organization*, Oxford: Oxford University Press.

Hossain, M. (1984) 'Credit for the Rural Poor: The Experience of the Grameen Bank', *Bangladesh Institute of Development Studies Research Monograph*, 4, Dhaka: Bangladesh Institute of Development Studies (BIDS).

Howes, S. (1992) 'Purchasing Power, Infant Mortality and Literacy in China and India: An Inter-Provincial Analysis'. *Working Paper: CP No. 19*, Suntory-Toyota International Centre for Economics and Related Disciplines (STICERD), London School of Economics.

—— (1993a) 'Income Inequality in Urban China in the 1980s: Levels, Trends and Determinants', *STICERD Discussion Paper EF-3*, London: London School of Economics.

—— (1993b) 'Mixed Dominance: A New Criterion for Poverty Analysis', *Distributional Analysis Research Programme Working Paper 3*, London: London School of Economics.

Howes, S. and Hussain, A. (1994) 'Regional Growth and Inequality in Rural China', *STICERD Discussion Paper no. 11*, London: London School of Economics.

Huang, Qinghuo (1985) 'On the Prospect of Catching up with Liaoning Province through Collaboration between Guizhou and Guangxi', *Social Sciences in Guizhou*, 6.

Huang, W., Yu, H. Wang, F. and Li, G. (1997) 'Infant Mortality among Various Nationalities in the Middle Part of Guizhou, China', *Social Science and Medicine*, 45, 7.

Hudson, C. (ed.), (1997) *The China Handbook*, Chicago: Fitzroy Dearborn.

Hulme, D. and Shepherd, A. (2003) 'Conceptualizing Chronic Poverty', *World Development*, 31, 3.

Hunnum, E. and Yu, Xie (1998) 'Ethnic Stratification in Northwest China', *Demography*, August.

Hussain, Athar (1988) 'The People's Livelihood and the Incidence of Poverty', in Reynolds, B. (ed.), *Chinese Economic Reform: How Far? How Fast?*, Boston, MA: Academic Press.

Hussain, A. and Stern, N. (1990) *On the Recent Increase in Death Rates in China*, London: London School of Economics.

Hussain, A., Lanjouw, P. and Stern, N. (1991) 'Income Inequalities in China: Evidence from Household Survey Data', *STICERD Discussion Paper CP 18*, London: London School of Economics.

Iceland, J. (2003) *Poverty in America: A Handbook*, Berkeley, CA: University of California Press.

Iliffe, J. (1987) *The African Poor*, Cambridge: Cambridge University Press.

Institute of Agricultural Economics of the Yunnan Academy of Social Sciences (1997) *Rural Micro-Credit – Road to Success for Poverty Alleviation*, Kunming: Yunnan Educational Publishing House.

Institute of Economic Affairs (1972) *The Long Debate on Poverty*, London: Unwin.

International Fund for Agricultural Development (IFAD) (1992) *The State of World Poverty: An Enquiry into Causes and Consequences*, New York: Oxford University Press.

Iredale, R. and Guo, F. (2000) 'Contemporary Minority Mobility in China and Its Implications', paper presented at the Conference on Social Transformation in the Asia Pacific Region, 4-6 December 2000, University of Wollongong, Australia.

Iredale, R., Bilik, N. and Guo, F. (2003a) *China's Minorities on the Move: Selected Case Studies*, Cheltenham: Edward Elgar.

—— (2003b) 'Ethnic Minority Labour Out-migrants from Guizhou Province and Its Impacts on Sending Areas', in Iredale *et al.* (2003a).

Iredale, R., Bilik, N., Wang, S., Guo, F. and Hoy, C. (2001) *Contemporary Minority Migration, Education and Ethnicity in China*, Cheltenham: Edward Elgar.

Jain, L.R. and Tendulkar, S.D. (1988) 'Dimensions of Rural Poverty: An Interregional Profile', *Economic and Political Weekly*, November 1989.

Jain, P.S. (1996) 'Managing Credit for the Rural Poor: Lessons from the Grameen Bank', *World Development*, 24, 1.

Jalan, J. and Ravallion, M. (1998a) 'Transient Poverty in Post-reform Rural China', *Journal of Comparative Economics*, June.

—— (1998b) 'Are There Dynamic Gains from a Poor Area Development Program?', *Journal of Public Economics*, 67, 1.

—— (1999) 'Are the Poor Less Well Insured? Evidence on Vulnerability to Income Risk in Rural China', *Journal of Development Economics*, February.

Jia, Liqun and Tisdell, Clem A. (1995–96) 'Resource Transfers and Trade within China: Economic Efficiency and Regional Inequality Consequences', *Regional Development Studies*, 2.

Jian, T., Sachs, J. and Warner, A.M. (1996) 'Trends in Regional Inequality in China', *China Economic Review*, 7, 1.

Johnson, B. and Chhetri, N. (2000) 'Exclusionary Policies in Chinese Minority Education', *Current Issues in Comparative Education*, 2, 2.

Jones, M.E. (1994) 'Poverty, Inequality and Living Standards in Rural China 1978–90:A Comparative Study of Anhui and Yunnan', Ph.D. Thesis of the School of Oriental and African Studies: London University.

Kakwani, N. (1980a) 'Alternative Measures of Poverty', in Kakwani, N., *Income Inequality and Poverty: Methods of Estimation and Policy Application*, Oxford: Oxford University Press.

—— (1980b) 'On a Class of Poverty Measures', *Econometrica*, 48, 2.

—— (1984) 'Issues in Measuring Poverty', in Basman, R.L. and Rhodes, G.F. (eds), *Advances in Econometrics*, 3.

Kanbur, R. (1987) 'Measurement and Alleviation of Poverty', *International Monetary Fund (IMF) Staff Papers*, 34, 1.

—— (1990) 'Poverty and Development: The Human Development Report and the World Development Report', *Working Paper Series WPS 618*,Washington, DC: World Bank.

Kanbur, R. and Zhang, X. (1999) 'Which Regional Inequality? The Evolution of Rural–Urban and Inland–Coastal Inequality in China from 1983 to 1995', *Journal of Comparative Economics*, 27, 4.

Kanbur, R., Keen, M. and Tuomala, M. (1994) 'Labour Supply and Targeting in Poverty Alleviation Programs', in van de Walle, D. and Nead, K. (eds), *Public Spending and the Poor: Theory and Evidence*, Baltimore, MD: Johns Hopkins University Press.

Kang, Mingzhong (1984) 'Reminiscences and Forecast of Guizhou Economy – In Commemoration of the 35th Anniversary of the Founding of the People's Republic of China', *Social Sciences in Guizhou*, 5.

Kelaher, David and Dollery, Brian (2003) 'Health Reform in China: An Analysis of Rural Health Care Delivery', *University of New England (School of Economics) Working Paper Series in Economics*, No. 2003–17.

Kelley, A.C. (1991) 'The Human Development Index: Handle with Care', *Population and Development Review*, June.

Khan, A.R. (1993) 'Employment and Wages in Rural China', *Asian Regional Team for Employment Promotion (ARTEP) Working Papers*, New Delhi: ILO, February.

Khan, A.R. and Riskin, C. (1998) 'Income and Inequality in China: Composition, Distribution and Growth of Household Income, 1988 to 1995', *China Quarterly*, June.

—— (2001) *Inequality and Poverty in China in the Age of Globalization*, New York: Oxford University Press.

Khan, A.R., Griffin, K., Riskin, C. and Zhou, Renwei (1993) 'Sources of Income Inequality in Post-reform China', *China Economic Review*, 4, 1.

Khusro, A.M. (1999) *The Poverty of Nations*, London: Macmillan.

Kilpatrick, R.W. (1973) 'The Income Elasticity of the Poverty Line', *The Review of Economics and Statistics*, 55, 3.

Kiminami, Lily Y. (1999) 'A Basic Analysis of the Poverty Problem in China', *International Development Research Institute (IDRI) Occasional Paper* no. *13*, Tokyo: IDRI.

Knack, S. (2002) 'Social Capital, Growth and Poverty: A Survey of Cross-country Evidence', in Grootaert and van Bastelaer, *The Role of Social Capital*, op. cit.

Knight, J. and Song, L. (1993) 'The Spatial Contribution to Income Inequality in Rural China', *Cambridge Journal of Economics*, 17, 2.

—— (1999) *The Rural–Urban Divide: Economic Disparities and Interactions in China*, Oxford: Oxford University Press.

Kravis, I. (1981) 'An Approximation of the Relative Real Per Capita GDP of the People's Republic of China', *Journal of Comparative Economics*, 5, 1.

Kravis, I., Heston, A. and Summers, R. (1978) 'Real GDP Per Capita for More Than 100 Countries', *Economic Journal*, 88, 350.

Kuznets, S. (1955) 'Economic Growth and Income Inequality', *American Economic Review*, XLV, 1.

—— (1971) *The Economic Growth of Nations*, Cambridge, MA: Harvard University Press.

Lakshmanan, T.R. and Hua, Chang-I. (1987) 'Regional Disparities in China', *International Regional Science Review*, 11, 1.

Lal, D. (1988) *Cultural Stability and Economic Stagnation: India c500 BC–AD 1980*, Oxford: Clarendon Press.

Lamontagne, Jacques and Ma, Rong (1998) 'Guest Editors' Introduction (to Fieldwork Reports of Rural Education Surveys)', *Chinese Education and Society*, 31, 3.

Lampman, R.J. (1971) *Ends and Means of Reducing Income Poverty*, Institute for Research in Poverty Monograph Series, Chicago: Markham Publishing Company.

Lansley, S. (1980) 'Changes in Inequality and Poverty in the UK, 1970–1976', *Oxford Economic Papers*, 32, 1.

Lardy, N. (1982) 'Prices, Markets and the Chinese Peasant', *Economic Growth Center Discussion Paper no. 428*, December, New Haven: Yale University.

—— (1984) 'Consumption and Living Standards in China 1978–83', *China Quarterly*, 100.

Leading Group Office of Poverty Alleviation and Development (LGOPAD) (1996) *Poverty Monitoring Report 1996* (World Bank Poverty Alleviation Project Area in Southwest China), Beijing, December.

—— (1997) *Poverty Monitoring Report 1997* (World Bank Poverty Alleviation Project Area in Southwest China), Beijing, December.

—— (1998) *Poverty Monitoring Report 1998* (World Bank Poverty Alleviation Project Area in Southwest China), Beijing, December.

—— (1999) *Poverty Monitoring Report 1999* (World Bank Poverty Alleviation Project Area in Southwest China), Beijing.

Lewis, G.W. and Ulph, D.T. (1988) 'Poverty, Inequality and Welfare', *Economic Journal*, 98, 390.

Lewis, O. (1969) 'The Culture of Poverty', in Moyniham, D. (ed.), *On Understanding Poverty*, New York: Basic Books.

Li, Shi and Gustafsson, B. (1996) 'The Structure of Chinese Poverty at End 1980s', *Social Sciences in China*, 6.

—— (1998) 'The End of the 1980s – An Estimate of the Scale and Extent of Poverty in China', *Social Sciences in China*, spring.

Li, W. and Lu, A. (1993) 'Labour Service Export: An Option for National Minority Areas', *Zhongyang minzu xueyuanxuebao*, 1.

Lin, G.C.S. (1998) 'State Policy and Spatial Restructuring in Post-Reform China: Toward a Synthesis', *University of British Columbia Centre for Chinese Research (CCR) Discussion Paper Series*, 98–4, March, Vancouver: University of British Columbia.

Lin, Justin, Cai, Fang and Li, Zhou (1998) 'Social Consequences of Economic Reform in China:An Analysis of Regional Disparity in the Transition Period', paper prepared for the International Conference on 'Openness and Disparities in China', Clermont-Ferrand (France), 22–26 October 1998, organized by the Centre d'Etudes et de Recherches sur le Développement International.

Lin, Justin, Wang, Gewei and Zhao, Yaohui (2004) 'Regional Inequality and Labour Transfers in China', *Economic Development and Cultural Change*, 52, 3.

Lipton, M. (1977) *Why Poor Stay Poor*, London: Temple Smith.

—— (1983a) 'Poverty, Undernutrition and Hunger', *World Bank Staff Paper no. 597*, Washingdon, DC: World Bank.

—— (1983b) 'Labour and Poverty', *World Bank Staff Working Paper no. 616*, Washington, DC: World Bank.

—— (1997a) 'Defining and Measuring Poverty', in *UNDP Human Development Papers*, New York: UNDP.

—— (1997b) 'Editorial: Poverty – Are There Holes in the Consensus?', *World Development*, 25, 7.

—— (1998) *Successes in Anti-Poverty*, Geneva: ILO.

Lipton, M. and Gaag, van der J. (eds) (1991) *Including the Poor*,Washington, DC: World Bank.

Lipton, M. and Ravallion, M. (1995) 'Poverty and Policy', in Behrman, J. and Srinivasan, T.N. (eds), *Handbook of Development Economics*, 3, Amsterdam: North-Holland.

Liu, S., Yi, G., Qiang, L. and You, W. (1996) 'China's Regional Income Disparities: Measurement, Analyses, and Policy Recommendations', in Chan *et al.*, *China's Regional Economic Development*, op. cit.

Longworth, J., Brown, C. and Williamson, G. (1997) 'Second Generation Problems Associated with Economic Reform in the Pastoral Region of China', *International Journal of Social Economics*, 24, 1/2.

Lu, A.G. (1996) 'Welfare Changes in China during the Economic Reforms', *Research for Action Paper no. 26*, Helsinki: UNU/WIDER.

Lu, Guangtian (1986) 'Review of Demographic Research on China's Minorities Nationalities', translation of article: *Zhongguo Shehui Kexue* (Social Sciences in China), January.

Lu, Qingyu (1985) 'Intelligence Development and the Minority Economy', *Social Sciences in Guizhou*, 6.

Luchters, G. and Menkhoff, L. (1996) 'Human Development as Statistical Artifact', *World Development*, August.

Lyons, T. (1991) 'Interprovincial Disparities in China: Output and Consumption 1952–1987', *Economic Development and Cultural Change*, 39, 3.

Ma, Rong (1999) 'Population Growth and Urbanization', in Gamer, Robert E. (ed.), *Understanding Contemporary China*, Boulder: Lynne Rienner.

Ma, Yiu (1985) *China's Minority Nationalities*, Beijing: New World Press.

McCulloch, N. and Calandrino, M. (2003) 'Vulnerability and Chronic Poverty in Rural Sichuan', *World Development*, 31, 3.

McGillivray, M. (1991) 'The Human Development Index: Yet Another Redundant Composite Development Indicator?', *World Development*, October.

McGillivray, M. and White, H. (1993) 'Measuring Development? The UNDP's Human Development Index', *Journal of International Development*, 5, 2.

McKay, A. and Lawson, D. (2003) 'Assessing the Extent and Nature of Chronic Poverty in Low-income Countries: Issues and Evidence', *World Development*, 31, 3.

Mackerras, C. (1985) 'The Minority Nationalities: Modernization and Integration', in Young, G. (ed.), *China: Dilemmas of Modernization*, London: Croom Helm.
—— (1994) *China's Minorities: Integration and Modernization in the Twentieth Century*, Hong Kong: Oxford University Press.
—— (1995) *China's Minority Cultures: Identities and Integration since 1912*, New York: St. Martin's Press.
—— (1998) 'The Impact of Economic Reform on China's Minority Nationalities', *Journal of the Asia Pacific Economy*, 3, 1.
Mackerras, C. and Palmer, K. (1997) 'China's Nationalities and Nationality Areas', in Hudson, C. (ed.), *The China Handbook*, Chicago: Fitzroy Dearborn.
McMillan, J., Whalley, J. and Zhu, L. (1989) 'The Impact of China's Economic Reforms on Agricultural Productivity Growth', *Journal of Political Economy*, 97, 4.
Malthus, T. (1798/1960) *Essay on the Principle of Population*, ed. Farb, G. Himmel, New York: Modern Library.
Marshall, A. (1946) *Principles of Economics*, Eighth edition, London: Macmillan.
Marshall, T. (1972) 'Value Problems of Welfare Capitalism', *Journal of Social Policy*, 1, 1.
Martin, M.F. (1990) 'Bias and Inequality in Rural Incomes in Post-Reform China', *Journal of Peasant Studies*, 17, 2.
Marx, K. (1867) *Capital: A Critical Analysis of Capitalist Production*, 1, London: Allen and Unwin.
Matson, Jim and Selden, Mark (1992) 'Poverty and Inequality in China and India', *Economic and Political Weekly*, 4 April.
Mazumdar, K. (1996) 'An Analysis of Causal Flow between Social Development and Economic Growth: The Social Development Index', *American Journal of Economics and Sociology*, July.
Mellor, J.W. and Desai, G.M. (eds) (1985) *Agricultural Change and Rural Poverty*, Baltimore, MD: Johns Hopkins University Press.
Meng, X. and Wu, H.X. (1998) 'Household Income Determination and Regional Income Differential in Rural China', *Asian Economic Journal*, 12, 1.
Meng, Zingguo and Hu Angang (2000) 'Health Poverty Reduction: A Strategic Priority of China's Rural Health Reform', *Proceedings of the Conference on Rural Health Reform and Development in China*, Beijing, November.
Minhas, B., Jain, L. and Tendulkar, S. (1991) 'Declining Incidence of Poverty in the 1980s: Evidence vs. Artifacts', *Economic and Political Weekly*, 6–13 July.
Mitra, Ashok (ed.), (1988) *China: Issues in Development* (chapter on minorities), New Delhi: Tulika.
Mizoguchi, T. and Matsuda, Y. (eds) (1997) *Analysis of Income Distribution and Poverty Ratio in China*, Tokyo: Taga Shuppan.
Moinuddin, K.H. (1992) 'Poverty in the People's Republic of China: Recent Developments and Scope for Bank Assistance', *Economics and Development Resource Center (EDRC) Occasional Papers no. 1*, November, Manila: Asian Development Bank.
Moon, Marilyn and Smolensky, Eugene (eds) (1977) *Improving Measures of Economic Well-being*, New York: Academic Press.
Morduch, J. (1994) 'Poverty and Vulnerability', *American Economic Review*, 84, 2.
—— (1999) 'The Role of Subsidies in Micro Finance: Evidence from the Grameen Bank', *Journal of Development Economics*, 60, 1.
Morris, M. (1979) *Measuring the Condition of the World's Poor: The Physical Quality of Life* (PQLI) Index, Oxford: Pergamon.
Muellbauer, J.N. (1974) 'Household Consumption, Engel Curves, and Welfare Comparisons between Households', *European Economic Review*, 5, 2.

—— (1977) 'Testing the Barten Model of Household Composition Effects and the Cost of Children', *Economic Journal*, 87, 347.

Mukherjee, A. (1997) 'Public Works Programmes: Some Issues', *Indian Journal of Labour Economics*, 40, 2.

Mukhopadhya, S. and Cameron, J. (eds) (1995) *Rural Poverty and Inequality in Post-Reform China*, Delhi: Oxford University Press.

Murray, Charles (1984) *Losing Ground: American Social Policy 1950–1980*, New York: Basic Books.

Murray, Richard (1996) *Poverty and Social Exclusion in North and South*, Seminar Series, Brighton, Institute of Development Studies (IDS), University of Sussex.

Musgrave, Philip (1986) 'Measurement of Equity in Health', *World Health Statistics Quarterly*, 39, 4.

Myrdal, G. (1968) *Asian Drama: An Inquiry into the Poverty of Nations*, London: Penguin Press, 3 vols.

—— (1970) *The Challenge of World Poverty: A World Anti-Poverty Program in Outline*, New York: Random House.

Neelakantan, M. (1994) '*Jawahar Rozgar Yojana*: An Assessment through Current Evaluation', *Economic and Political Weekly*, 3 December.

Nelson, J.A. (1993) 'Household Equivalence Scales: Theory vs. Policy', *Journal of Labour Economics*, 11, 2.

Newby, L.J. (1988) 'The Pure and True Religion in China', *Third World Quarterly*, April.

Nissan, E. and Shahmoon, R. (1993) 'An Assessment of "Human Development" by Region and Country', *Journal of Economics and Finance*, spring.

Nolan, Peter (1992) 'Economic Reform, Poverty and Migration in China', *Economic and Political Weekly*, 26 June.

Nolan, P. and Sender, J. (1992) 'Death Rates, Life Expectancy and China's Economic Reform: A Critique of A. K. Sen', *World Development*, 20, 9.

Noorbaksh, F. (1998a) 'The Human Development Index: Some Technological Issues and Alternative Indices', *Journal of International Development*, July–August.

—— (1998b) 'A Modified Human Development Index', *World Development*, March.

Nussbaum, M.C. and Sen, A. (1993) *The Quality of Life*, Oxford: Clarendon Press.

O'Brien, D., Wilkes, J., de Haan, A. and Maxwell, S. (1997) 'Poverty and Social Exclusion in North and South', *IDS Working Paper no. 55*, May, Brighton: IDS.

OECD (1976) *Public Expenditures on Income Maintenance Programs*, Studies in Resource Allocation, 3, Paris: OECD.

Orshansky, M. (1969) 'How Poverty Is Measured', *Monthly Labour Review*, 2, 3.

Osmani, S.R. (1982) *Economic Inequality and Group Welfare*, Oxford: Oxford University Press.

Overseas Economic Cooperation Fund (OECF) (1997) 'The Major Issues of the Regional Development Strategies in China', *OECF Research Papers no. 18*, Research Institute of Development Assistance (RIDA), Tokyo: OECF, July.

Pal, S. (2000) 'Economic Reform and Household Welfare in Rural China: Evidence from Household Survey Data', *Journal of International Development*, 12, 2.

Palazzi, P. and Lauri, A. (1998) 'The Human Development Index: Suggested Corrections', *Banca Nazionale del Lavoro Quarterly Review*, June.

Palmer, K. (1997) 'China's Nationalities and Nationality Areas', in Hudson, C. (ed.), *The China Handbook*, Chicago, IL, Fitzroy Dearborn.

Park, A. and Ren, C. (2001) 'Microfinance with Chinese Characteristics', *World Development*, 29, 1.

Park, A. and Wang, S. (2001) 'China's Poverty Statistics', *China Economic Review*, 12, 4.

Park, A., Wang, S. and Wu, G. (2002) 'Regional Poverty Targeting in China', *Journal of Public Economics*, 86, 1.

Parris, K. (1993) 'Local Initiative and National Reform: The Wenzhou Model of Development', *China Quarterly*, 134.

Parthasarthy, G. (1991) 'Lease Market, Poverty Alleviation and Policy Options', *Economic and Political Weekly*, 30 March.

Paul, S. (1996) 'A Modified Human Development Index and International Comparison', *Applied Economics Letters*, October.

Piazza, A. and Liang, E.H. (1997) *The State of Poverty in China: Its Causes and Remedies*, paper presented at the Conference on Unintended Social Consequences of Chinese Economic Reform, Cambridge, MA: Harvard School of Public Health and Fairbank Center for East Asian Research.

Pollak, R.A. and Wales, T.J. (1979) 'Welfare Comparisons and Equivalence Scales', *American Economic Review*, 69, 2.

Postiglione, G. (1992a) 'China's National Minorities and Educational Change', *Journal of Contemporary Asia*, 22,1.

—— (1992b) 'The Implications of Modernization for the Education of China's National Minorities', in Hayhoe, R. (ed.), *Education and Modernization – The Chinese Experience*, New York: Pergamon Press.

—— (ed.) (1999) *China's National Minority Education: Culture, Schooling and Development*, New York: Falmer Press.

Poston, D.L., Jr. and Shu, J. (1987) 'The Demographic and Socioeconomic Composition of China's Ethnic Minorities', *Population and Development Review*, December.

Poston, D.L., Jr. and Yaukey, D. (eds) (1992) *The Population of Modern China*, New York: Plenum Press.

Poverty – A Problem Facing Human Beings, A Study of Poverty Types in the Minority Areas of Yunnan Province, supported by the Ford Foundation, Beijing: China Science and Technology Press.

Provincial Government of Guizhou (several years) *Statistical Yearbook of Guizhou*, Guiyang.

Provincial Government of Sichuan, Workfare Office (1999) *Basic Data on Poverty Counties in Sichuan*, Chengdu, March.

Provincial Government of Tibet (several years) *Tibet Statistical Yearbook*, Lhasa.

Psacharapoulos, G. (1988) 'Education and Development: A Review', *World Bank Research Observer*, 3, 1.

Qiu, Hong (1996) *Openness and Economic Growth in China*, M.Phil. thesis, Hong Kong: Chinese University of Hong Kong.

Quibria, M.G. (1993) *Rural Poverty in Asia: Priority Issues and Policy Options*, Hong Kong: Oxford University Press.

Raiser, M. (1998) 'Subsidising Inequality: Economic Reforms, Fiscal Transfers and Convergence across Chinese Provinces', *Journal of Development Studies*, February.

Rao, C.H.H. (1994) 'Policy Issues Relating to Irrigation and Rural Credit in India', in Bhalla, G.S. (ed.), *Economic Liberalisation and Indian Agriculture*, New Delhi: Institute for Studies in Industrial Development.

Rao, V.V. B. (1981) 'Measurement of Deprivation and Poverty Based on the Proportion Spent on Food: An Exploratory Exercise', *World Development*, 9, 4.

Ravallion, M. (1988) 'Expected Poverty under Risk-induced Welfare Variability', *Economic Journal*, December.

—— (1991a) 'Employment Guarantee Schemes: Are They a Good Idea?', *Indian Economic Journal*, 39, 2.

—— (1991b) 'Reaching the Rural Poor through Public Employment: Arguments, Evidence and Lessons from South Asia', *World Bank Research Observer*, 6, 2.

—— (1994) 'Poverty Comparisons', in *Fundamentals of Pure and Applied Economics*, 56, Chur, Switzerland: Harwood Academic Press.

—— (1995) 'Growth and Poverty: Evidence for Developing Countries in the 1980s', *Economics Letters*, 48, 3–4.

—— (1996) 'Issues in Measuring and Modelling Poverty', *Economic Journal*, September.

—— (1997) 'Measuring Aggregate Welfare in Developing Countries: How Well Do National Accounts and Surveys Agree?', *World Bank Policy Research Working Paper*, Washington, DC: World Bank.

—— (1999) 'Appraising Workfare', *World Bank Research Observer*, 14, 1.

Ravallion, M. and Bidani, B. (1994) 'How Robust Is a Poverty Profile?', *World Bank Economic Review*, 8, 1.

Ravallion, M., and Datt, G. (1994) 'Is Targeting through a Work Requirement Efficient?', in van de Walle, D. and Nead, K. (eds), *Public Spending and the Poor: Theory and Evidence*, Baltimore, MD: Johns Hopkins University Press.

Ravallion, M. and Jalan, J. (1999) 'China's Lagging Poor Areas', *American Economic Review – Papers and Proceedings*, May.

Ravallion, M., Datt, G. and Walle, van de D. (1991) 'Quantifying Absolute Poverty in the Developing World', *Review of Income and Wealth*, Series 37, 4.

Rawski, T.G. (2001) 'What Is Happening to China's GDP Statistics?', *China Economic Review*, 12, 4.

Rein, M. (1971) 'Problems in the Definition and Measurement of Poverty', in Townsend, P. (ed.), *The Concept of Poverty*, London: Heinemann Educational Books.

Reutlinger, S. and Selowsky, M. (1976) *Malnutrition and Poverty: Magnitude and Policy Options*, Baltimore, MD: Johns Hopkins Press.

Riskin, C. (1987) *China's Political Economy: The Quest for Development since 1949*, Oxford: Oxford University Press.

—— (1991) 'Rural Poverty in Post-reform China', paper presented at the Conference on China's Reform and Growth, Canberra: Australian National University.

—— (1993a) 'Poverty in China's Countryside: Legacy and Change', in Bardhan, P., Datta-Chaudhuri, M. and Krishnan, T.N. (eds), *Development and Change – Essays in Honour of K.N. Raj*, Bombay: Oxford University Press.

—— (1993b) 'Income Distribution and Poverty in Rural China', in Griffin, Keith and Zhao, Renwei (eds), *The Distribution of Income in China*, London: Macmillan Press.

—— (1994) 'Chinese Rural Poverty: Marginalized or Dispersed?', *American Economic Review – Papers and Proceedings*, May.

—— (1996) 'Rural Poverty in Post-reform China', in Garnaut, R., Guo, S. and Ma, G. (eds), *The Third Revolution in Chinese Countryside*, Melbourne: Cambridge University Press.

—— (1998) 'Social Development and China's Changing Development Strategy', in Ghai, Dharam (ed.), *Social Development and Public Policies*, London: Macmillan.

Riskin, C. and Li, Shi (2001) 'Chinese Rural Poverty inside and outside the Poor Regions', in Riskin, C. *et al.* (eds), *China's Retreat from Equality*, op. cit.

Riskin, C., Zhao, Renwei and Li, Shi (eds) (2001) *China's Retreat from Equality*, New York: ME Sharpe.

Rong, Xue Lan and Shi, Tianjian (2001) 'Inequality in Chinese Education', *Journal of Contemporary China*, 10, 26.

Rosenhouse, S. (1989) 'Identifying the Poor: Is Headship a Useful Concept?', *Living Standards Measurement Survey, Working Paper no. 58*, Washington, DC: World Bank.

Rowntree, S. (1901) *Poverty: A Study of Town Life*, London: Macmillan.

Rozzelle, S., Park, A., Bezineger, V. and Ren, Changqing (1998) 'Targeted Poverty Investment and Economic Growth in China', *World Development*, December.

Safran, W. (ed.) (1998) *Nationalism and Ethnoregional Identities in China*, London: Frank Cass.

Sagar, A.D. and Najam, A. (1998) 'The Human Development Index: A Critical Review', *Ecological Economics*, June.

Sagar, S. (1989) 'Poverty Measurement: Some Issues', *Indian Economic Journal*, April–June.

Sangay, L. (1998) 'Education Rights for Tibetans in Tibet and India', in Montgomery, J.D. (ed.), *Human Rights: Positive Policies in Asia and the Pacific Rim*, Hollis, NH: Hollis Publishing Company.

Sautman, Barry (1998) 'Preferential Policies for Ethnic Minorities in China: The Case of Xinjiang', in Safran, William (ed.), *Nationalism and Ethnoregional Identities in China*, London: Frank Cass.

—— (1999) 'Expanding Access to Higher Education for China's National Minorities – Policies for Preferential Admissions', in Postiglione, G. (ed.), *China's National Minority Education: Culture, Schooling and Development*, New York: Falmer Press.

Schiff, M. and Valdes, A. (1990) 'Poverty, Food Intake and Nutrition', *American Journal of Agricultural Economics*, 72, 5.

Selowsky, M. (1981) 'Public Action and the Quality of Life in Developing Countries', *Oxford Bulletin of Economics and Statistics*, 43, 4.

Sen, A.K. (1973a) 'Poverty, Inequality and Unemployment', in Srinivasan, T.N. and Bardhan, P. (eds), *Poverty and Income Distribution in India*, Calcutta: Statistical Publishing Society.

—— (1973b) *On Economic Inequality – The Radcliffe Lectures Delivered in the University of Warwick 1972*, Oxford: Clarendon Press.

—— (1976) 'Poverty: An Ordinal Approach to Measurement', *Econometrica*, 44, 2.

—— (1979) 'Issues in the Measurement of Poverty', *Scandinavian Journal of Economics*, 81.

—— (1980) 'Levels of Poverty: Policy and Change', *World Bank Staff Papers no. 401*, Washington, DC: World Bank.

—— (1981) *Poverty and Famines*, Oxford: Clarendon Press.

—— (1983) 'Poor Relatively Speaking', *Oxford Economic Papers*, 35, 2.

—— (1985) 'A Sociological Approach to the Measurement of Poverty: A Reply', *Oxford Economic Papers*, December.

—— (1992) *Economic Inequality Re-examined*, Oxford: Clarendon Press.

—— (1993) 'Life Expectancy and Inequality: Some Conceptual Issues', in Bardhan, P., Datta-Chaudhuri, M. and Krishnan, T.N. (eds), *Development and Change – Essays in Honour of K.N. Raj*, Bombay: Oxford University Press.

—— (1994) 'Well Being, Capability and Public Policy', *Giornale-degli-Economisti-e-Annali-di-Economia*, July–September.

—— (1995) 'Varieties of Deprivation: Comment', in Kuiper, E. and Sap, J. (eds), *Out of the Margin: Feminine Perspectives on Economics*, London: Routledge.

—— (1996) 'Equality of What?', in Hamlin, A.P. (ed.), *Ethics and Economics*, 2, Cheltenham: Edgar Reference Collection.

—— (1997a) 'Human Capital and Human Capability', *World Development*, December.

—— (1997b) 'Quality of Life and Economic Evaluation', *Academia – Economic Papers*, September.

—— (1997c) 'From Income Inequality to Economic Inequality', *Southern Economic Journal*, October.

Shariff, A. (1999) *India: Human Development Report* (a joint study by the NCAER and the UNDP), Delhi: Oxford University Press.

Shi, Zheng (1982) 'A General Plan for the Economic Development of the Minority National Regions in Guizhou', *Social Sciences in Guizhou*, 3.

—— (1985) 'On the Strategic Position of Guizhou in China's Economy', *Social Sciences in Guizhou*, 7.

Shi, Zheng, Tan Zhongxin, Fu Ramao and Xu Yong (1982) 'An Inquiry into Developing Guizhou's Economy', *Social Sciences in Guizhou*, 1.

Shi, Zhengyi (1996) 'On Studying Methods of the Economic Situation of the Minorities', *Social Sciences in Yunnan*, 3.

'Sidelights of How Educational Labour Union of Liupanshui Municipality in Guizhou Province Helped the Poor' (1998) *Chinese Education and Society*, 31, 5.

Sinha, K.K. (1977) 'The Poverty Concept and Rural Strategies: A Critique', *Indian Economic Journal*, 25, 2.

Smith, A. (1776) *An Inquiry into the Nature and Causes of the Wealth of Nations*, fifth edition, London: Methuen.

Squire, Lyn (1993) 'Fighting Poverty', *American Economic Review*, 83, 2.

Srinivasan, T.N. (1993) 'Rural Poverty: Conceptual, Measurement and Policy Issues', in Quibria, *Rural Poverty in Asia*, op. cit.

Stewart, F. (1985) *Basic Needs in Developing Countries*, Baltimore, MD: Johns Hopkins University Press.

Streeten, P., Burki, S.J., ul Haq, M., Hicks N. and Stewart, F. (1981) *First Things First: Meeting Basic Needs in Developing Countries*, New York: Oxford University Press.

Subbarao, K. (1997) 'Public Works and Anti-Poverty Program: An Overview of Cross-country Experience', *American Journal of Agricultural Economics*, May.

Subbarao, K., Bannerjee, A., Braithwite, J., Carvalho, S., Ezemenari, K. Graham, C. and Thompson, A. (1997) *Safety Net Programs and Poverty Reduction: Some Lessons from Cross-country Experience*, Directions in Development Series, Washington, DC: World Bank.

Summers, R. and Heston, A. (1988) 'A New Set of International Comparisons of Real Product and Price Levels – Estimates for 130 Countries, 1950–1985', *Review of Income and Wealth*, 34, 1.

Sun, Haishan and Dutta, Dilip (1997) 'China's Economic Growth during 1984–93: A Case of Regional Dualism', *Third World Quarterly*, 18, 5.

Suryanarayana, M.H. (1995) 'Growth, Poverty and Levels of Living: Hypotheses, Methods and Policies', *Journal of Indian School of Political Economy*, April–June.

Takayama, N. (1979) 'Poverty, Income Inequality, and Their Measures: Professor Sen's Axiomatic Approach Reconsidered', *Econometrica*, 47, 3.

Tang, J. (1996) 'Determinants of the Minimum Living Security Line in Urban China', in White, G. and Shang, X.Y. (eds), *Reforms in Chinese Social Assistance and Community Services in Comparative Perspective*, Brighton: Institute of Development Studies.

Tang, Yufang (1984) 'On the Specific Characteristics of Guizhou's Economy and Its Countermeasure', *Social Sciences in Guizhou*, 6.

Tang, Z. and Lu, D. (1996) 'China's Region-oriented Preferential Policies at the Crossroads', *Asia-Pacific Development Journal*, December.

Tarp, F., Simler, K., Matusse, C., Heltberg, R. and Dava, G. (2002) 'The Robustness of Poverty Profiles Reconsidered', *Economic Development and Cultural Change*, 51, 1.

Thampapillai, D.J. (1989) 'The Elimination of Absolute Poverty: Approaches to Monetary Valuation', *Indian Economic Journal*, April–June.

Thon, D. (1979) 'On Measuring Poverty', *Review of Income and Wealth*, 25, 4.

Thorbecke, E. and Jung, H.-S. (1996) 'A Multiplier Decomposition Method to Analyse Poverty Alleviation', *Journal of Development Economics*, 48, 2.

Tomlinson, S. (1997) 'Diversity, Choice and Ethnicity: The Effects of Educational Markets on Ethnic Minorities', *Oxford Review of Education*, 23, 1.

Tong, Fei Xiao (1980), 'Ethnic Identification in China', *Social Sciences in China*, March.

Tong, Xing and Lin, Mingang (1995) 'A Study of Poverty Lines in Rural Areas', *Social Sciences in China*, summer.

Tong, Ya-ming (1991) 'Poverty Issues and Policies in China: The Case of Luliang District in Shanxi Province', National Centre for Development Studies, Research School of Pacific Studies, Australian National University, Canberra.

Townsend, P. (1971) *The Concept of Poverty*, London: Heinemann Educational Books.

Townsend, P. (1974) 'Poverty as Relative Deprivation', in Wedderburn, Dorothy (ed.), *Poverty, Inequality and Class Structure*, Cambridge: Cambridge University Press.
—— (1979) *Poverty in the United Kingdom*, London: Penguin Books.
Tsakalogu, P. (1988) 'Development and Inequality Revisited', *Applied Economics*, 20, 4.
Tsui, Kai-yuen (1996a) 'Measurement of Multidimensional Interprovincial Inequality with an Application Using Chinese Data', in Chan, R.C.K, Hsueh, T. and Luk, C., *China's Regional Economic Development*, op. cit.
—— (1996b) 'The Measurement of China's Regional Inequalities: Some Issues and Problems', in Chan *et al.*, ibid.
—— (1998) 'Trends and Inequalities of Rural Welfare in China: Evidence from Rural Households in Guangdong and Sichuan', *Journal of Comparative Economics*, 26, 4.
United Nations (1954) *International Definition and Measurement of Standards and Levels of Living*, New York: UN.
United Nations Development Programme (UNDP) (1990, 1992, 1993) *Human Development Report*, New York: Oxford University Press.
—— (1997a) *China: Human Development Report*, Beijing.
—— (1997b) *Poverty Alleviation in China: A Compendium of Programmes Supported by International Donors*, Beijing: UNDP, July.
—— (1999) *China Human Development Report – Transition and the State*, Beijing.
Upton, J.L. (1999) 'The Development of Modern School-Based Tibetan Language Education in the PRC', in Postiglione, *China's National Minority Education*, op. cit.
Wahid, A.N.M. (1994) 'The Grameen Bank and Poverty Alleviation in Bangladesh: Theory, Evidence, Limitations', *American Journal of Economics and Sociology*, January.
Walker, K.R. (1984) *Foodgrain Procurement and Consumption in China*, Cambridge: Cambridge University Press.
Wang, De (1995–96) 'Spatial Structure of Internal Migration in Modern China: An Analysis Based on the 1990 Population Census', *Regional Development Studies*, 2.
Wang, F. (1998) *Gong tong fuyu zhi lu* (Road to Common Prosperity), Beijing: Publishing House of Economic Science.
Wang, Lianfang (1989)'The Problem of Developing Minority Education in Yunnan Province', *Chinese Education*, 22, 1.
Wang, S. (1994) 'On the Possible Approaches to the Achievement of Modernisation for the Minority Nationalities in Yunnan', *Journal of Yunnan Institute for Nationalities*, 2.
—— (1997) 'Institutional Innovation is Needed for Increasing Efficiency in the Utilization of Poverty Alleviation Funds', in Zhao, J. (ed.), *The Theory and Practice of Poverty Alleviation in China*, Kunming: Yunnan Scientific Publishing House.
Wang, S. and Zhu, X. (1997) 'Distribution and Management of Loans for Poverty Alleviation and Poor Area Development with Special reference to Zhijin County (Guizhou)', ibid.
Watts, H.W. (1967) 'The Iso-prop Index: An Approach to the Determination of Differential Poverty Income Thresholds', *The Journal of Human Resources*, II, 1.
—— (1968) 'An Economic Definition of Poverty', in Moynihan, D.P. (ed.), *On Understanding Poverty*, New York: Basic Books.
Wei, Qiguang (1986) 'A Study of the Relation between the Agricultural Population and Economic Development in Guizhou Province', *Social Sciences in Guizhou*, 11.
Weiner, M. (1991) *The Child and the State in India*, Princeton, NJ: Princeton University.
Weiss, J. (2002) 'Explaining Trends in Regional Poverty in China', Asian Development Bank Institute, Tokyo, December (mimeo draft).
World Bank (1985) *World Development Report*, New York: Oxford University Press.
—— (1990) *World Development Report*, New York: Oxford University Press.
—— (1992a) *China: Strategies for Reducing Poverty in the 1990s*, Washington, DC: World Bank.

World Bank (1992b) *Poverty Reduction Handbook*, Washington, DC: World Bank.
—— (1993) *World Development Report 1993 – Investing in Health*, New York: Oxford University Press.
—— (1995) *Staff Appraisal Report, China: Southwest Poverty Reduction Project Report No. 13968-CHA*, Washington, DC: World Bank, 18 May.
—— (1996) *Poverty in China: What Do the Numbers Say? A Background Note*, Washington, DC: World Bank.
—— (1997a) *Staff Appraisal Report, China: Qinba Mountains Poverty Reduction Project Report no. 16390-CHA*, Washington, DC: World Bank, 15 May.
—— (1997b) *China 2020: Sharing Rising Incomes – Disparities in China*, Washington, DC: World Bank.
——(1999) *China: Weathering the Storm and Learning the Lessons – Country Economic Memorandum*, East Asia and Pacific Region Department, Washington, DC: World Bank.
—— (2000) *World Development Report*, New York: Oxford University Press.
—— (2001) *China: Overcoming Rural Poverty*, A World Bank Country Study, Washington, DC: World Bank.
Wu, Guodong (1994) 'Research Report on Credit Policies for Poverty Alleviation', paper presented at the International Workshop on Anti-Poverty Strategies of China, Beijing, 4–7 December.
Wu, Shimin (1998) *China's Ethnic Minorities Policies* (in Chinese), Beijing: Central Minority University Publishing House.
Wu, Y. (2000) 'Productivity Growth and Economic Integration in the Southern China Region', *Asian Economic Journal*, March.
Xie, Y. and Hannum, E. (1996) 'Regional Variation in Earnings Inequality in Reform-Era Urban China', *American Journal of Sociology*, 101.
Xu, X. (1997) 'Review of the Poverty Alleviation Policy of the Chinese Government: The Subsidized Loans', in Zhao, J. (ed.), *The Theory and Practice of Poverty Alleviation in China*, Kunming: Yunnan Scientific Publishing House.
Yang, Dennis Tao (2002) 'What Has Caused Regional Inequality in China?', *China Economic Review*, 13, 4.
Yang, D.T. and Cai, F. (2003) 'The Political Economy of China's Rural–Urban Divide', in Hope, N., Yang, D.T. and Yang, M. (eds), *How Far Across the River? Chinese Policy Reform at the Millennium*, Stanford, CA: Stanford University Press.
Yang, Shijie (1990) 'Exploration into Labour Quality among the Minority Nationalities in Yunnan', *Social Sciences in Yunnan*, 3.
Yao, S. (1997) 'Industrialization and Spatial Income Inequality in China 1986–1992', *Economics of Transition*, 5, 1.
—— (1999a) 'On the Decompositions of the Gini Coefficient by Population Class and Income Source: A Spreadsheet Approach', *Applied Economics*, 34.
—— (1999b) 'Economic Growth, Income Inequality and Poverty in China under Economic Reforms', *Journal of Development Studies*, 35, 6.
—— (2000) 'Economic Development and Poverty Reduction in China over 20 Years of Reform', *Economic Development and Cultural Change*, 48, 3.
Yao, S. and Liu, J. (1998) 'Economic Reforms and Spatial Income Inequality in China', *Regional Studies*, 32, 8.
Yao, S. and Zhang, Z. (2001a) 'On Regional Inequality and Diverging Clubs: A Case Study of Contemporary China', *Journal of Comparative Economics*, 29, 3.
—— (2001b) 'Regional Growth in China under Economic Reforms', *Journal of Development Studies*, 38, 2.
Yao, S. and Zhu L. (1999) 'Understanding Income Inequality in China: A Multi-Angle Perspective', Economic Department, University of Portsmouth (mimeo).

Yaqub, S. (1999a) *Poverty Dynamics in Developing Countries: An Annotated Bibliography*, Brighton: Institute of Development Studies.
—— (1999b) *Born Poor, Stay Poor? A Literature Review*, Brighton: Institute of Development Studies.
Ye, Xiaowen (1994) 'On Narrowing the Gap and Speeding Up Development in Minority Areas', *Minzu Yanjui*, 4.
Ying, Y. (1996) *Income, Poverty and Inequality in China During Transition to a Market Economy*, World Bank Transitional Economies Division, Research Paper Series no. 10, Washington, DC: World Bank.
Yu, Changjiang (1998a) 'Jinping Miao-yao-Dai Autonomous County (Yunnan Province)', *Chinese Education and Society*, 31, 3.
—— (1998b) 'Anning County (Yunnan Province)', *Chinese Education and Society*, 31, 3.
Yu, Hongmo (1986) 'Approaches to the Development of Minority Economy in Mountainous Areas', *Social Sciences in Guizhou*, 1.
Zai, Liang and White, Michael J. (1997) 'Market Transition, Government Policies, and Interprovincial Migration in China: 1983–1988', *Economic Development and Cultural Change*, 45, 2.
Zeren, L., Yaxiong, C. and Yingliang, J. (1990–91) 'The Affairs of Guizhou Province – Public Finance, Taxation, Finance and Auditing', *Chinese Economic Studies*, 24, 2.
Zhang, F. and Fuxing Yang (1994) 'On the Poverty Eradication Project and the Production and Circulation of Nationalities', *Journal of Yunnan Institute for Nationalities*, 2.
Zhang, T. (1984) 'Growth of China's Minority Population', *Beijing Review*, 27, 6.
—— (1987) 'Population Development and Changes of China's Minority Nationalities', in SSB, *A Census of One Billion People*, Beijing: Department of Population Statistics.
—— (1989) *Change in Tibetan Population*, Beijing: China's Tibetan Studies Publishing House.
Zhang, T. and Huang, R. (eds) (1993) *Development among China's Minorities* (in Chinese), Beijing: Haiyang Publishing House.
Zhang, Zhen-Dong (1982) 'Guizhou Shen Min Zhu Ren Kou Gai Kuang' (General Information on the Nationalities in Guizhou), in *Quan Guo Shao Shu Min Zhu Ren Ku Lun Wen Zi Liao Xuan Bian* (Selected Information on the Minority Populations in China), Beijing: Population Association of China.
Zhang, Z. and Yao, S. (2001) 'Regional Inequalities in Contemporary China Measured by GDP and Consumption', *Economic Issues*, 6, 2.
Zhang, Z., Liu, A. and Yao, S. (2001) 'Convergence of China's Regional Incomes, 1952–1997', *China Economic Review*, 12, 2–3.
Zhao, G. (1996) 'A Model of Decentralized Development: Border Trade and Economic Development in Yunnan', *Issues and Studies*, October.
Zhao, J.C. (1999) 'How to Deal with the Extremely Poor Population in the Next Century's Poverty Alleviation in China', in Zhao, Yaqiao and Dong, Di (eds), *An Action Research Focus on the Extremely Poor Population*, Yunnan Social Forestry Project Study Series 3, funded by the Ford Foundation, Kunming: Yunnan Science and Technology Press.
Zhao, R. and Li, Shi (1997) 'Enlargment of Household Income Disparity and Its Causes', *Economic Study*, China Social Sciences Academy Institute of Economic Studies, 9.
Zhao, T. (1993) 'A Comprehensive Study of Yunnan's Nationalities Scattering Across the Border', *Minzu Yanjui*, 2.
Zhao, Y. and Dong, D. (1999) *An Action Research Focus on the Extremely Poor Population*, Yunnan Social Forestry Project Study Series 3, Kunming: Yunnan Science and Technology Press.
Zhou, B. and Gao, H. (1993) 'Researches on Poverty and an Evaluation of Anti-poverty Practices', *Tribune of Economic Development*, 1.
Zhou, Fang (1996) 'On Using the Composite Indicator and the Single Indicator to Measure Regional Inequality', in Chan *et al.*, *China's Regional Economic Development*, op. cit.

Zhou, Gengxin (1989) 'Accelerate the Pace of Educational Reform in Minority Regions: Primary Education in the Four Counties of Southwestern Yunnan', *Chinese Education*, 22, 1.

Zhou, Haibo (1996) 'Special Revenue Sources and Their Impact on Yunnan Finances', *Chinese Economic Studies*, 29, 4.

Zhou, Ping (1994) 'Modernization and Immoralization: The Political Opinion of Minority Nationalities in China', *Social Sciences in Yunnan*, 5.

Zhou, Shaofu (1997) 'Development through Migration, Experience of the Mountain Areas in the Northern Guangdong Province', in Zhao, J. (ed.), *The Theory and Practice of Poverty Alleviation in China*, Kunming: Yunnan Scientific Publishing House.

Zhu, Ling (1991) *Rural Reform and Peasant Income in China: The Impact of China's Post-Mao Rural Reforms in Selected Regions*, London: Macmillan.

—— (1997) 'Poverty Alleviation During the Transition in Rural China', UNU/WIDER Research in Progress (RIP), April, Helsinki: WIDER.

Zhu, Ling and Jiang Zhongyi (1995) 'The *Yigong-daizen* Poverty Reduction Program and its Effects on the Employment, Income and Nutritional Status of Poor Households', in von Braun, J. (ed.), *Employment for Poverty Reduction and Food Security*, Washington, DC: International Food Policy Research Institute.

—— (1996) *Public Works and Poverty Alleviation in Rural China*, New York: Nova Science Publishers, Inc.

Zhu, Ling, Jiang Zhongyi and von Braun, Joachim (1997) *Credit Systems for the Rural Poor in China*, New York: Nova Science Publishers.

Zhu, M. Zhenjun (1995) 'China's Financial Policies for Minority Nationalities and Poor Areas', in Ahmad, E., Gao Qiang and Tanzi, Vito (eds), *Reforming China's Public Finances*, Washington, DC: IMF.

Zhuge, R. and Tisdell, C. (1998) 'Poverty and Its Alleviation in Yunnan Province, China: Sources, Policies and Solutions', *Current Politics and Economics of China*, 1, 4.

Zine, J. (2001) 'Negotiating Equity – The Dynamics of Minority and Community Engagement in Constructing Inclusive Educational Policy', *Cambridge Journal of Education*, 41, 2.

Zuo, Lu (1992) 'Rural Reforms in Guizhou', *China Report*, 28, 2.

Author/name index

Subject index

For Product Safety Concerns and Information please contact our EU
representative GPSR@taylorandfrancis.com
Taylor & Francis Verlag GmbH, Kaufingerstraße 24, 80331 München, Germany

www.ingramcontent.com/pod-product-compliance
Ingram Content Group UK Ltd.
Pitfield, Milton Keynes, MK11 3LW, UK
UKHW022255051225
465792UK00006B/54